Get It Together

I'M GONNA GET IT TOGETHER.
THEN GRADUALLY SLIDE BACK INTO MY OLD WAYS.
THEN GET IT TOGETHER AGAIN.

Empty

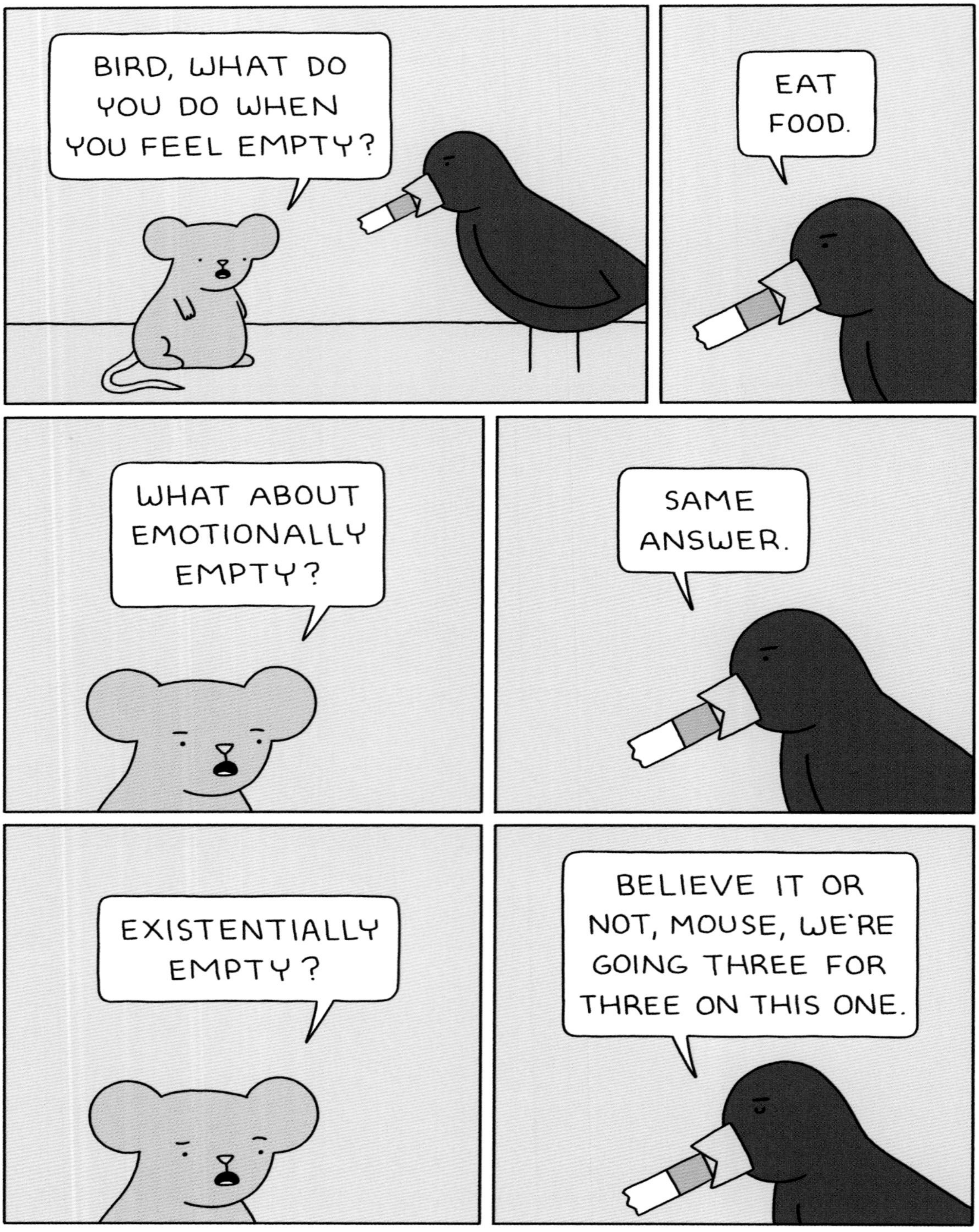
BIRD, WHAT DO YOU DO WHEN YOU FEEL EMPTY?
EAT FOOD.
WHAT ABOUT EMOTIONALLY EMPTY?
SAME ANSWER.
EXISTENTIALLY EMPTY?
BELIEVE IT OR NOT, MOUSE, WE'RE GOING THREE FOR THREE ON THIS ONE.

HOPE IT ALL WORKS OUT!

A "POORLY DRAWN LINES"
COLLECTION

REZA FARAZMAND

Andrews McMeel
PUBLISHING®

Work Hard

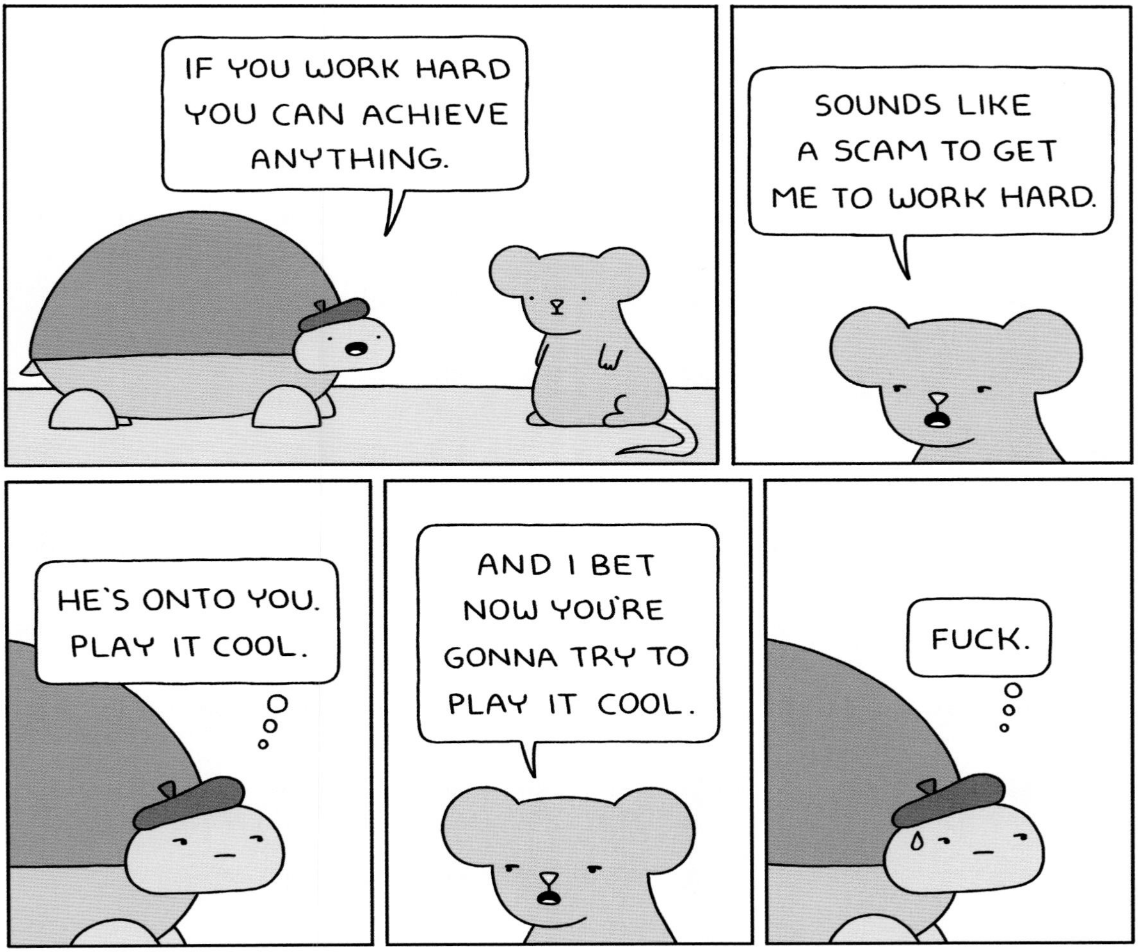
IF YOU WORK HARD YOU CAN ACHIEVE ANYTHING.
SOUNDS LIKE A SCAM TO GET ME TO WORK HARD.
HE'S ONTO YOU. PLAY IT COOL.
AND I BET NOW YOU'RE GONNA TRY TO PLAY IT COOL.
FUCK.

Come With Me

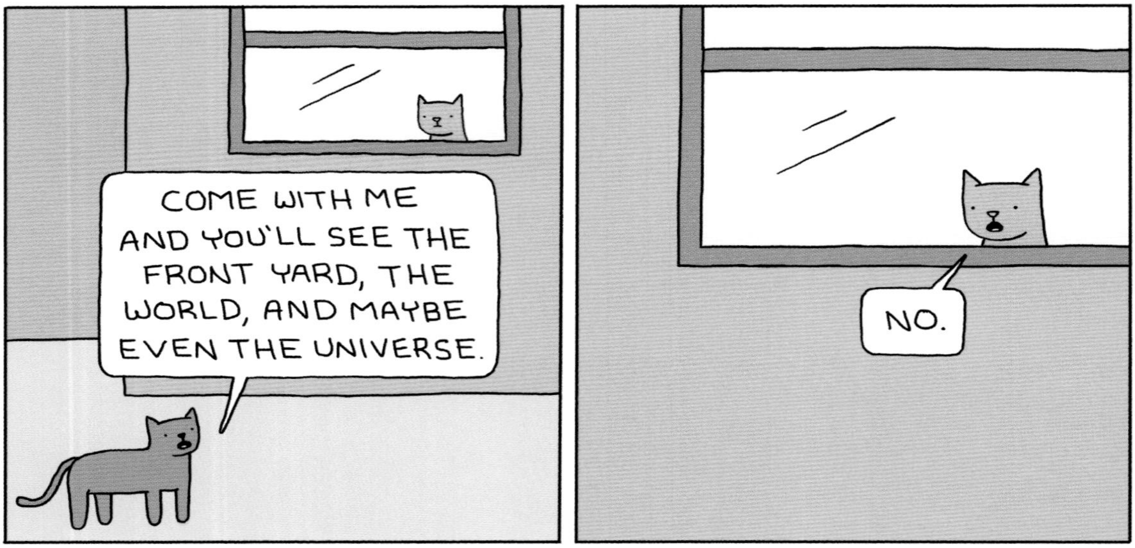
COME WITH ME AND YOU'LL SEE THE FRONT YARD, THE WORLD, AND MAYBE EVEN THE UNIVERSE.
NO.

Think Hard

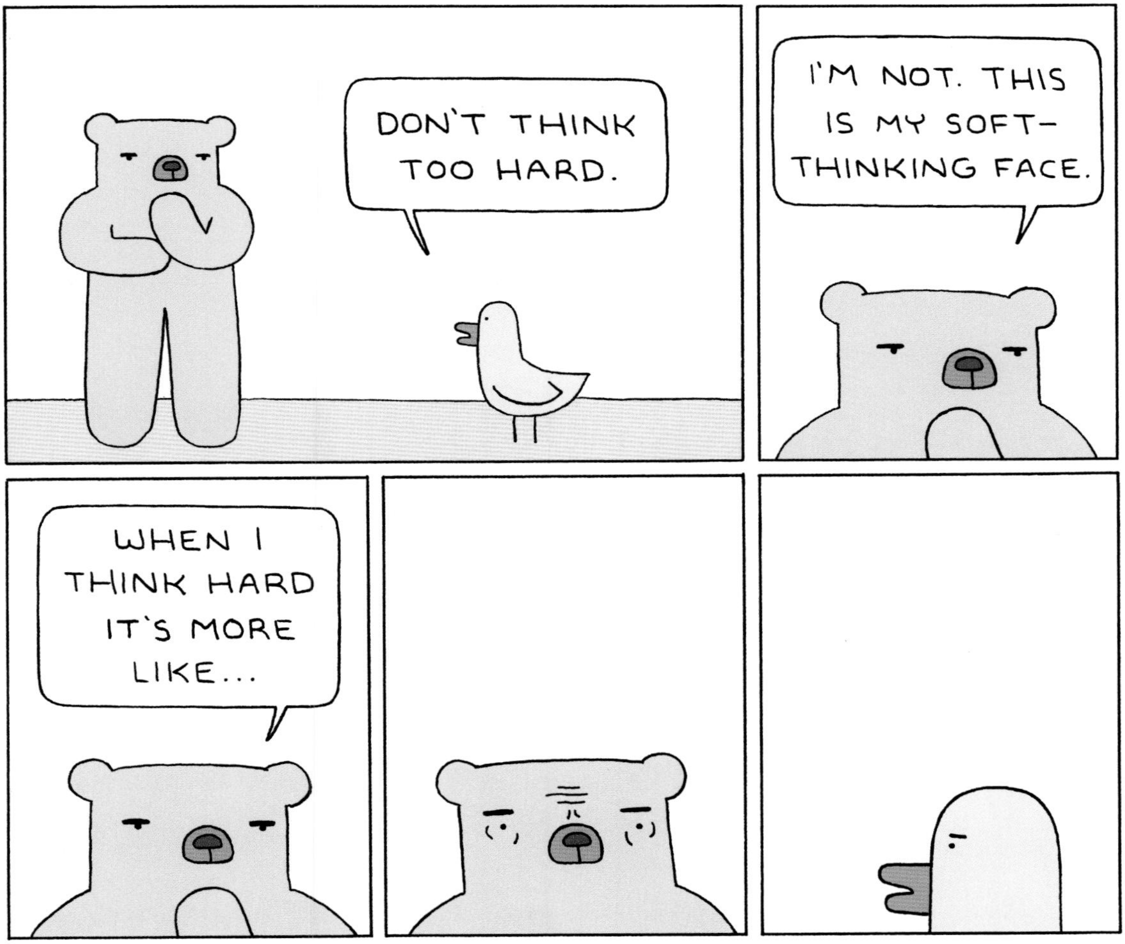
DON'T THINK TOO HARD.
I'M NOT. THIS IS MY SOFT-THINKING FACE.
WHEN I THINK HARD IT'S MORE LIKE...

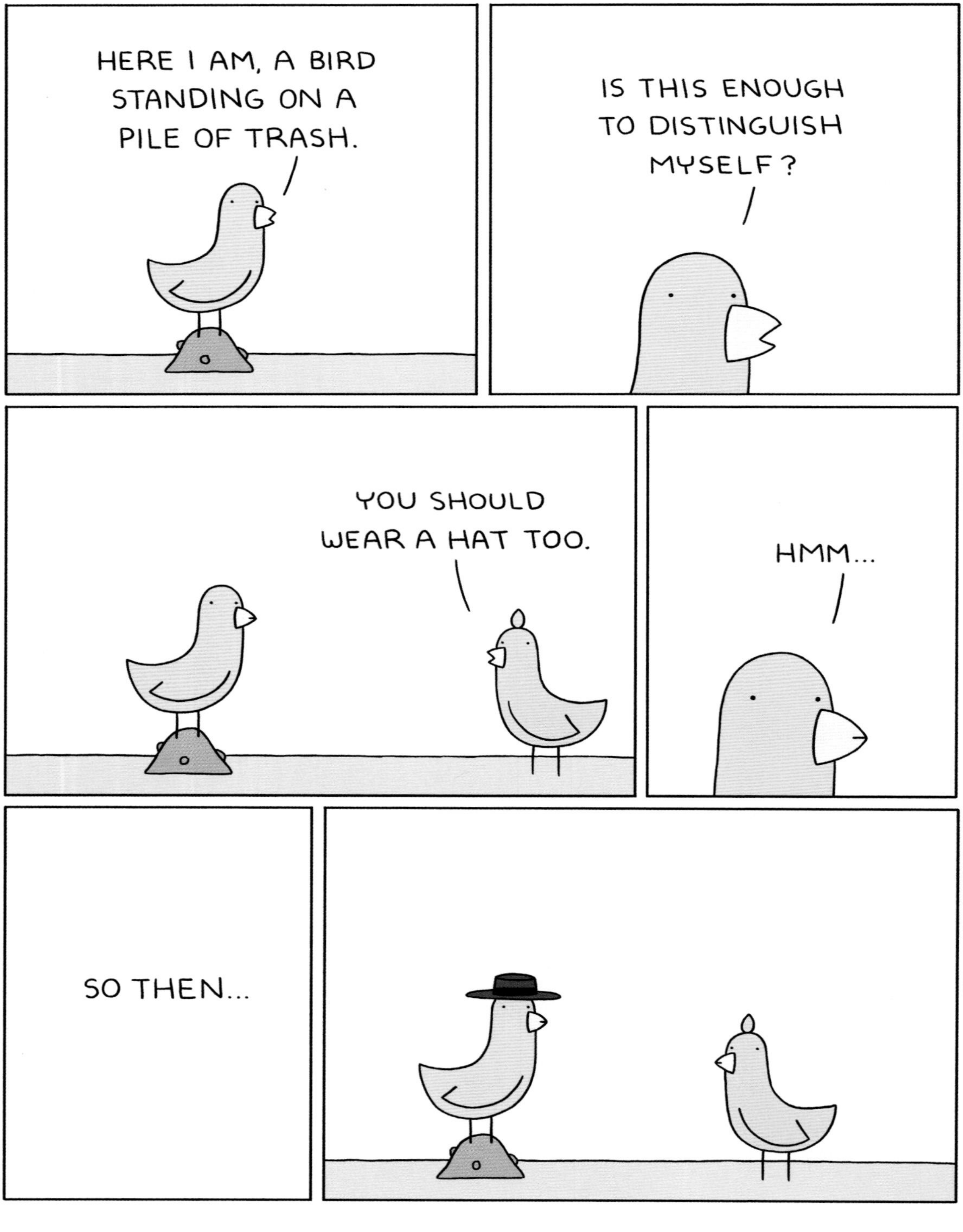
HERE I AM, A BIRD STANDING ON A PILE OF TRASH.
IS THIS ENOUGH TO DISTINGUISH MYSELF?
YOU SHOULD WEAR A HAT TOO.
HMM...
SO THEN...

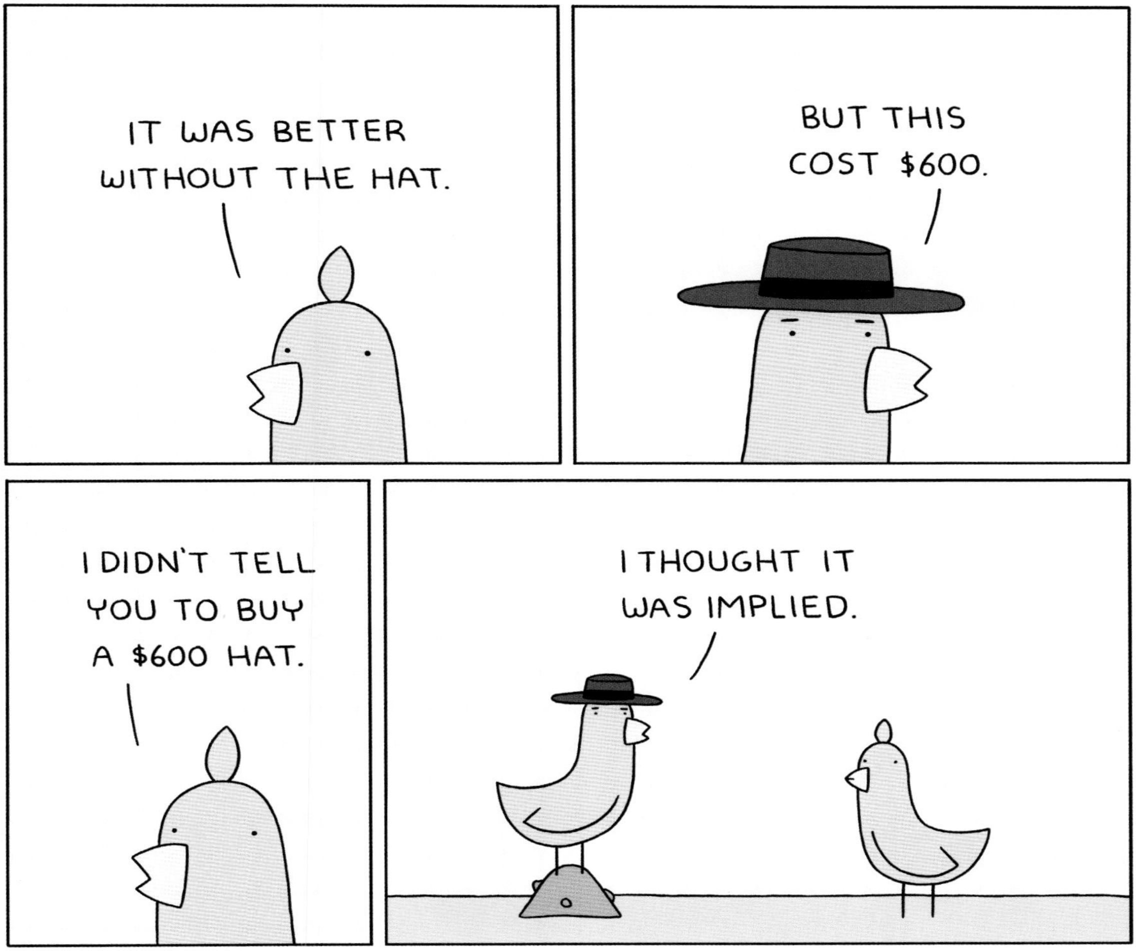
IT WAS BETTER WITHOUT THE HAT.
BUT THIS COST $600.
I DIDN'T TELL YOU TO BUY A $600 HAT.
I THOUGHT IT WAS IMPLIED.

Who We Are

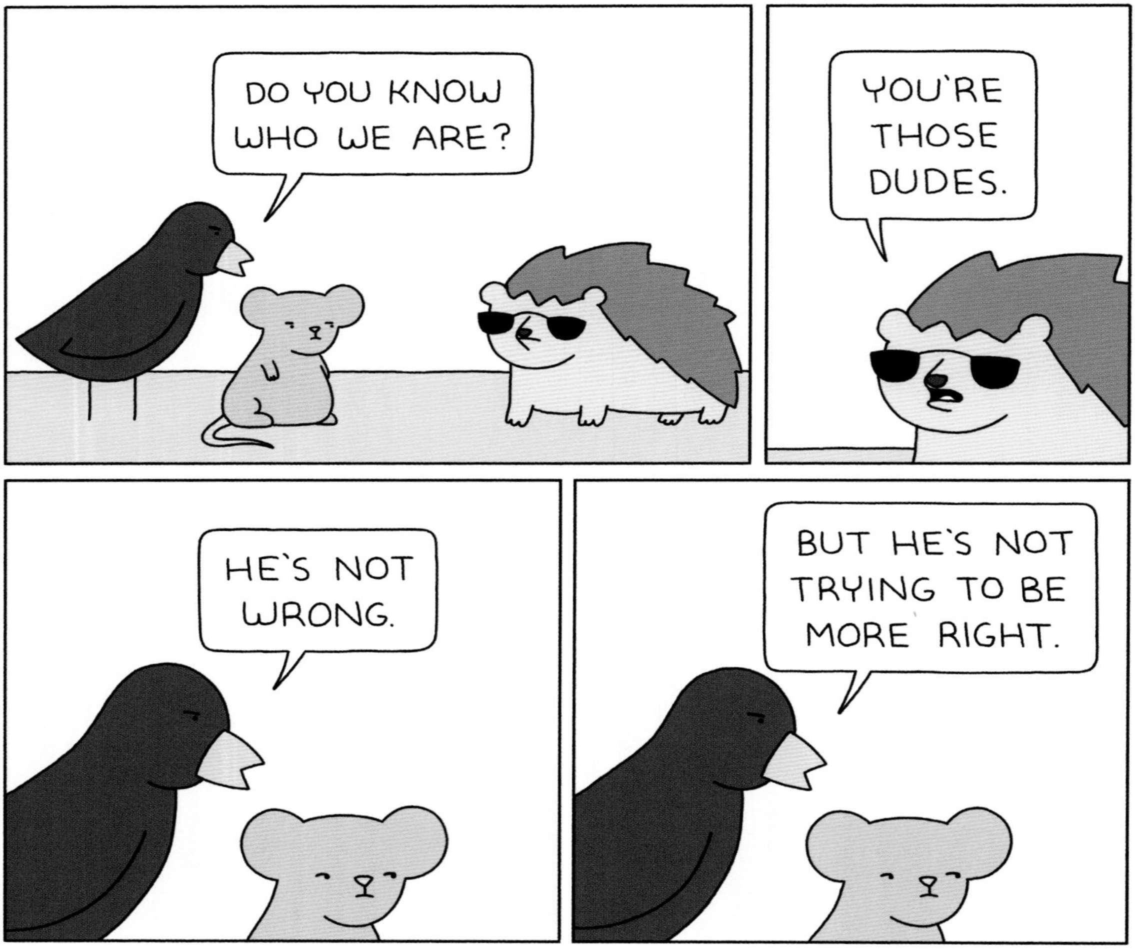

DO YOU KNOW WHO WE ARE?
YOU'RE THOSE DUDES.
HE'S NOT WRONG.
BUT HE'S NOT TRYING TO BE MORE RIGHT.

Retiring

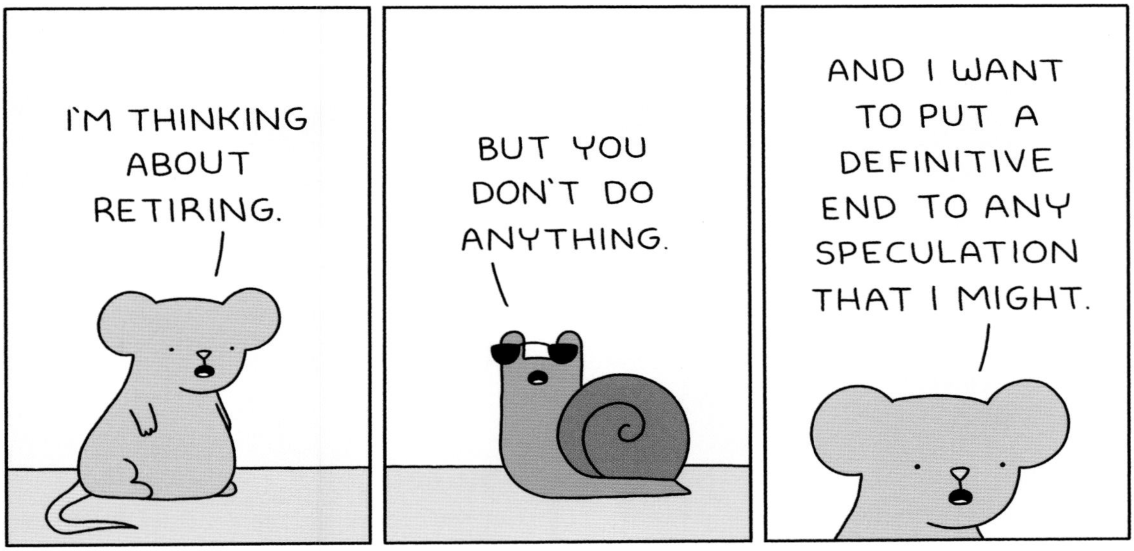
I'M THINKING ABOUT RETIRING.
BUT YOU DON'T DO ANYTHING.
AND I WANT TO PUT A DEFINITIVE END TO ANY SPECULATION THAT I MIGHT.

Notebook

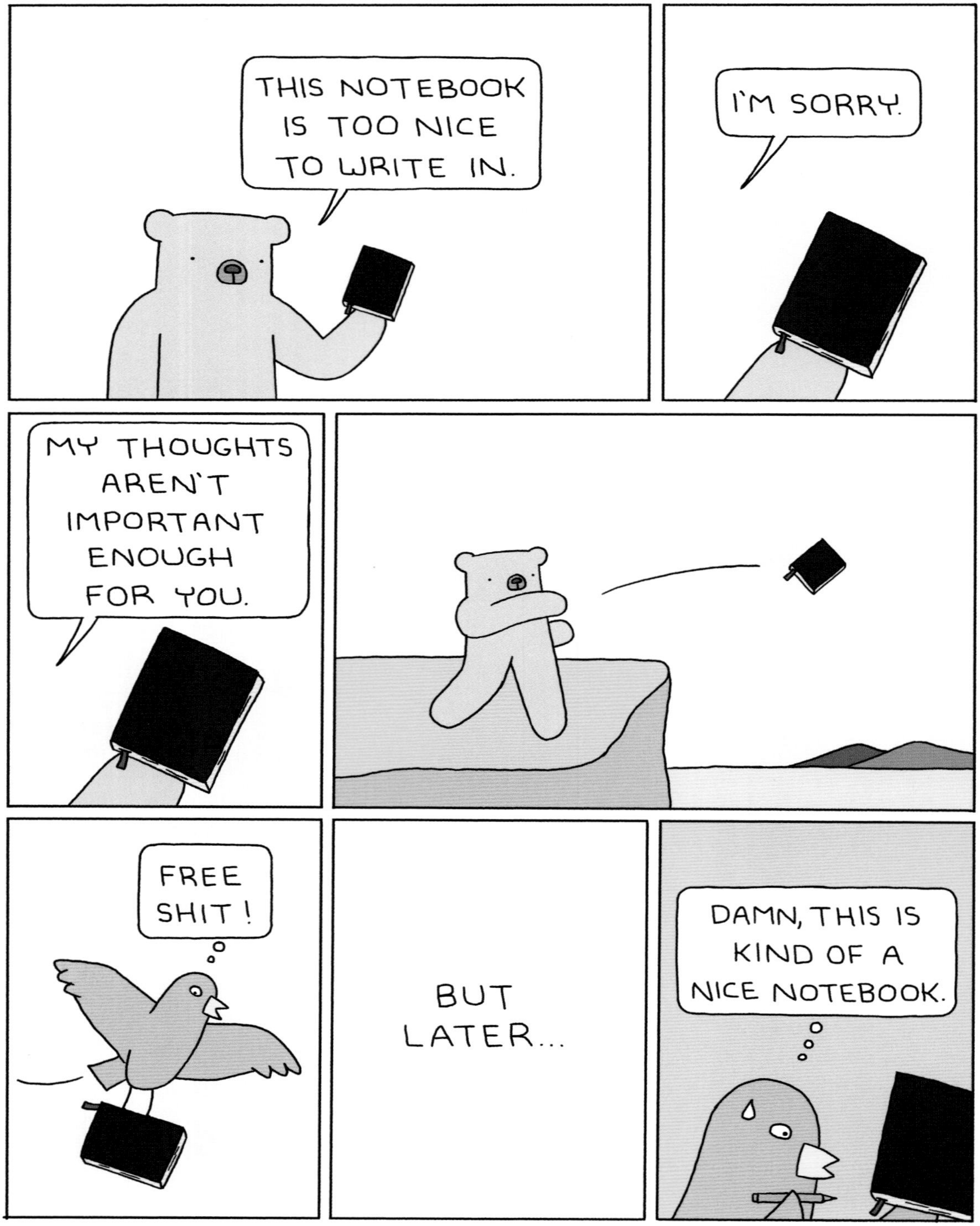
THIS NOTEBOOK IS TOO NICE TO WRITE IN.
I'M SORRY.
MY THOUGHTS AREN'T IMPORTANT ENOUGH FOR YOU.
FREE SHIT!
BUT LATER...
DAMN, THIS IS KIND OF A NICE NOTEBOOK.

Been Thinking

I'VE BEEN THINKING.
I'M SO SORRY TO HEAR THAT, MAN.

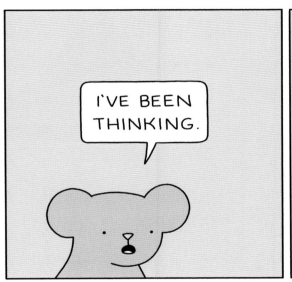

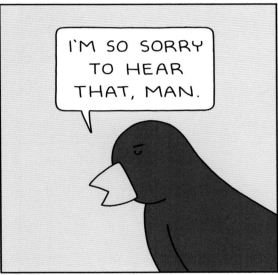

Ever Feel

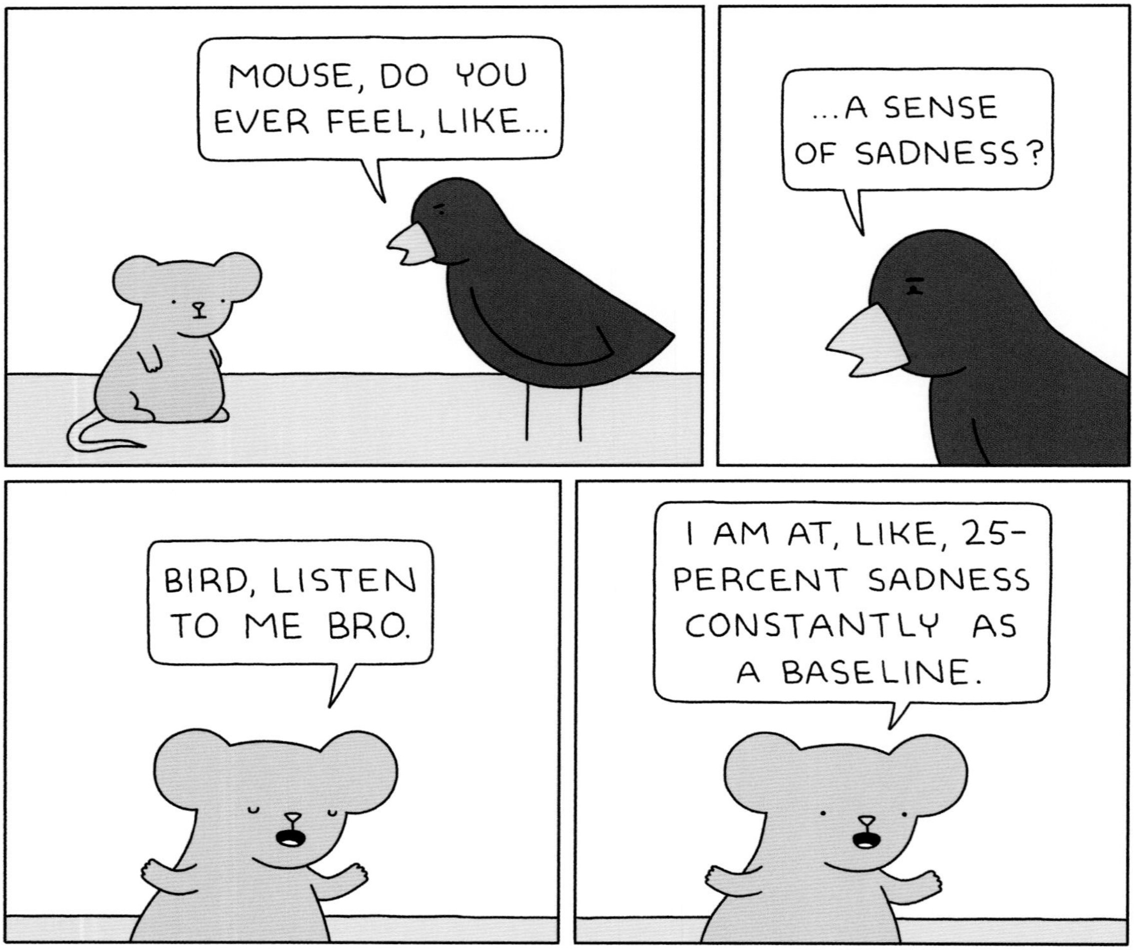
MOUSE, DO YOU EVER FEEL, LIKE...
...A SENSE OF SADNESS?
BIRD, LISTEN TO ME BRO.
I AM AT, LIKE, 25-PERCENT SADNESS CONSTANTLY AS A BASELINE.

The Past

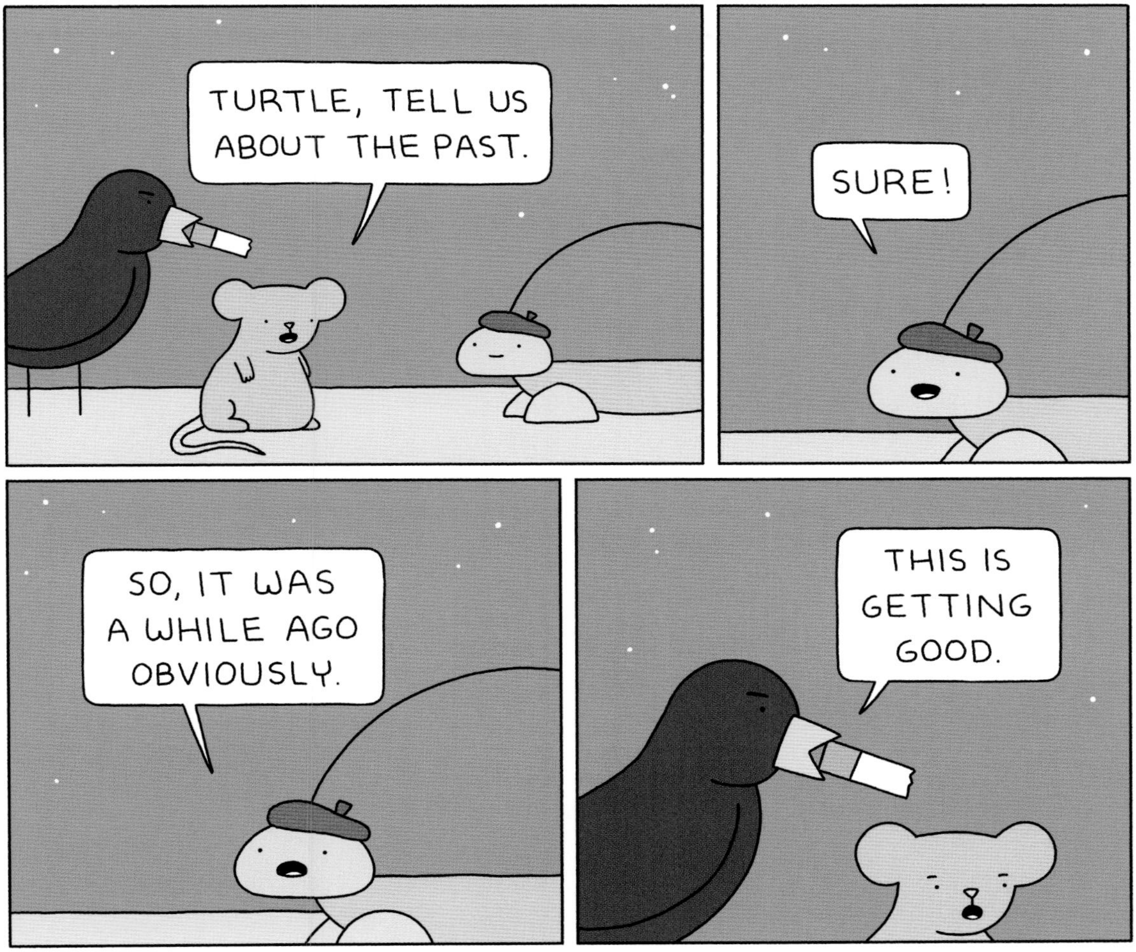
TURTLE, TELL US ABOUT THE PAST.
SURE!
SO, IT WAS A WHILE AGO OBVIOUSLY.
THIS IS GETTING GOOD.

Thank Me Later

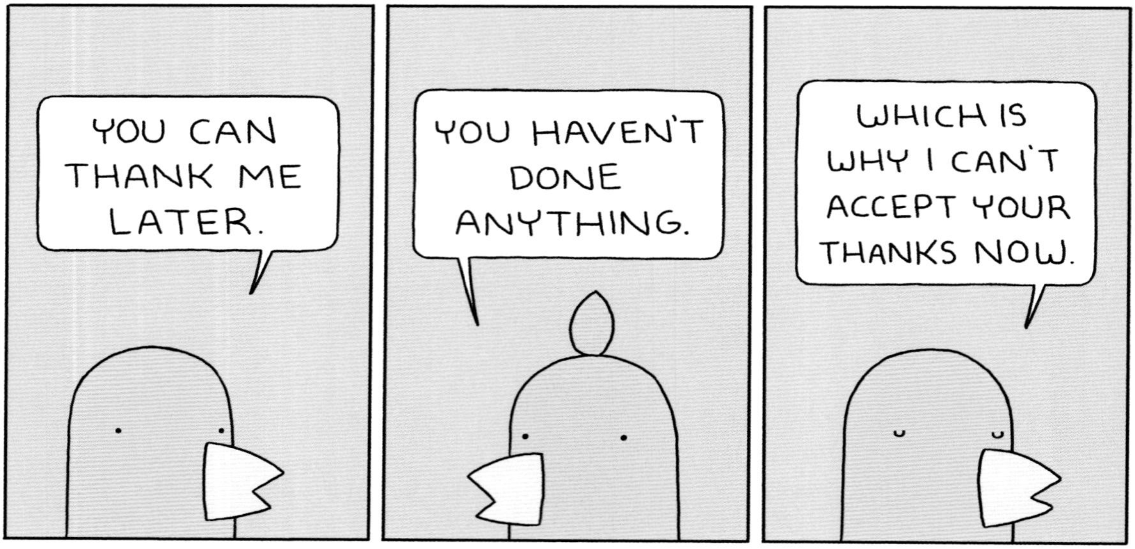

YOU CAN THANK ME LATER.
YOU HAVEN'T DONE ANYTHING.
WHICH IS WHY I CAN'T ACCEPT YOUR THANKS NOW.

Best Friend

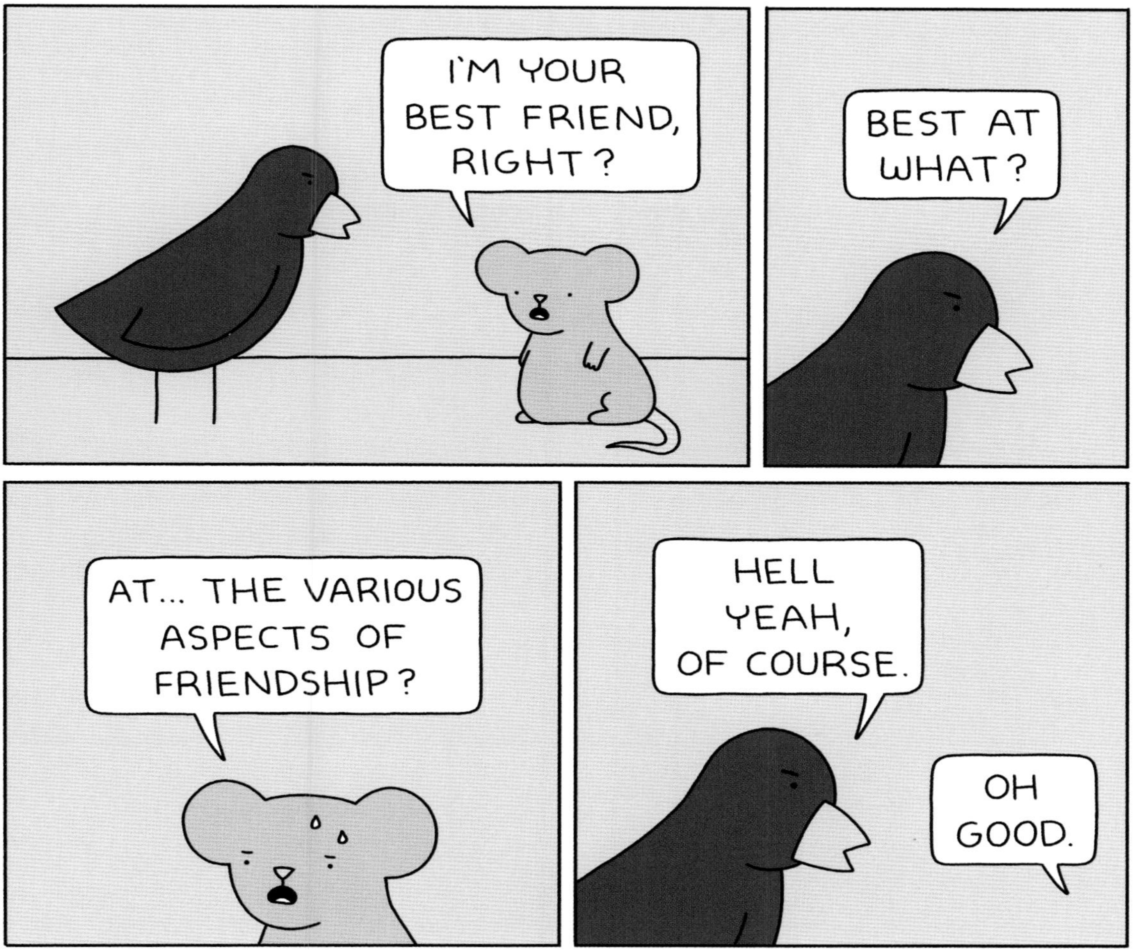
I'M YOUR BEST FRIEND, RIGHT?
BEST AT WHAT?
AT... THE VARIOUS ASPECTS OF FRIENDSHIP?
HELL YEAH, OF COURSE.
OH GOOD.

Alone

THIS IS WHERE I COME WHEN I WANT TO BE ALONE.
SO, I'M GONNA NEED YOU TO LEAVE.

Busy Day

WHAT A LONG AND BUSY DAY. LET ME THINK WHAT I GOT DONE...
Nothing.
YEAH, THAT SEEMS RIGHT.

That Hat

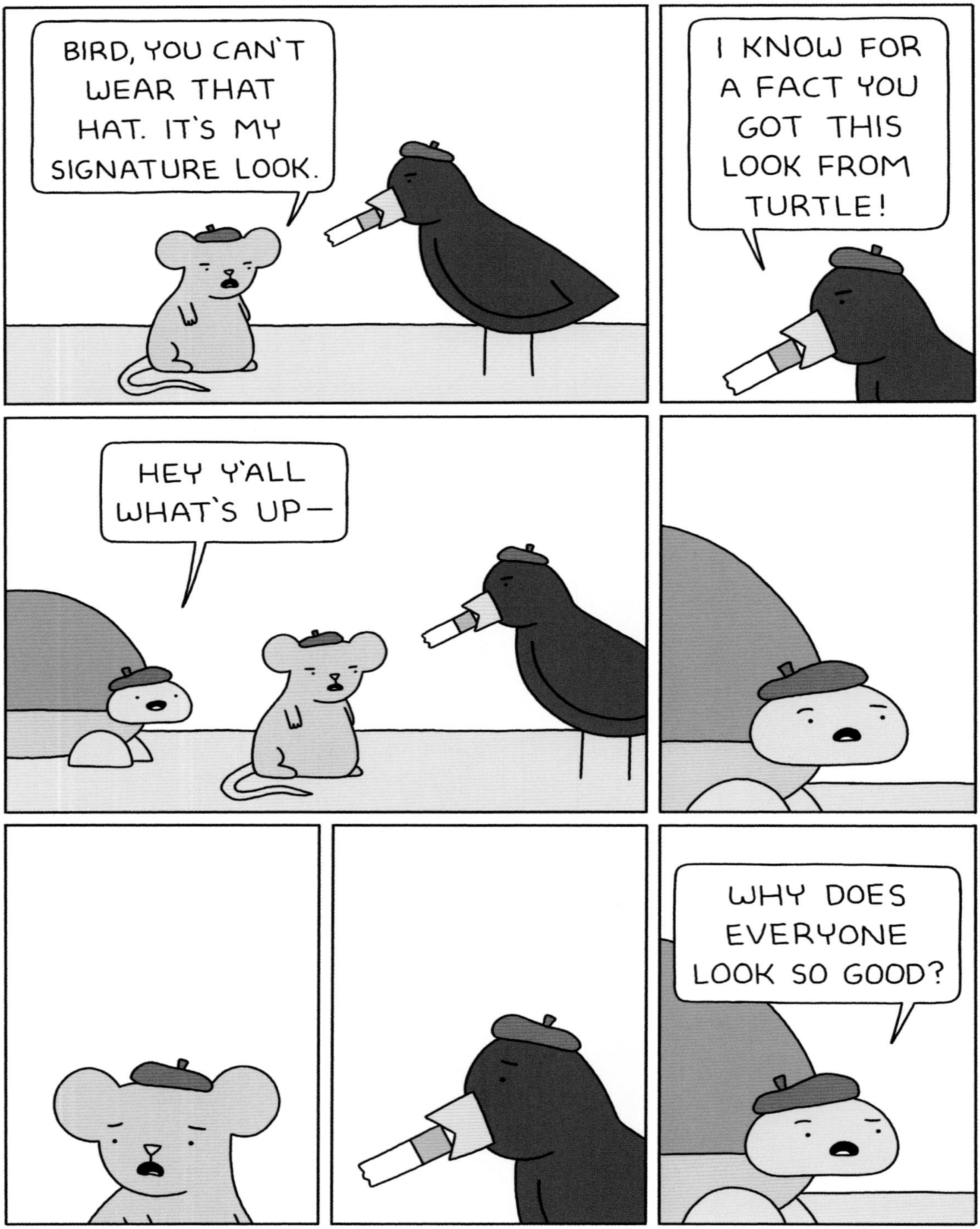
BIRD, YOU CAN'T WEAR THAT HAT. IT'S MY SIGNATURE LOOK.
I KNOW FOR A FACT YOU GOT THIS LOOK FROM TURTLE!
HEY Y'ALL WHAT'S UP—
WHY DOES EVERYONE LOOK SO GOOD?

Interesting People

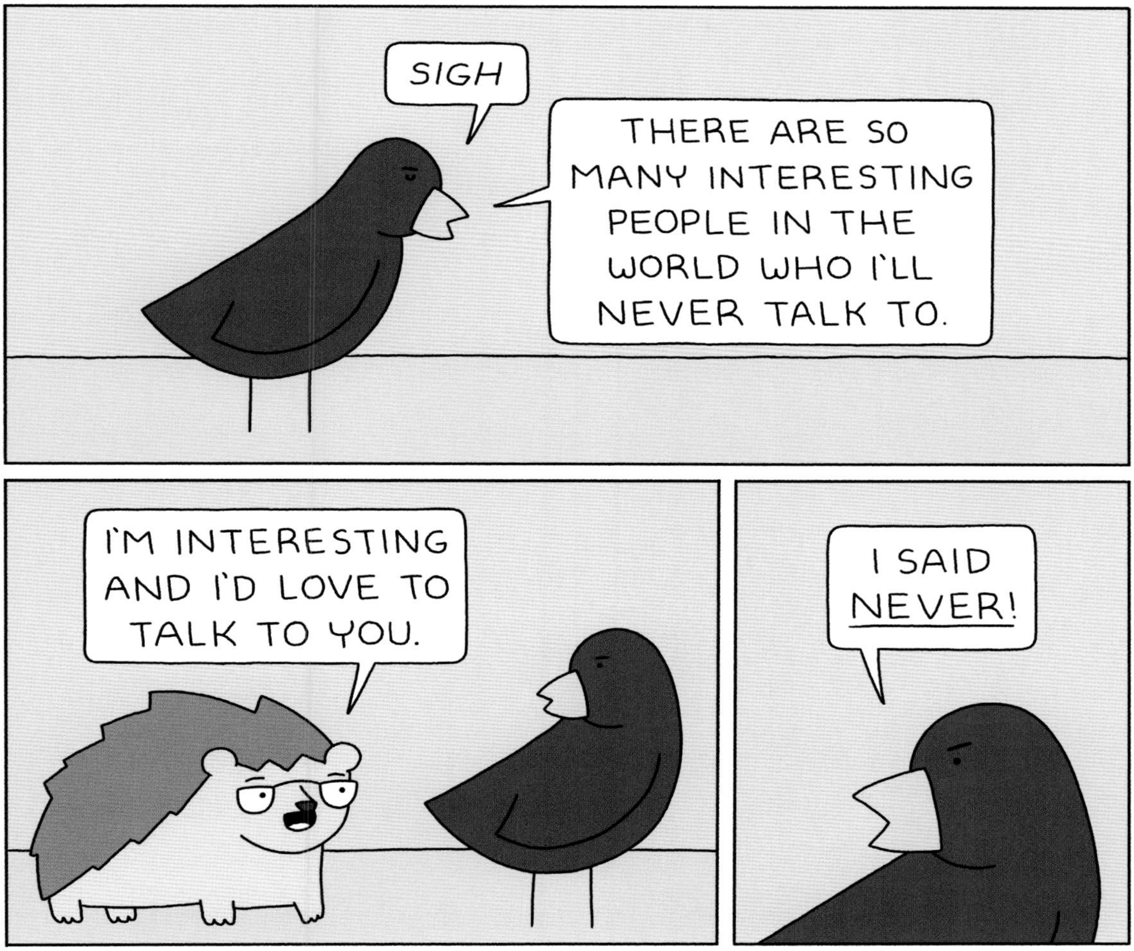
SIGH
THERE ARE SO MANY INTERESTING PEOPLE IN THE WORLD WHO I'LL NEVER TALK TO.
I'M INTERESTING AND I'D LOVE TO TALK TO YOU.
I SAID NEVER!

Running

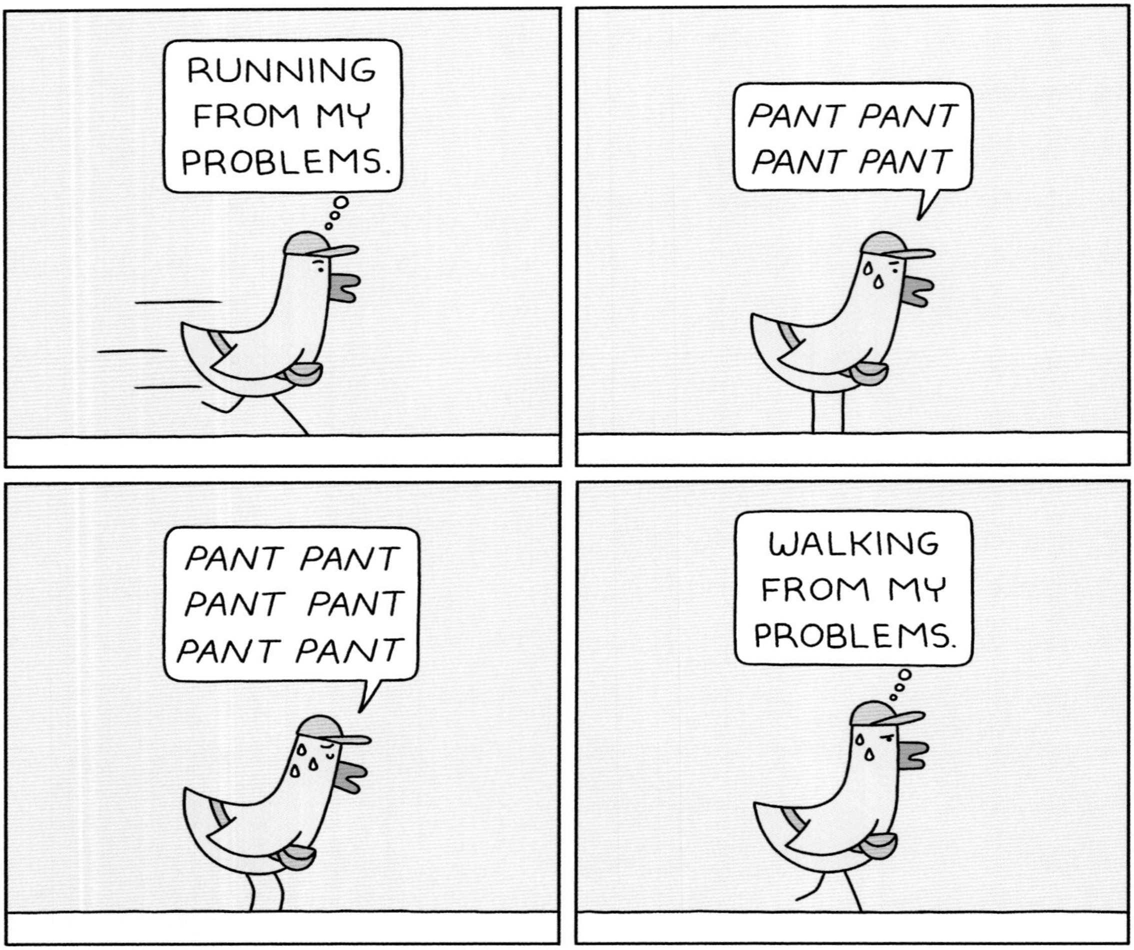
RUNNING FROM MY PROBLEMS.
PANT PANT PANT PANT
PANT PANT PANT PANT PANT PANT
WALKING FROM MY PROBLEMS.

Duties As Fish

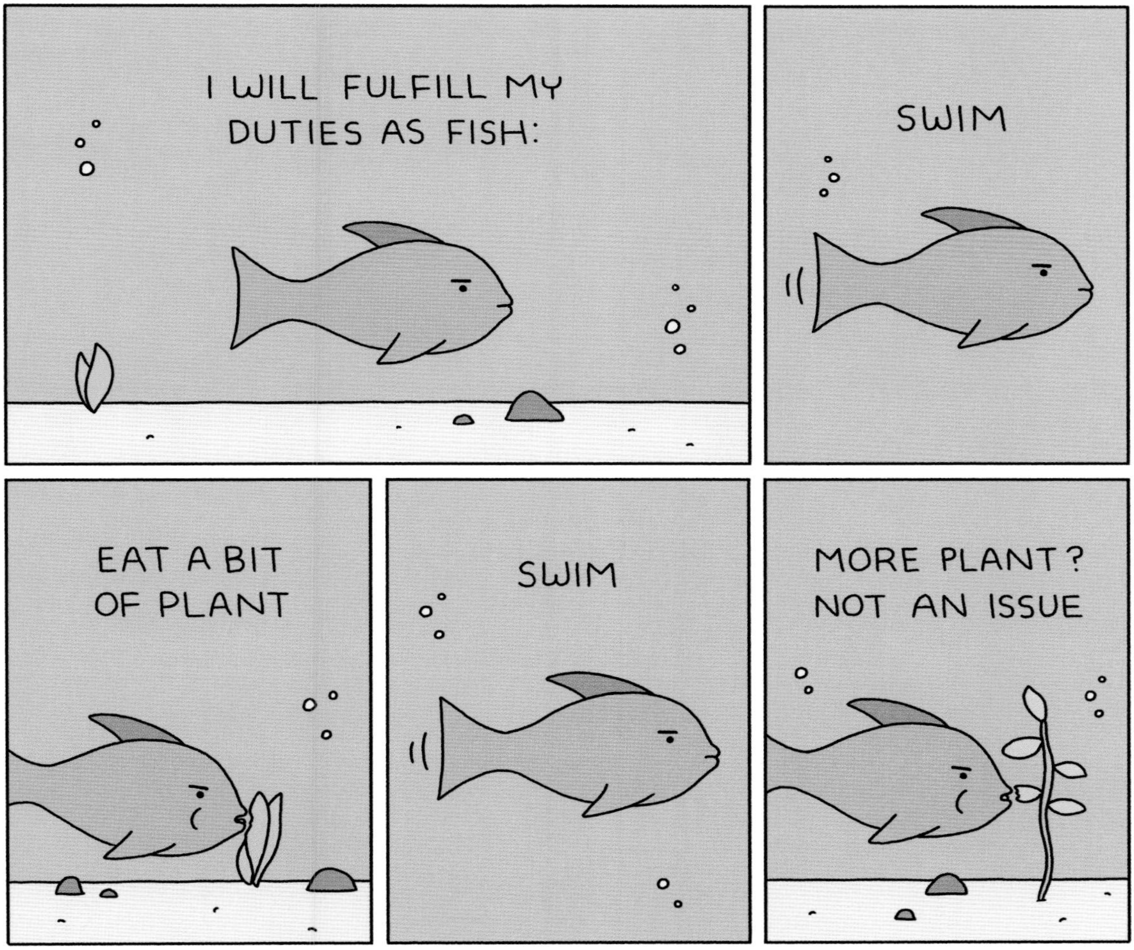
I WILL FULFILL MY DUTIES AS FISH:
SWIM
EAT A BIT OF PLANT
SWIM
MORE PLANT? NOT AN ISSUE

My Friends

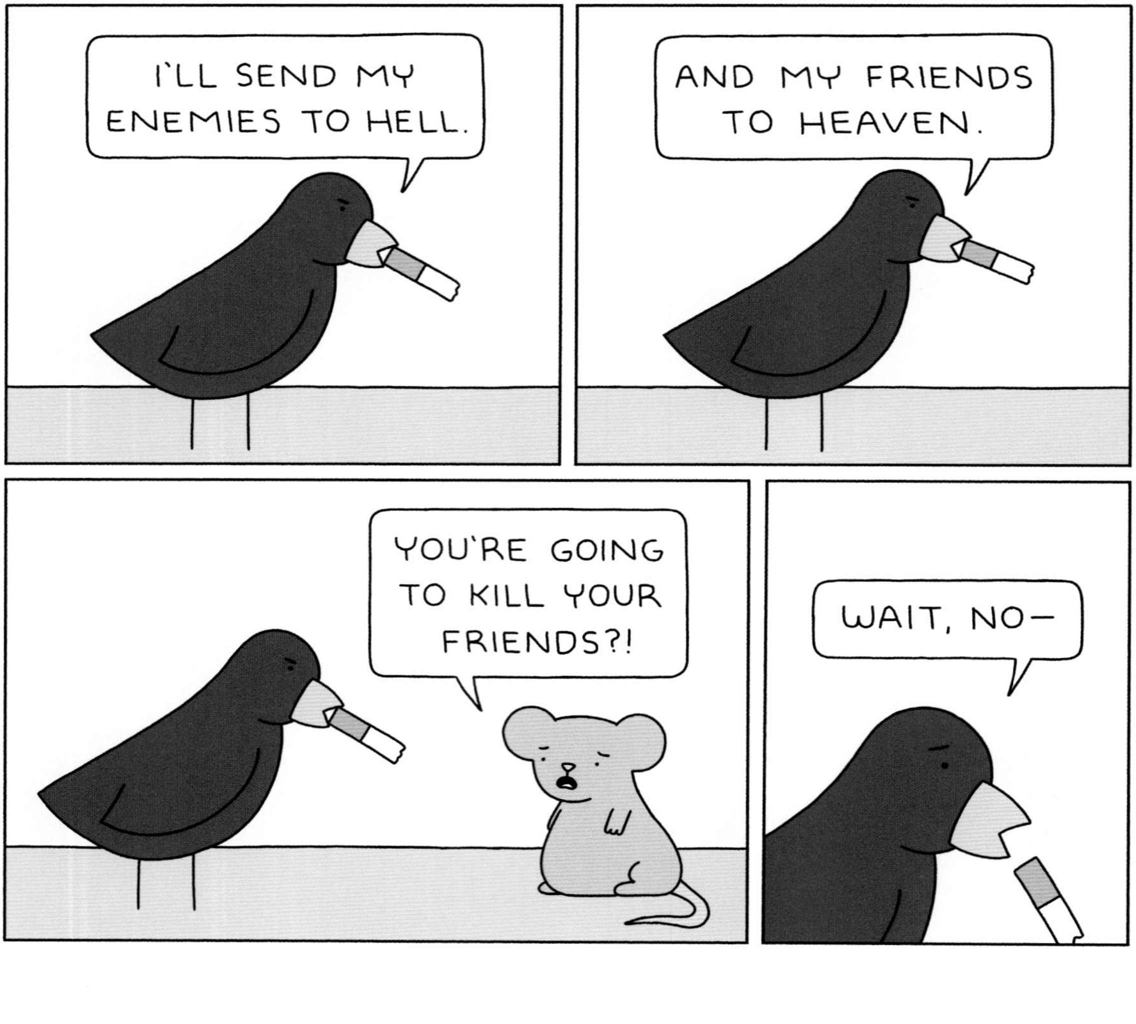
I'LL SEND MY ENEMIES TO HELL.
AND MY FRIENDS TO HEAVEN.
YOU'RE GOING TO KILL YOUR FRIENDS?!
WAIT, NO—

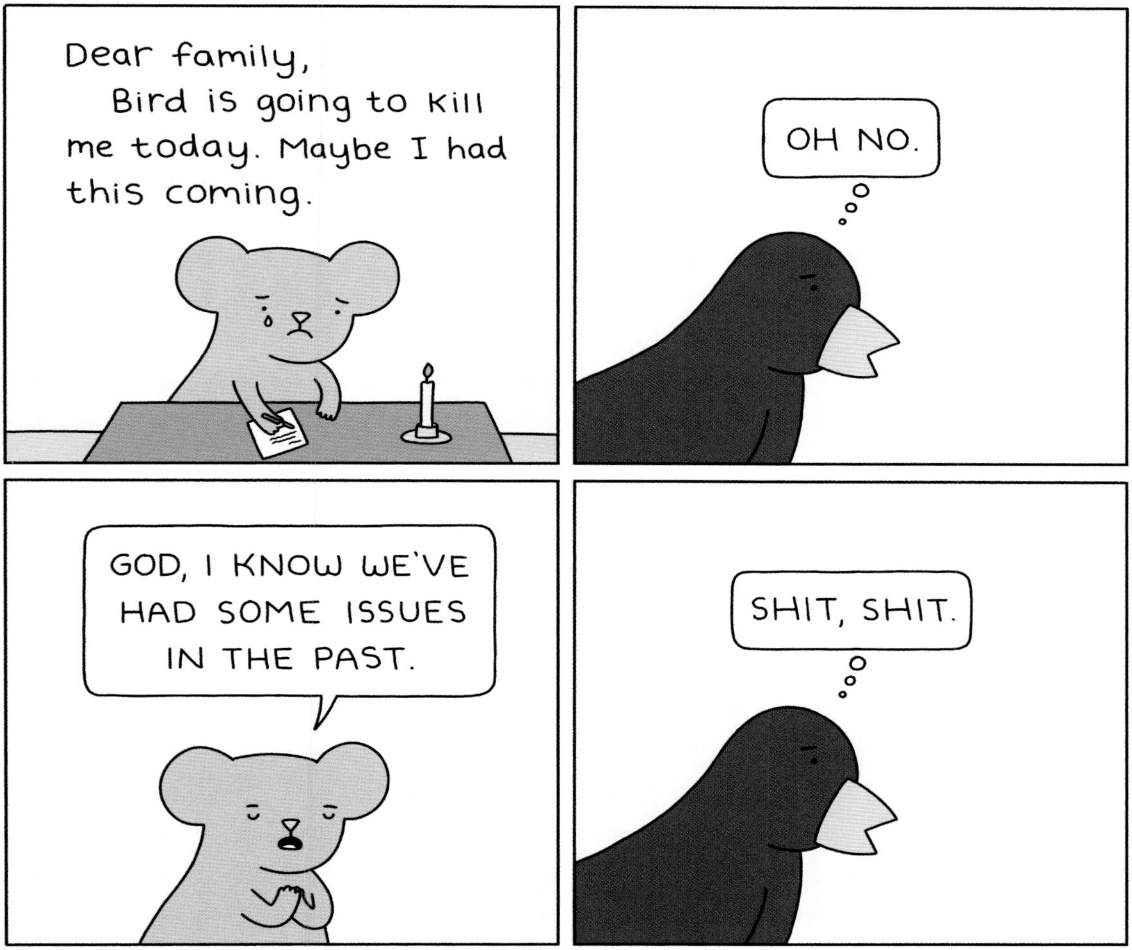
Dear family,
Bird is going to kill me today. Maybe I had this coming.
OH NO.
GOD, I KNOW WE'VE HAD SOME ISSUES IN THE PAST.
SHIT, SHIT.

Another Mess

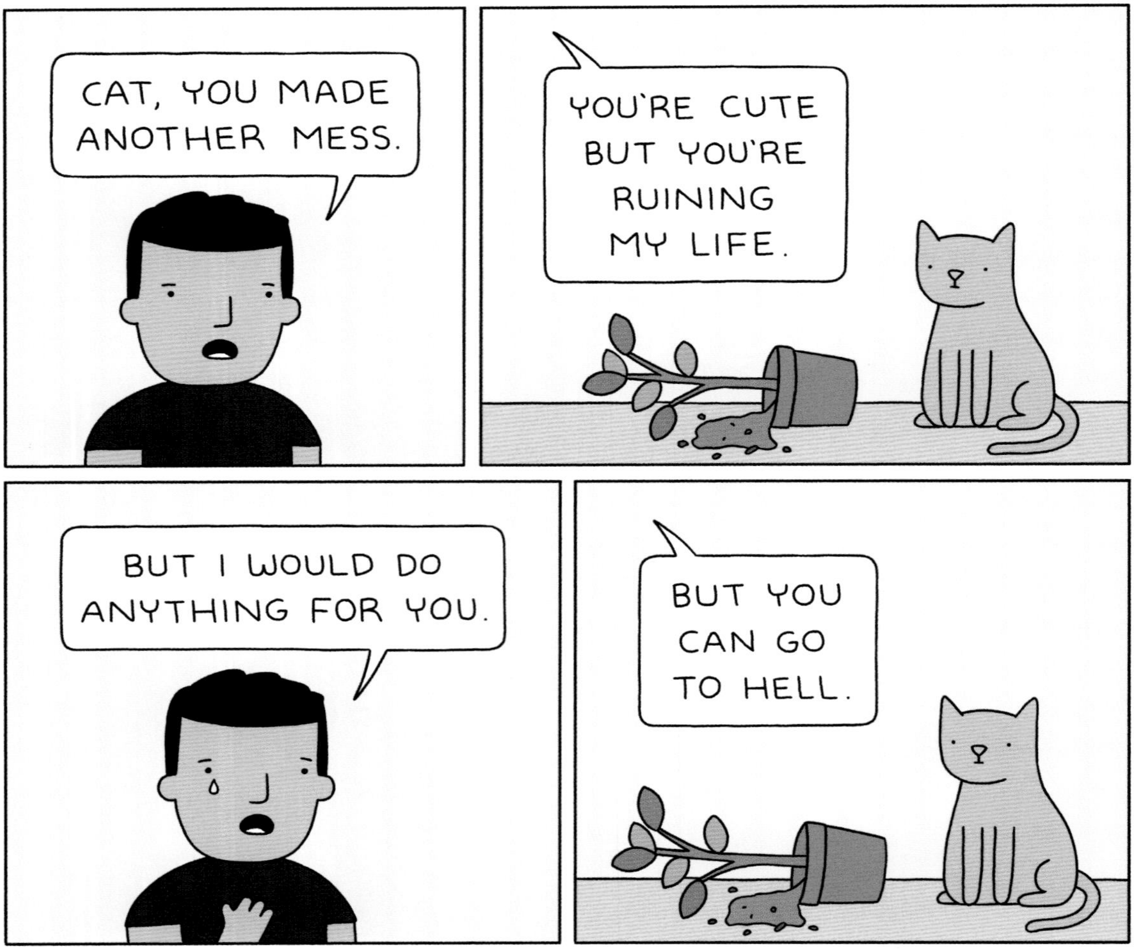
CAT, YOU MADE ANOTHER MESS.
YOU'RE CUTE BUT YOU'RE RUINING MY LIFE.
BUT I WOULD DO ANYTHING FOR YOU.
BUT YOU CAN GO TO HELL.

More Decisive

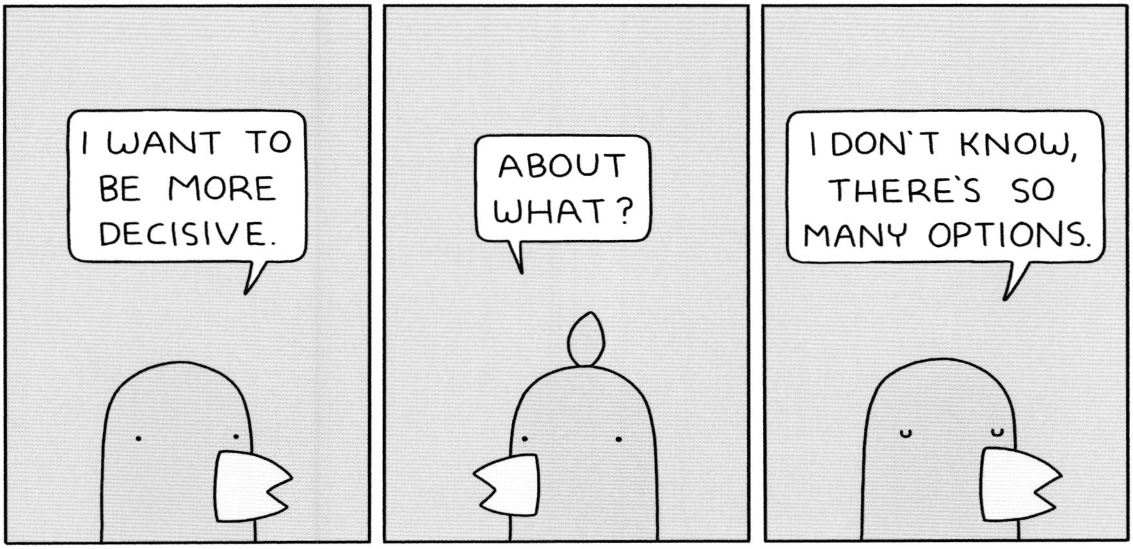
I WANT TO BE MORE DECISIVE.
ABOUT WHAT?
I DON'T KNOW, THERE'S SO MANY OPTIONS.

To-Do List

THIS IS MY TO-DO LIST.
IT'S WHERE I KEEP TRACK OF ALL THE THINGS I'M NOT DOING.

How's Life

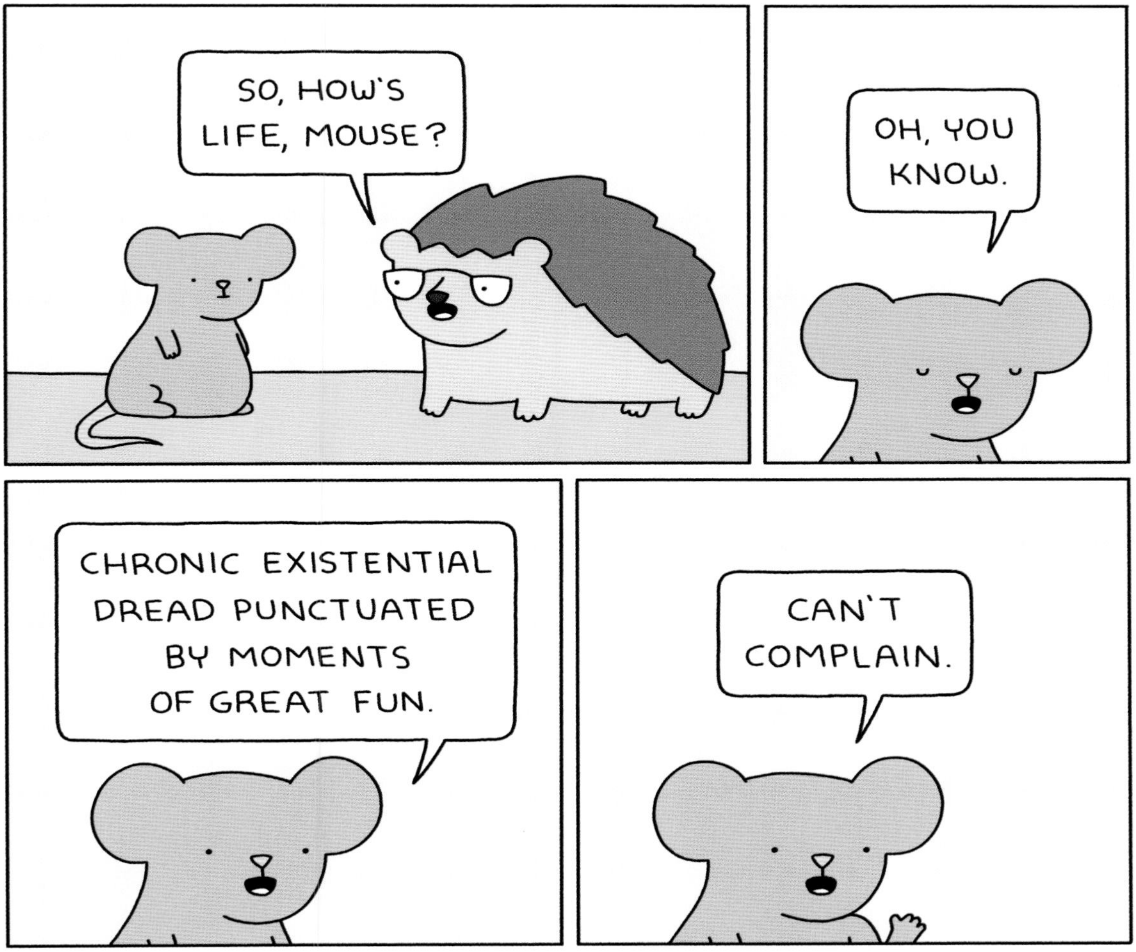
SO, HOW'S LIFE, MOUSE?
OH, YOU KNOW.
CHRONIC EXISTENTIAL DREAD PUNCTUATED BY MOMENTS OF GREAT FUN.
CAN'T COMPLAIN.

All My Clothes

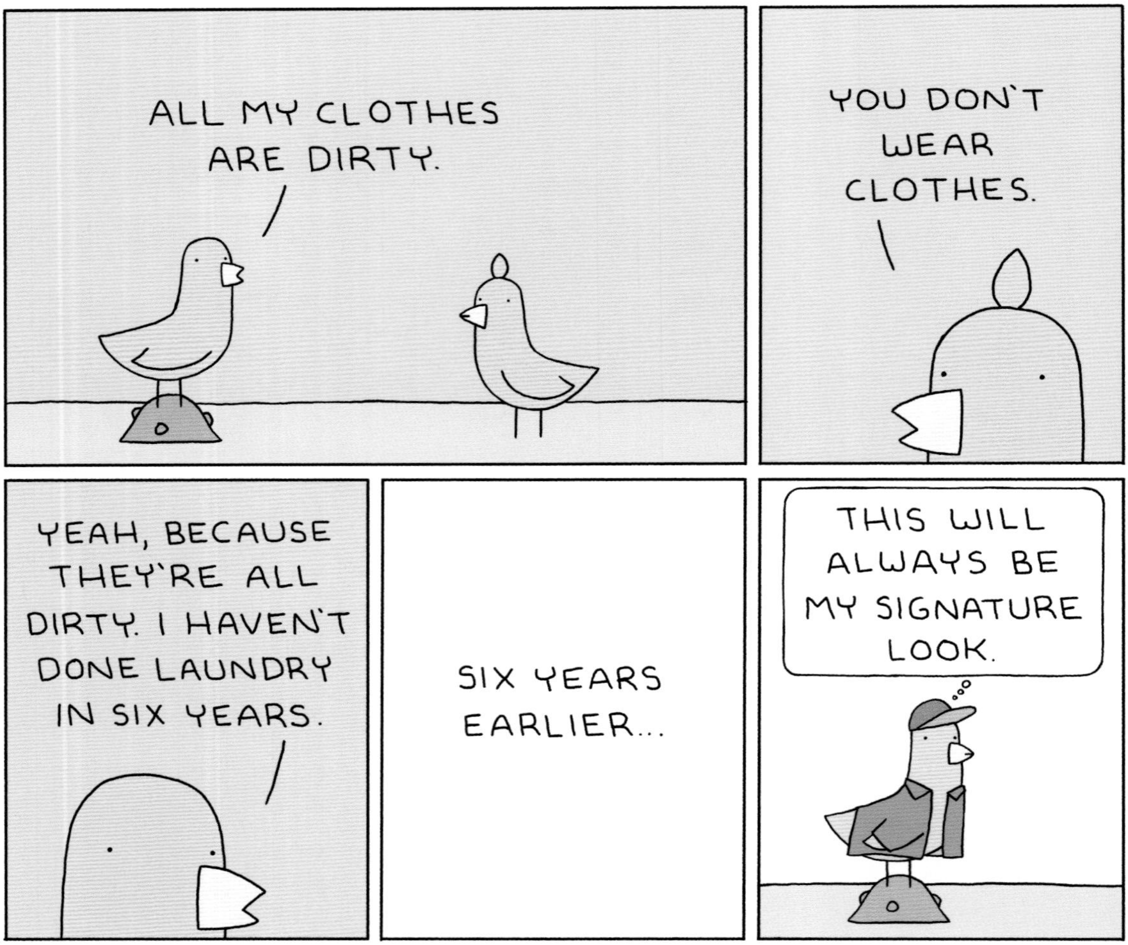
ALL MY CLOTHES ARE DIRTY.
YOU DON'T WEAR CLOTHES.
YEAH, BECAUSE THEY'RE ALL DIRTY. I HAVEN'T DONE LAUNDRY IN SIX YEARS.
SIX YEARS EARLIER...
THIS WILL ALWAYS BE MY SIGNATURE LOOK.

A Trip

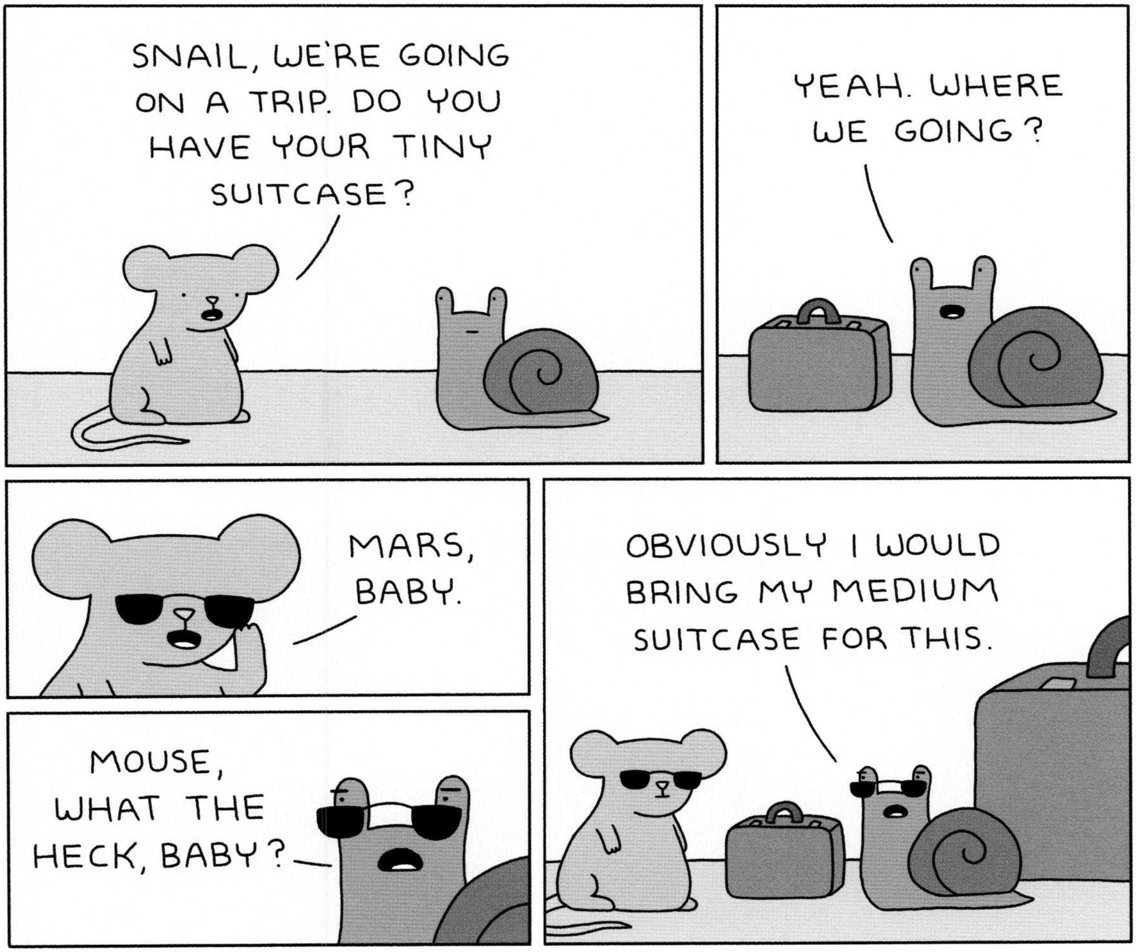
SNAIL, WE'RE GOING ON A TRIP. DO YOU HAVE YOUR TINY SUITCASE?
YEAH. WHERE WE GOING?
MARS, BABY.
MOUSE, WHAT THE HECK, BABY?
OBVIOUSLY I WOULD BRING MY MEDIUM SUITCASE FOR THIS.

We're Off

OKAY, WE'RE OFF TO MARS.
ARE YOU SURE THIS IS A SPACESHIP?
YEAH, SNAIL FOUND IT.
I ACQUIRED IT THROUGH AN ONLINE AUCTION WEBSITE.
DOESN'T IT NEED A ROOF?
SNAIL, DOES IT NEED A ROOF?
HONESTLY, I DON'T KNOW.

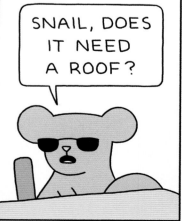

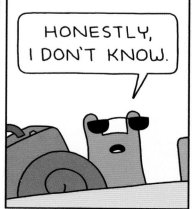

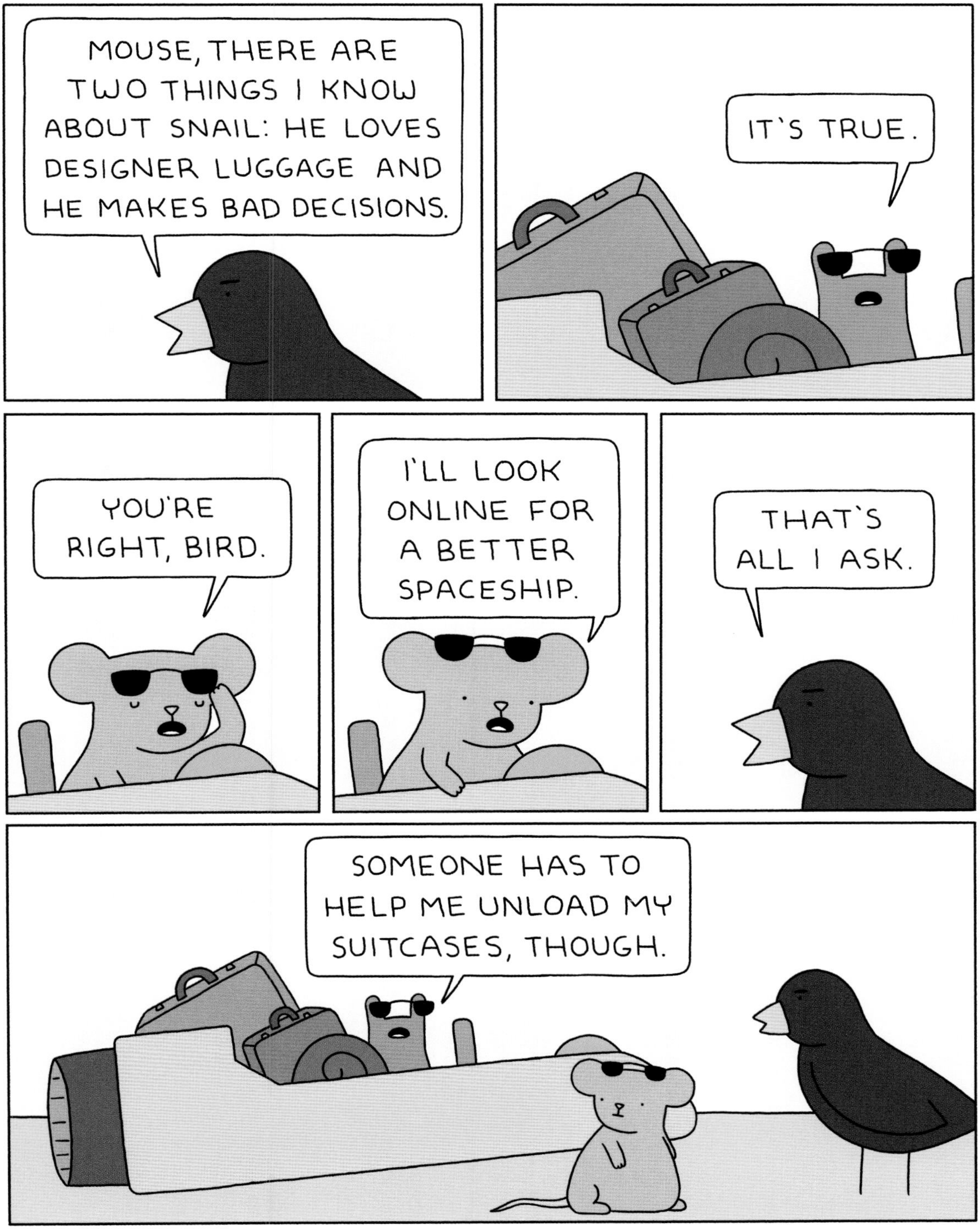
MOUSE, THERE ARE TWO THINGS I KNOW ABOUT SNAIL: HE LOVES DESIGNER LUGGAGE AND HE MAKES BAD DECISIONS.
IT'S TRUE.
YOU'RE RIGHT, BIRD.
I'LL LOOK ONLINE FOR A BETTER SPACESHIP.
THAT'S ALL I ASK.
SOMEONE HAS TO HELP ME UNLOAD MY SUITCASES, THOUGH.

Self-Doubt

SOMETIMES I HAVE MOMENTS OF SELF-DOUBT.
AM I... TOO INCREDIBLE?

Been Places

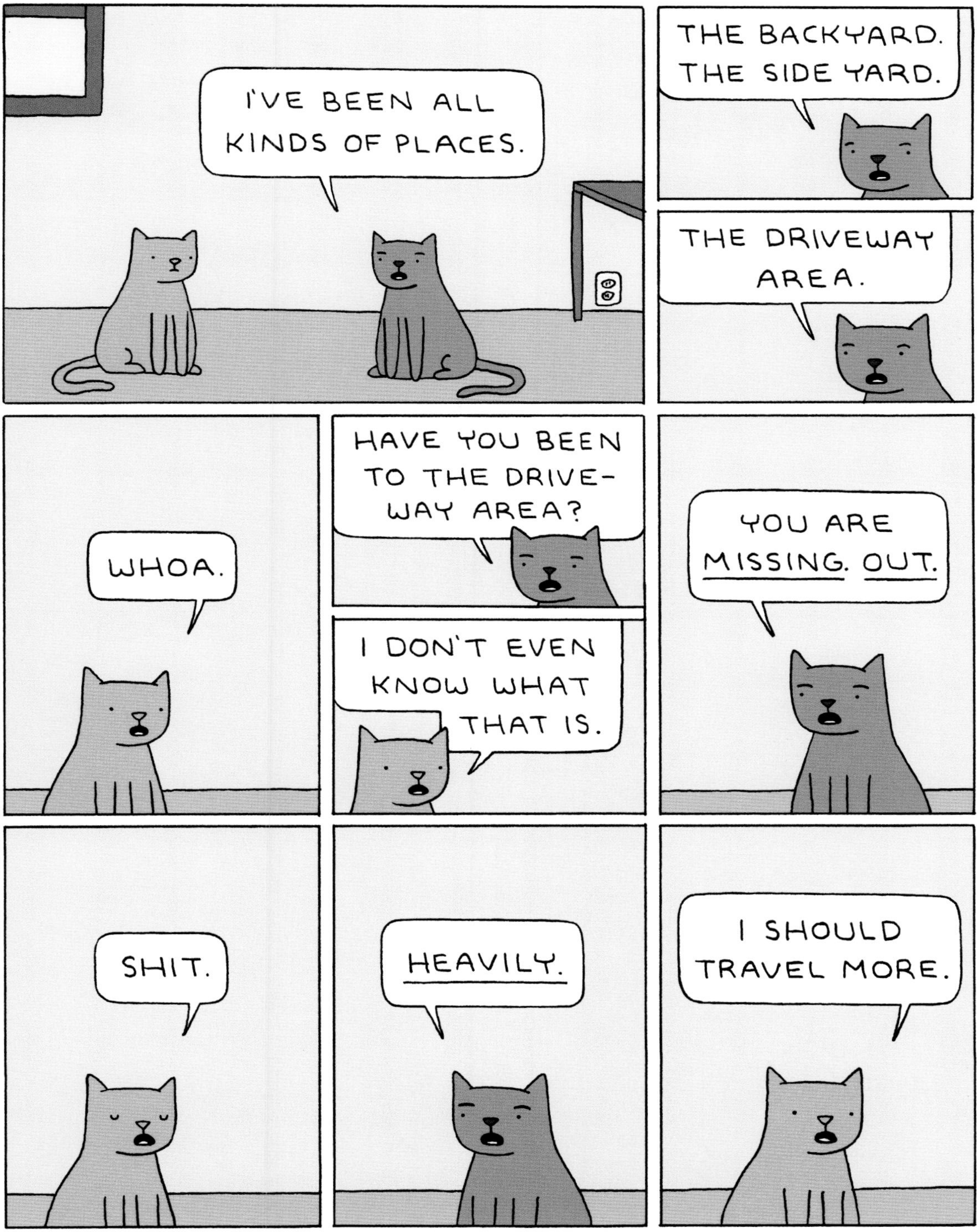
I'VE BEEN ALL KINDS OF PLACES.
THE BACKYARD. THE SIDE YARD.
THE DRIVEWAY AREA.
WHOA.
HAVE YOU BEEN TO THE DRIVE-WAY AREA?
I DON'T EVEN KNOW WHAT THAT IS.
YOU ARE MISSING. OUT.
SHIT.
HEAVILY.
I SHOULD TRAVEL MORE.

Okay

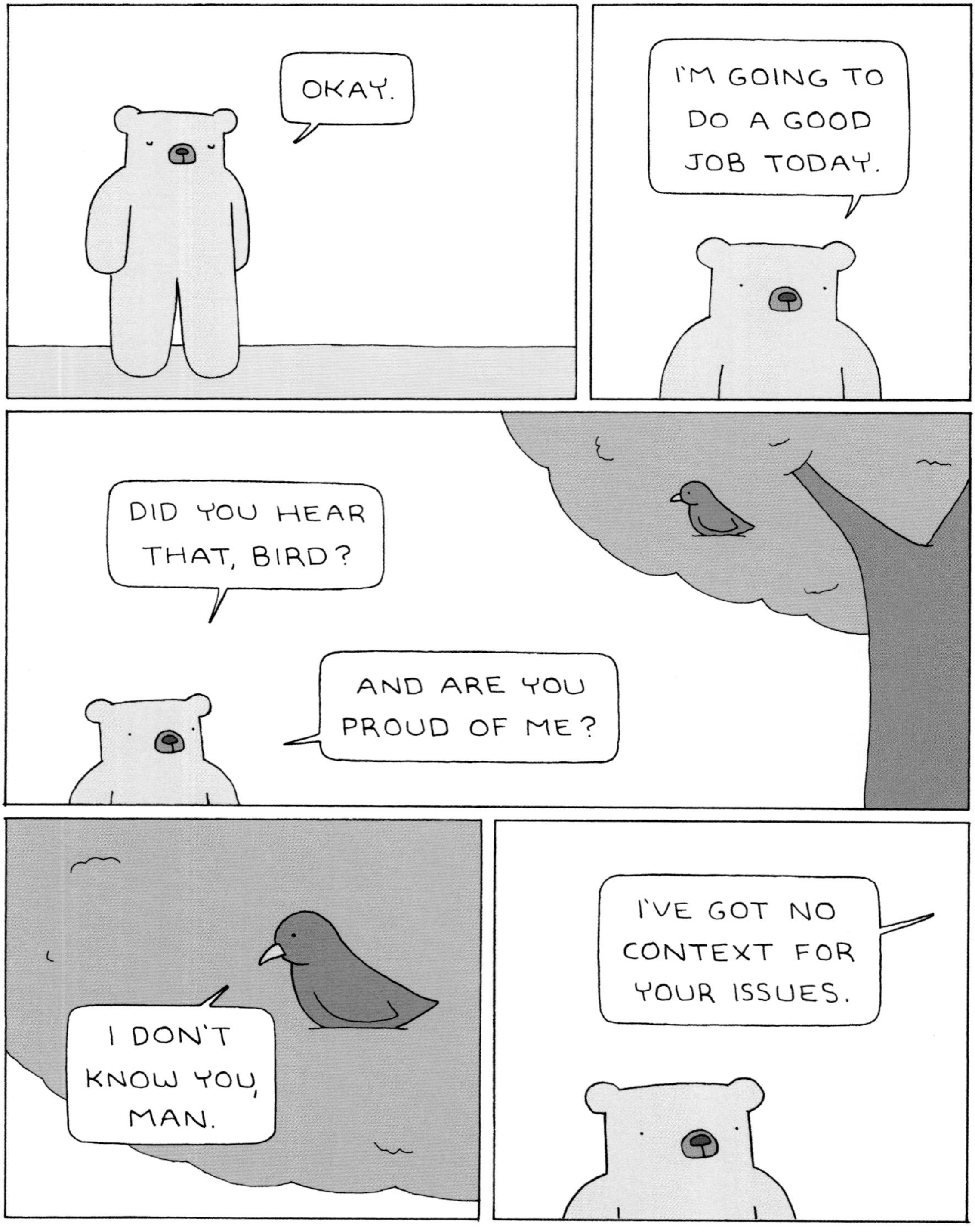
OKAY.
I'M GOING TO DO A GOOD JOB TODAY.
DID YOU HEAR THAT, BIRD?
AND ARE YOU PROUD OF ME?
I DON'T KNOW YOU, MAN.
I'VE GOT NO CONTEXT FOR YOUR ISSUES.

Been a Fish

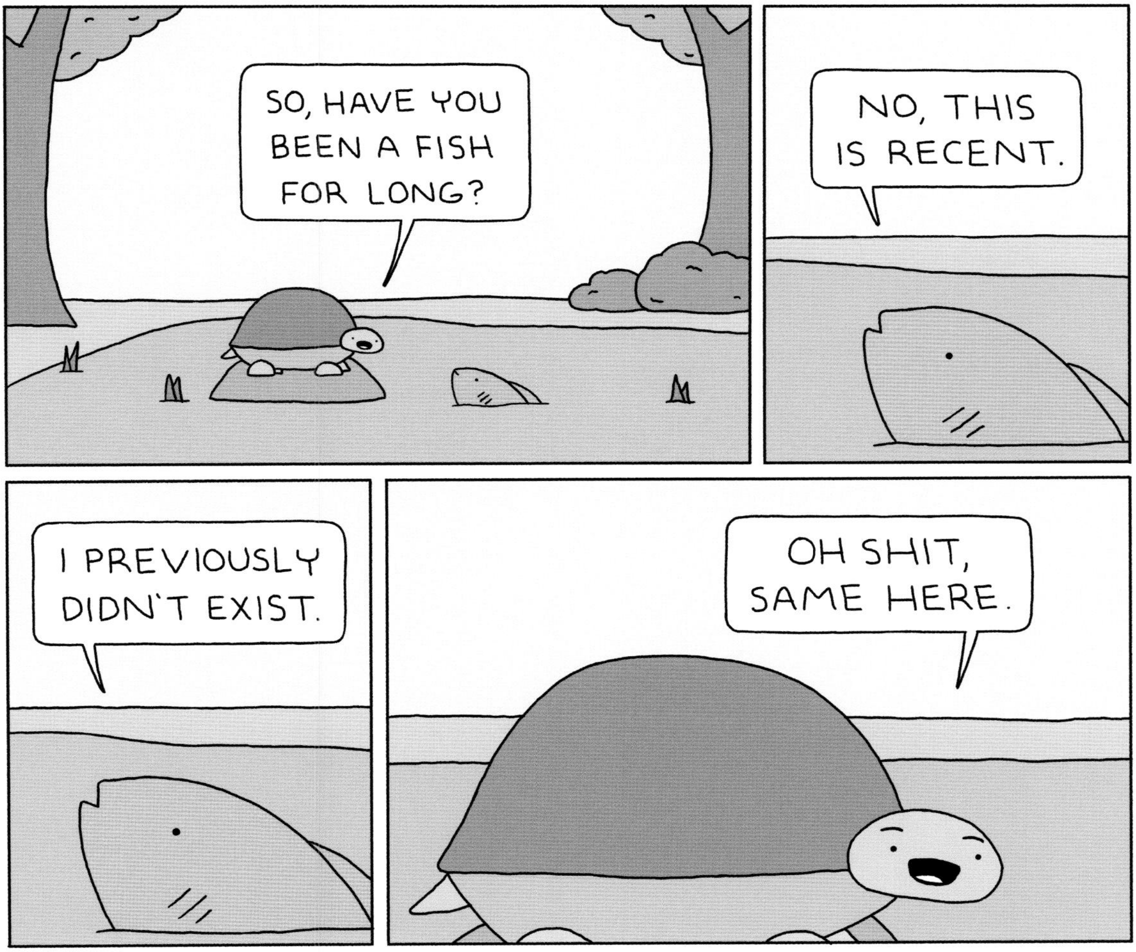
SO, HAVE YOU BEEN A FISH FOR LONG?
NO, THIS IS RECENT.
I PREVIOUSLY DIDN'T EXIST.
OH SHIT, SAME HERE.

Authenticity

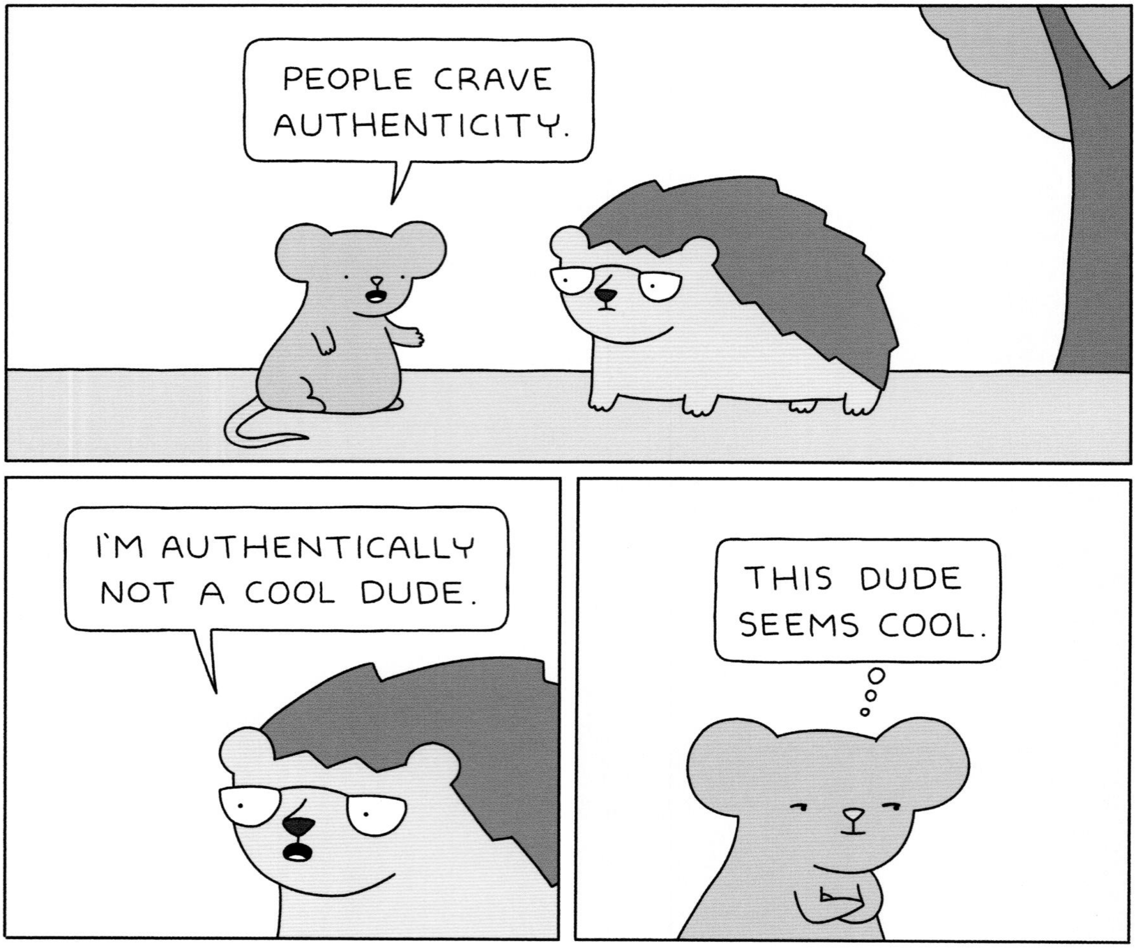
PEOPLE CRAVE AUTHENTICITY.
I'M AUTHENTICALLY NOT A COOL DUDE.
THIS DUDE SEEMS COOL.

Need to Focus

I JUST NEED TO FOCUS FOR, LIKE, FIVE MINUTES.
AND FIGURE OUT MY ENTIRE LIFE.

Found the Ocean

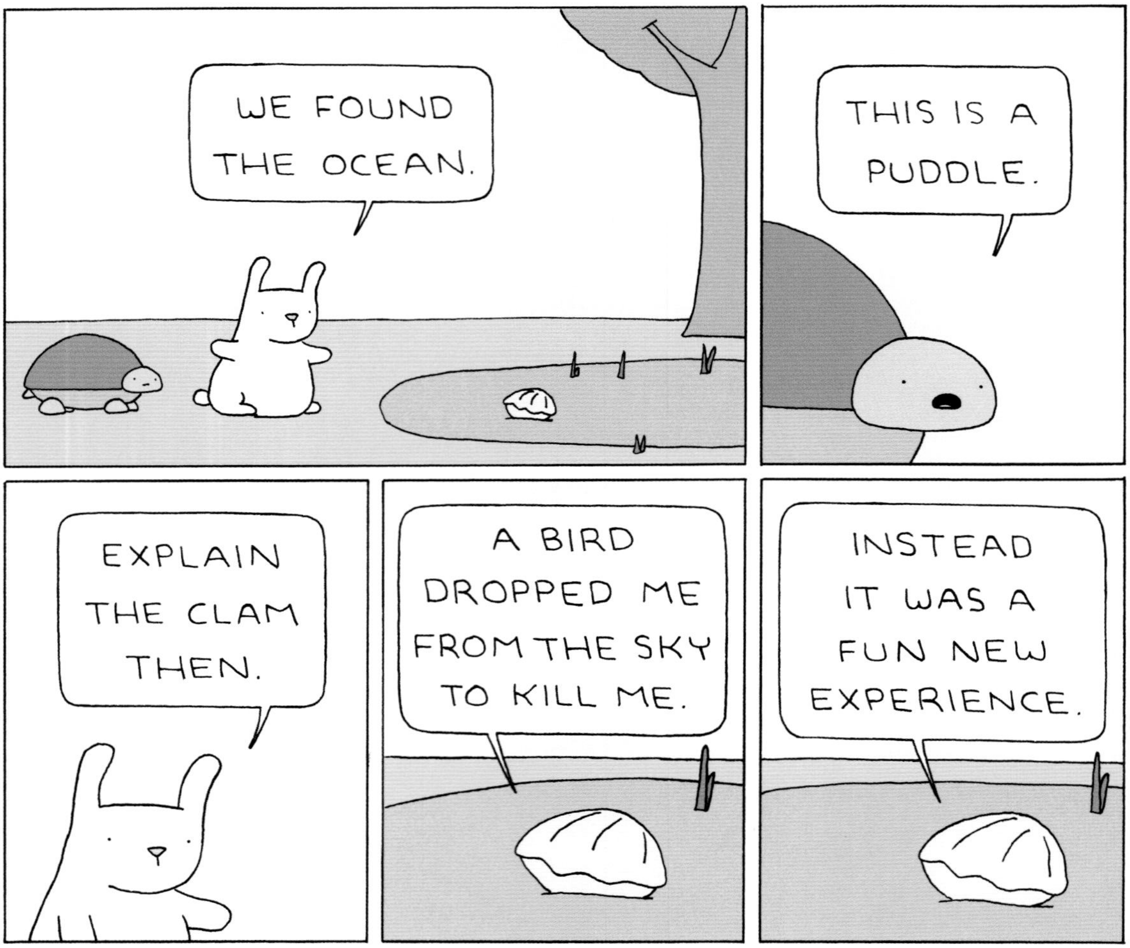
WE FOUND THE OCEAN.
THIS IS A PUDDLE.
EXPLAIN THE CLAM THEN.
A BIRD DROPPED ME FROM THE SKY TO KILL ME.
INSTEAD IT WAS A FUN NEW EXPERIENCE.

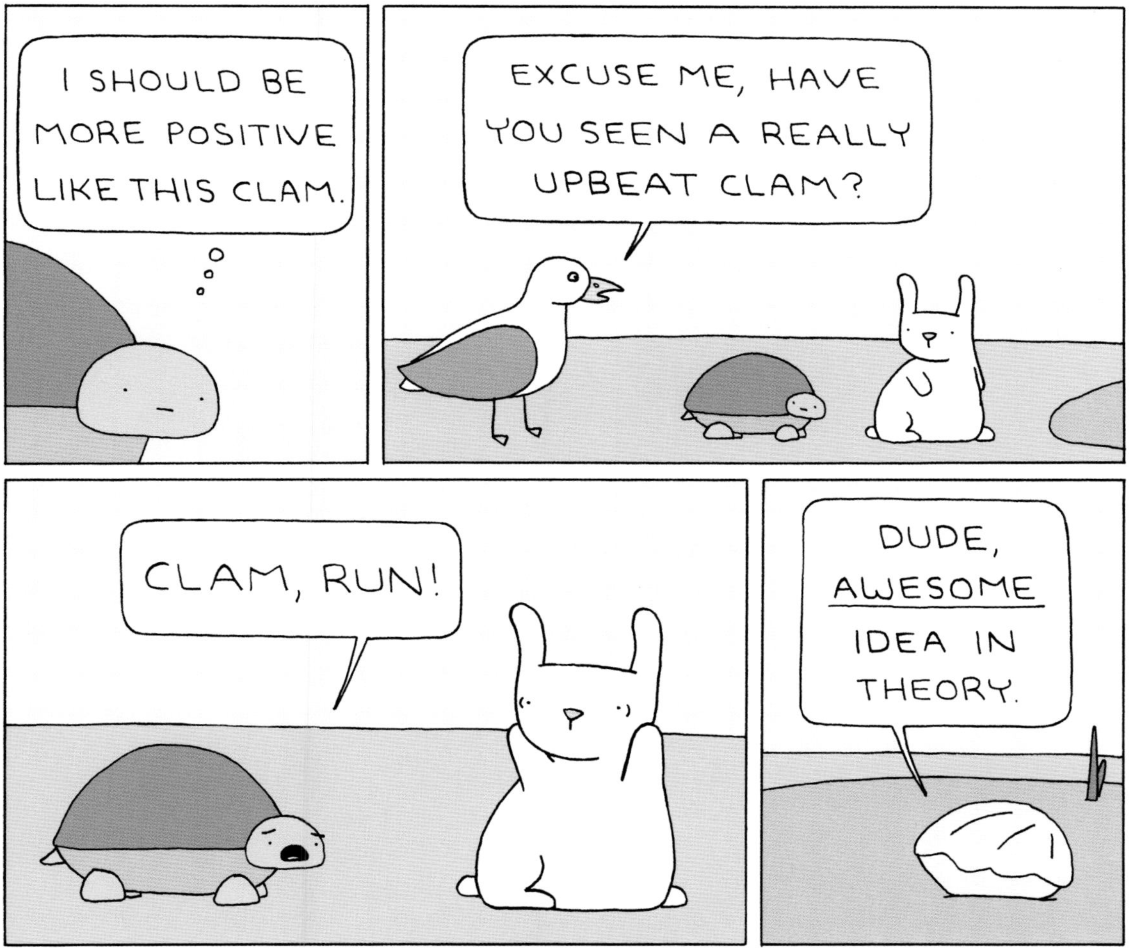
I SHOULD BE MORE POSITIVE LIKE THIS CLAM.
EXCUSE ME, HAVE YOU SEEN A REALLY UPBEAT CLAM?
CLAM, RUN!
DUDE, AWESOME IDEA IN THEORY.

Over This

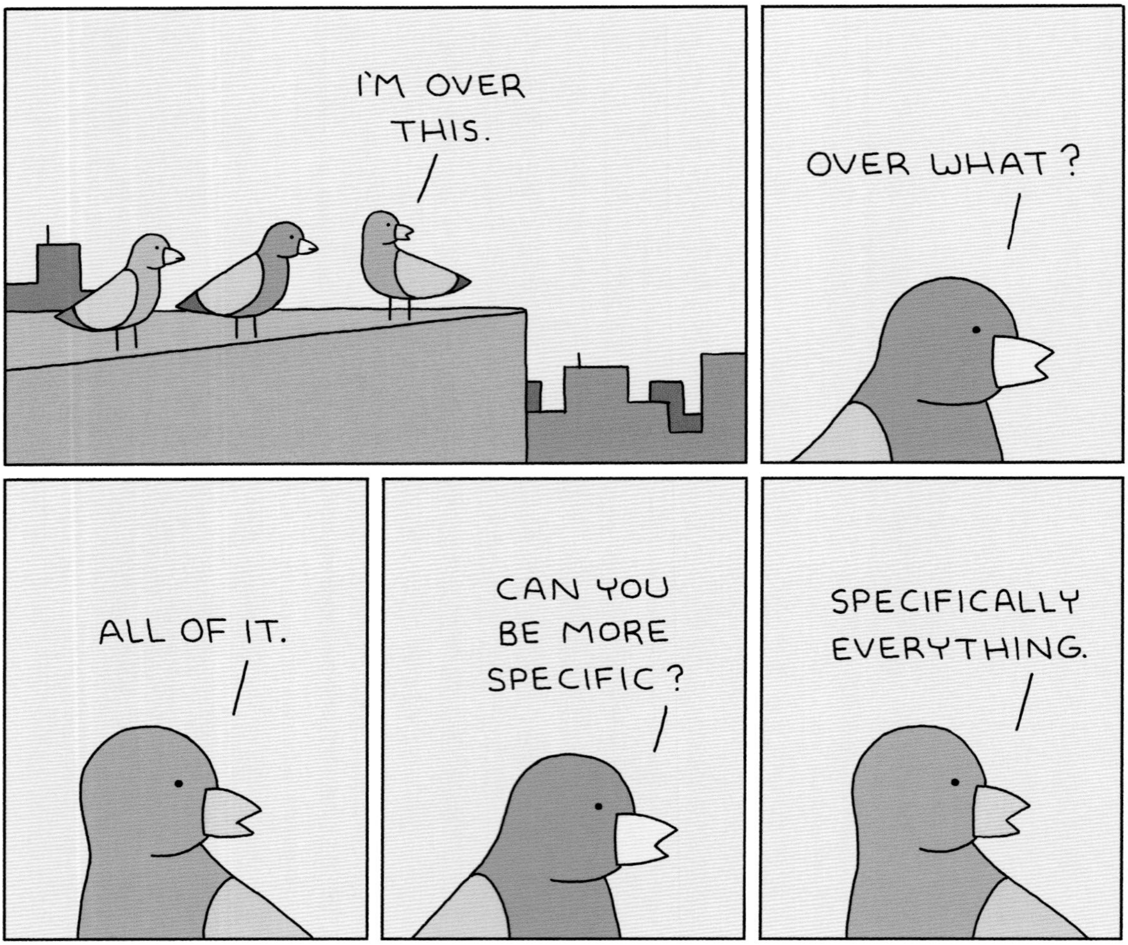
I'M OVER THIS.
OVER WHAT?
ALL OF IT.
CAN YOU BE MORE SPECIFIC?
SPECIFICALLY EVERYTHING.

Future Mouse

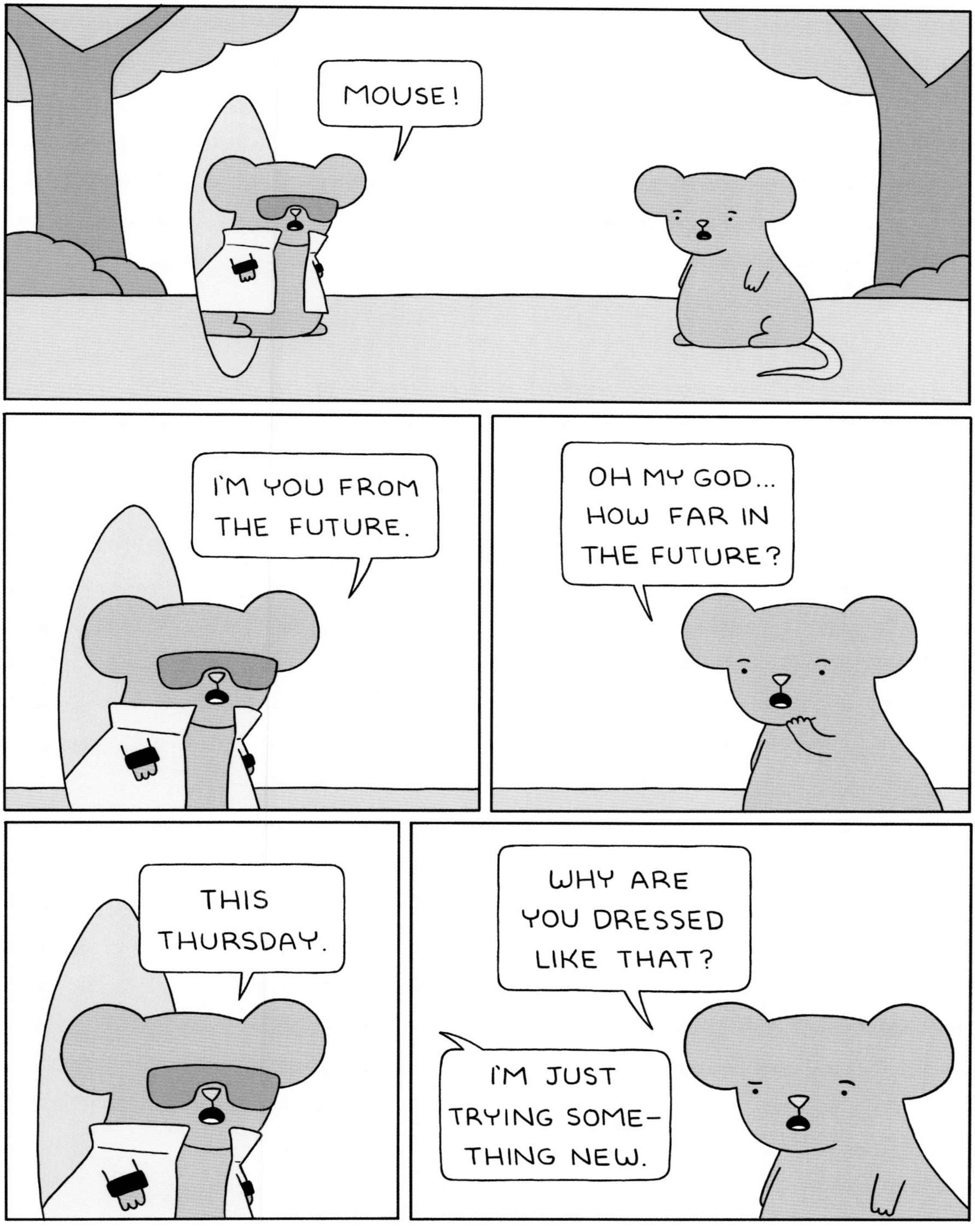
MOUSE!
I'M YOU FROM THE FUTURE.
OH MY GOD... HOW FAR IN THE FUTURE?
THIS THURSDAY.
WHY ARE YOU DRESSED LIKE THAT?
I'M JUST TRYING SOME-THING NEW.

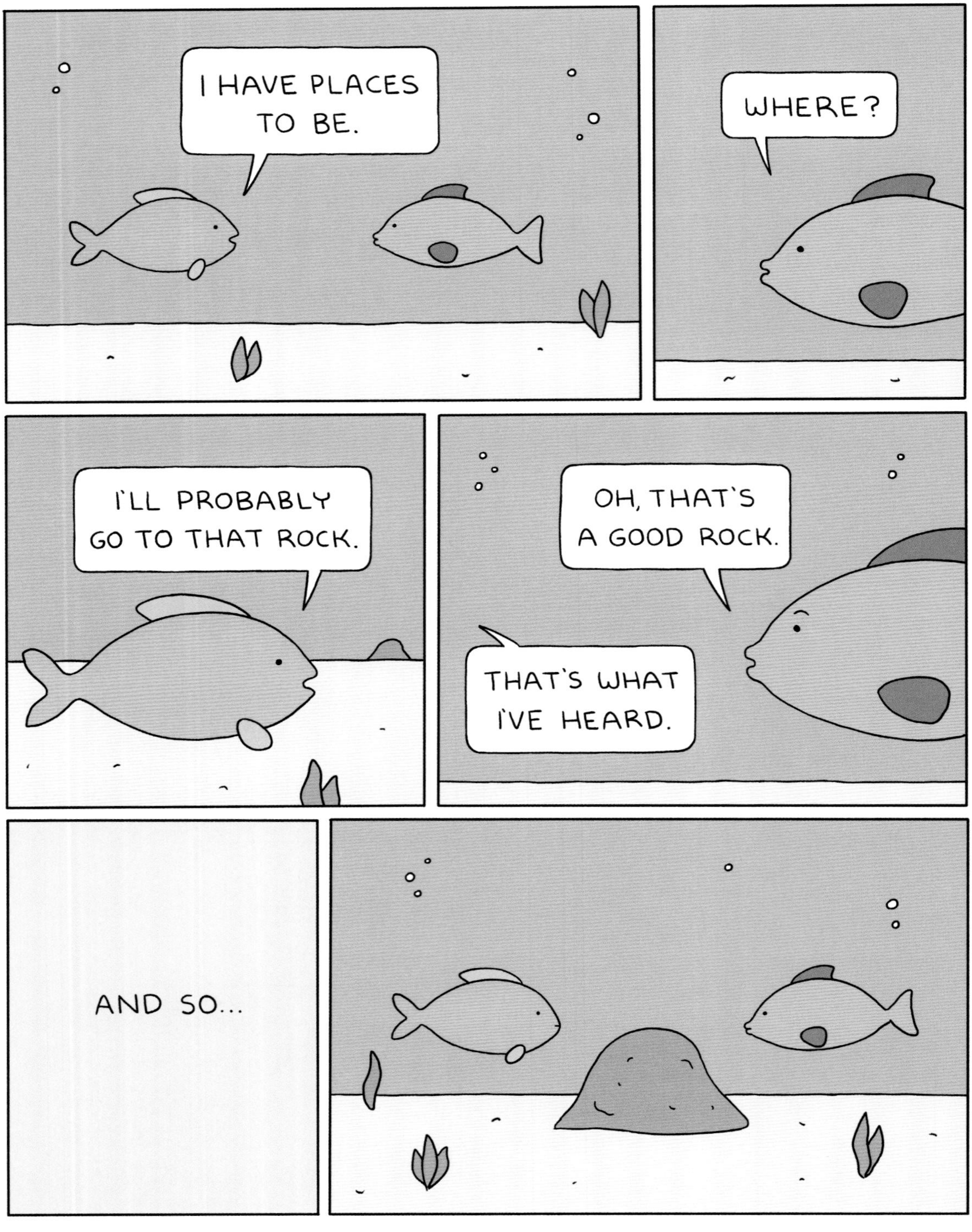
I HAVE PLACES TO BE.
WHERE?
I'LL PROBABLY GO TO THAT ROCK.
OH, THAT'S A GOOD ROCK.
THAT'S WHAT I'VE HEARD.
AND SO...

YEAH, THIS IS GREAT.
ONE OF THE NICER ROCKS.
DO YOU KEEP TRACK OF THE ROCKS YOU SEE?
LIKE, TAKE NOTE OF THEIR CHARACTERISTICS IN A SPECIAL JOURNAL?
NO, NO. IF I MAKE IT TOO TECHNICAL IT WON'T BE FUN ANYMORE.
YEAH, TOTALLY. I FEEL THAT.
I'M JUST GONNA WRITE DOWN A COUPLE THINGS.

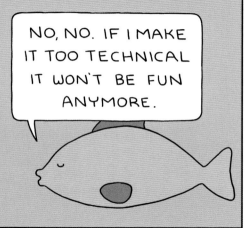

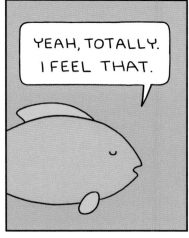

A Mistake

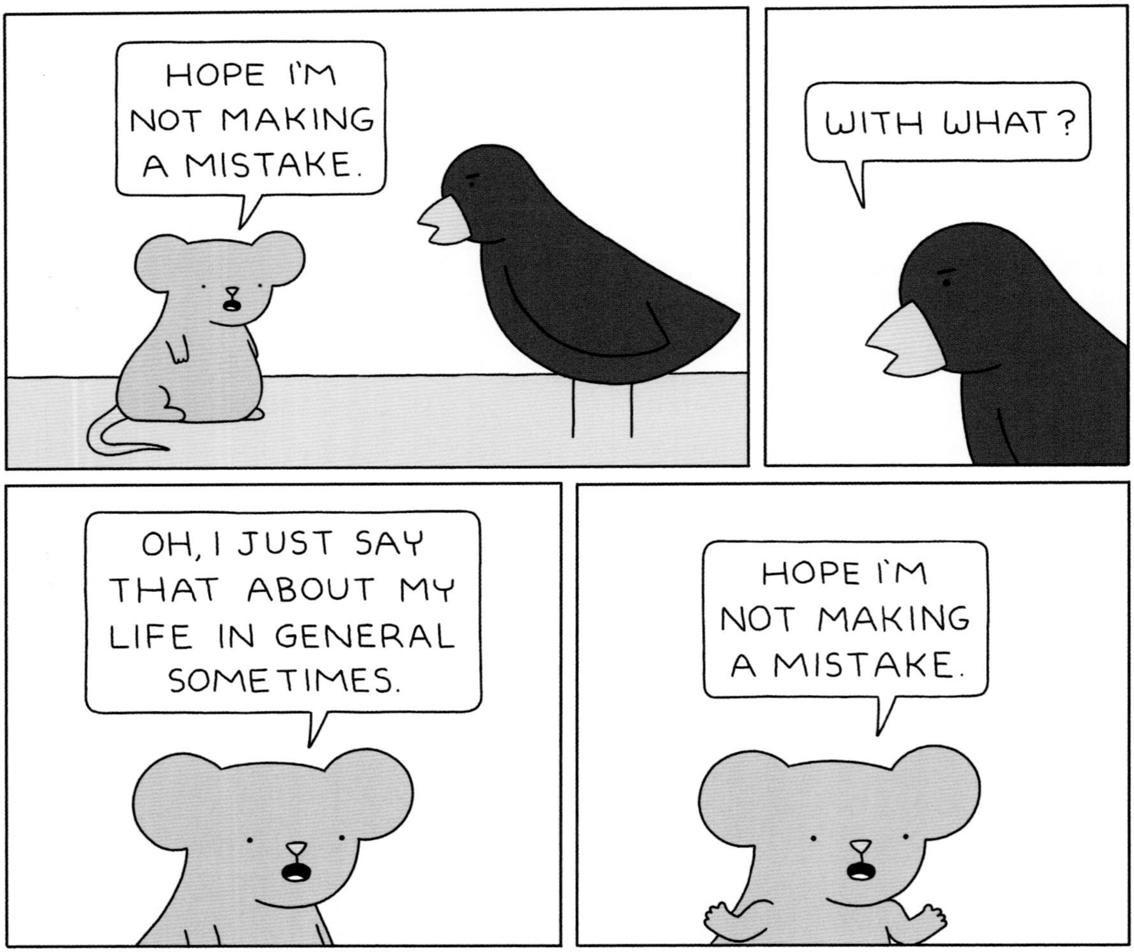
HOPE I'M NOT MAKING A MISTAKE.
WITH WHAT?
OH, I JUST SAY THAT ABOUT MY LIFE IN GENERAL SOMETIMES.
HOPE I'M NOT MAKING A MISTAKE.

Plan

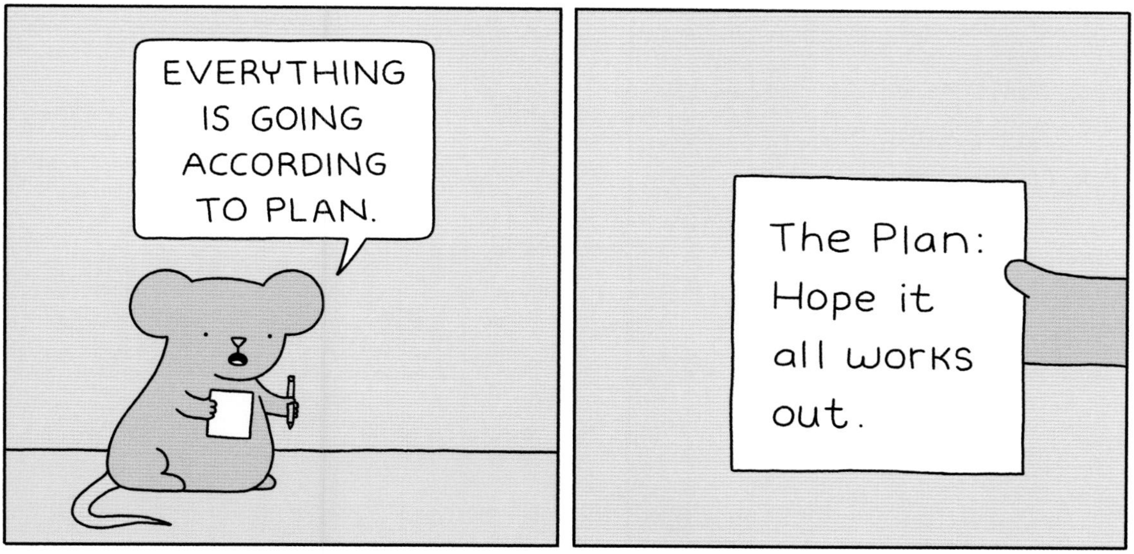
EVERYTHING IS GOING ACCORDING TO PLAN.
The Plan: Hope it all works out.

Ask Too Much

SOMETIMES YOU ASK TOO MUCH OF PEOPLE.
I DO?
GIVE ME 14 EXAMPLES.

Improve

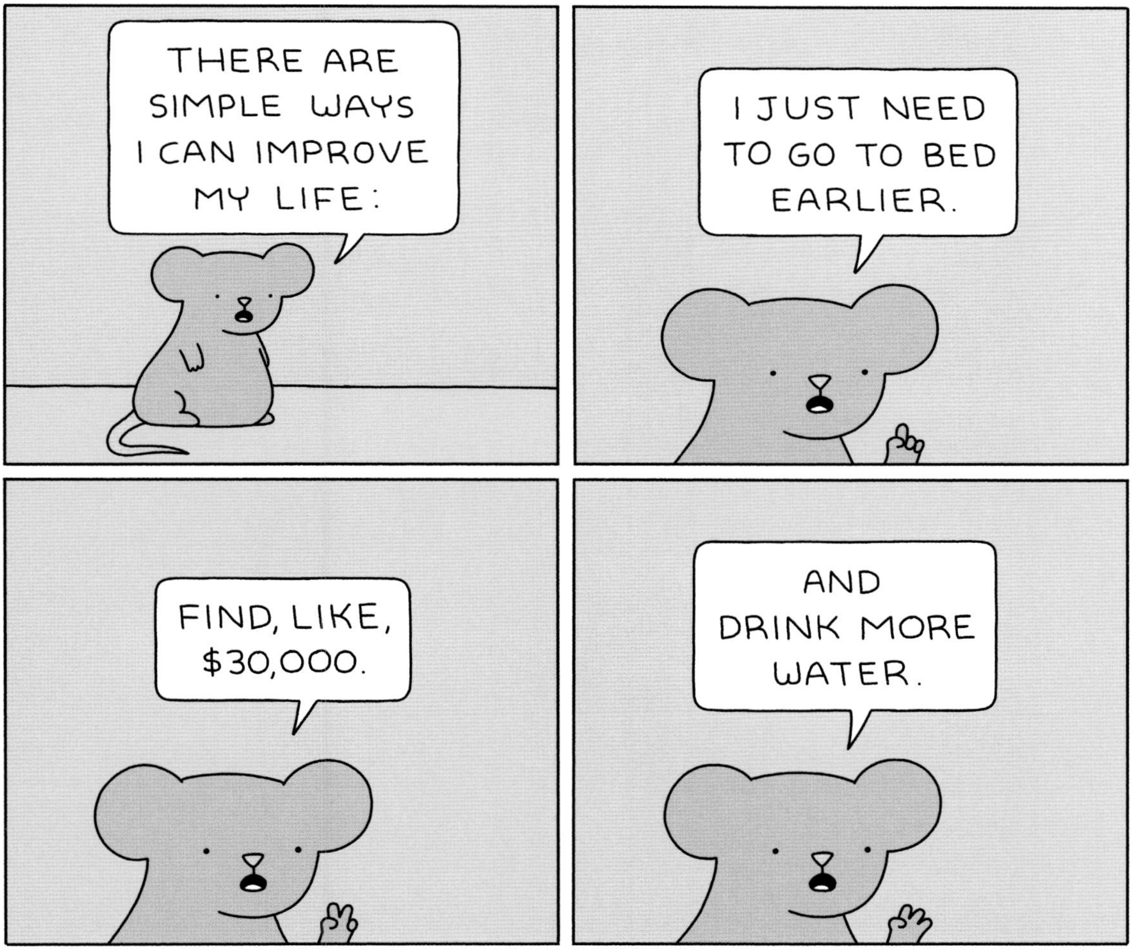
THERE ARE SIMPLE WAYS I CAN IMPROVE MY LIFE:
I JUST NEED TO GO TO BED EARLIER.
FIND, LIKE, $30,000.
AND DRINK MORE WATER.

Sunlight

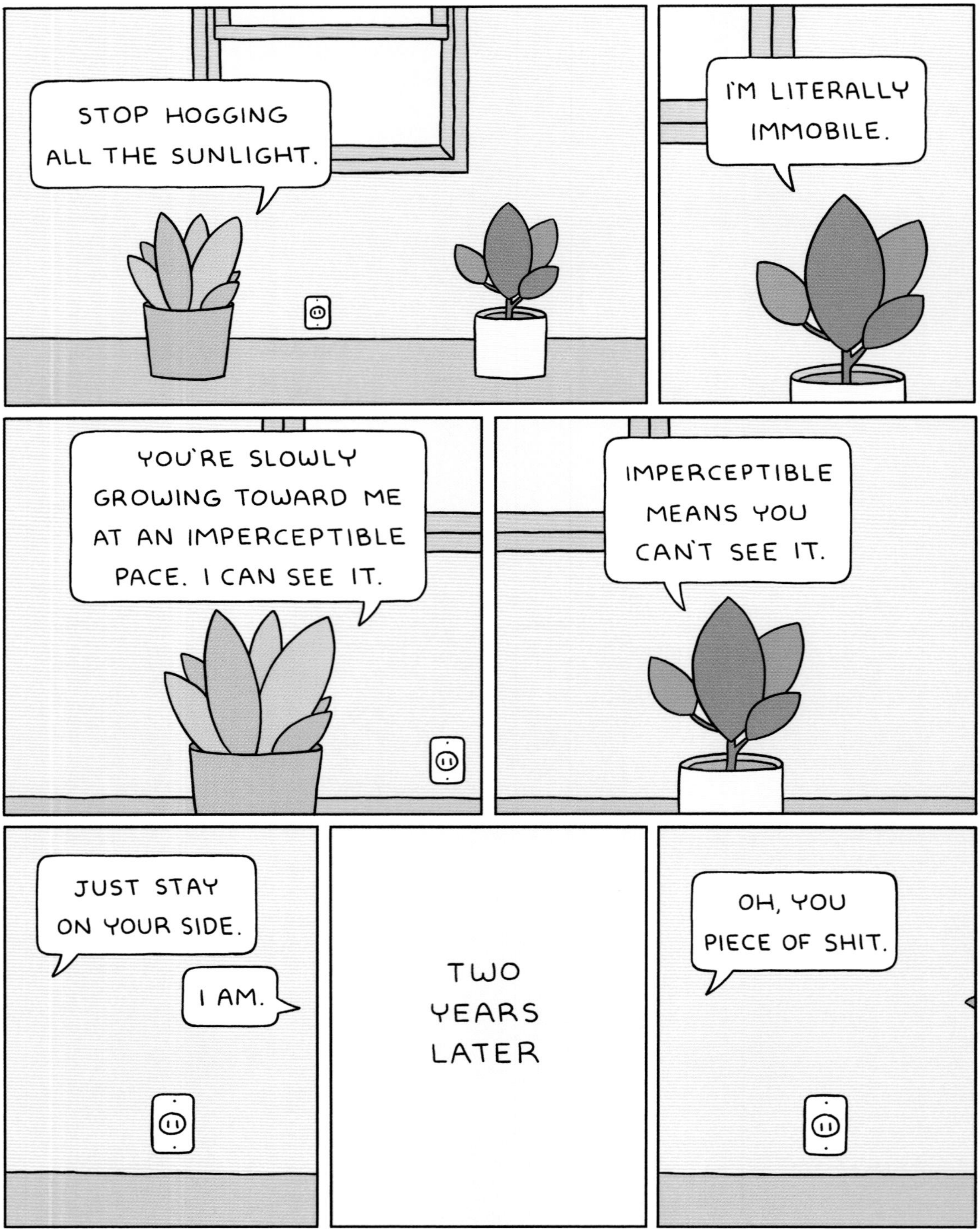
STOP HOGGING ALL THE SUNLIGHT.
I'M LITERALLY IMMOBILE.
YOU'RE SLOWLY GROWING TOWARD ME AT AN IMPERCEPTIBLE PACE. I CAN SEE IT.
IMPERCEPTIBLE MEANS YOU CAN'T SEE IT.
JUST STAY ON YOUR SIDE.
I AM.
TWO YEARS LATER
OH, YOU PIECE OF SHIT.

THE
COLLECTED
SAGA OF
DR. MOUNTAINSON

CHAPTER 1
INTRODUCTIONS

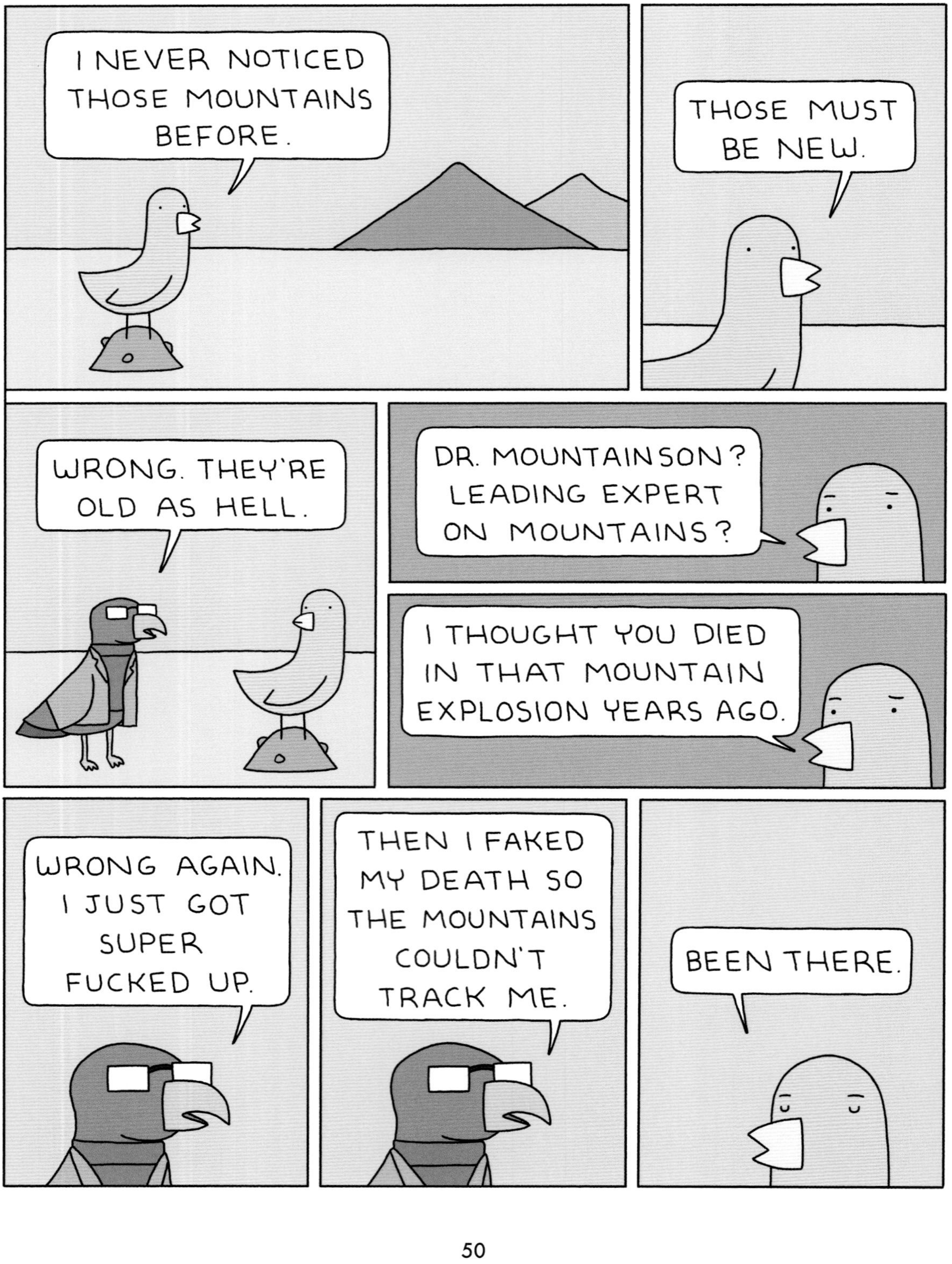
I NEVER NOTICED THOSE MOUNTAINS BEFORE.
THOSE MUST BE NEW.
WRONG. THEY'RE OLD AS HELL.
DR. MOUNTAINSON? LEADING EXPERT ON MOUNTAINS?
I THOUGHT YOU DIED IN THAT MOUNTAIN EXPLOSION YEARS AGO.
WRONG AGAIN. I JUST GOT SUPER FUCKED UP.
THEN I FAKED MY DEATH SO THE MOUNTAINS COULDN'T TRACK ME.
BEEN THERE.

CHAPTER 2
THE TEAM

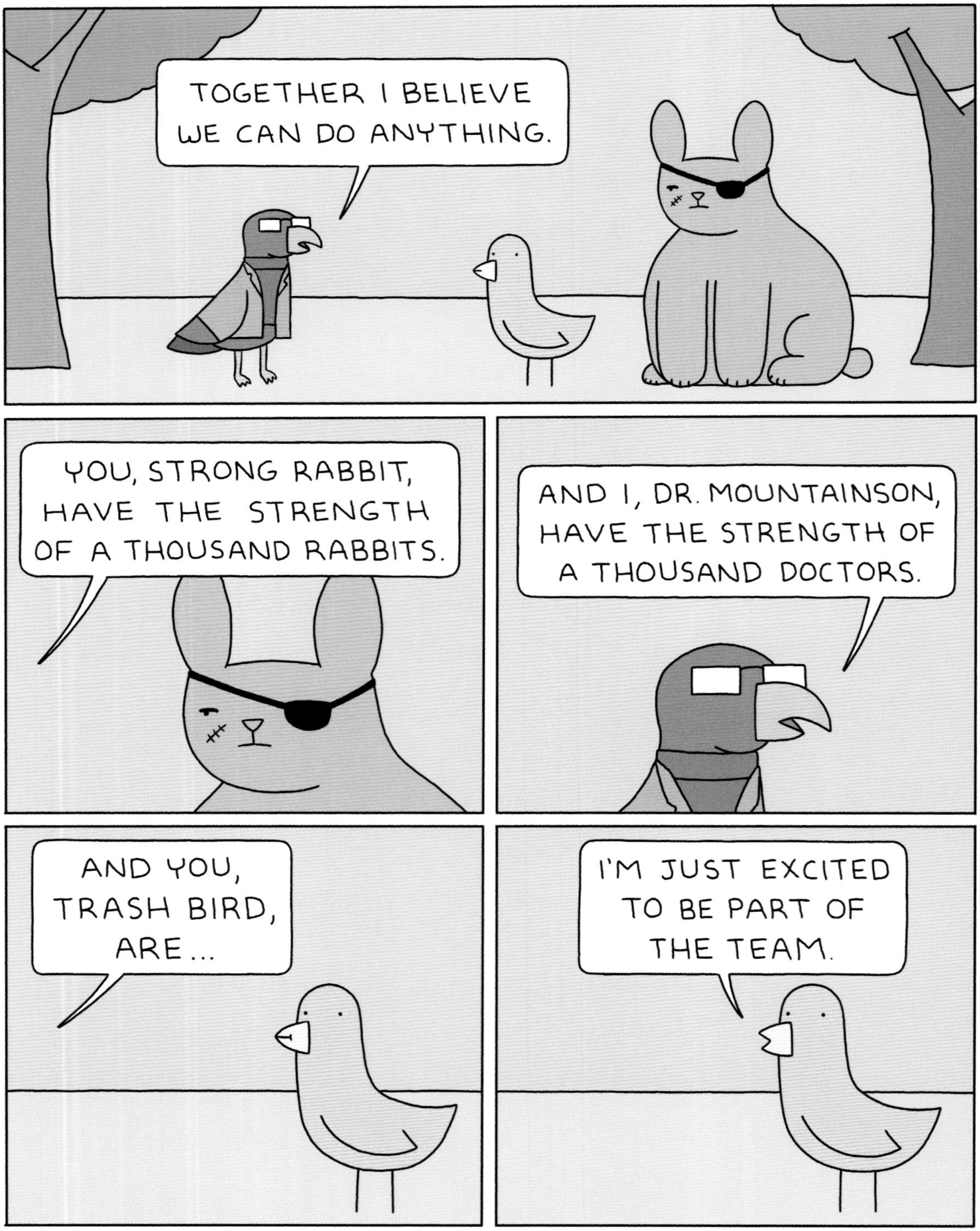
TOGETHER I BELIEVE WE CAN DO ANYTHING.
YOU, STRONG RABBIT, HAVE THE STRENGTH OF A THOUSAND RABBITS.
AND I, DR. MOUNTAINSON, HAVE THE STRENGTH OF A THOUSAND DOCTORS.
AND YOU, TRASH BIRD, ARE...
I'M JUST EXCITED TO BE PART OF THE TEAM.

CHAPTER 3

RETURN
TO THE
MOUNTAIN

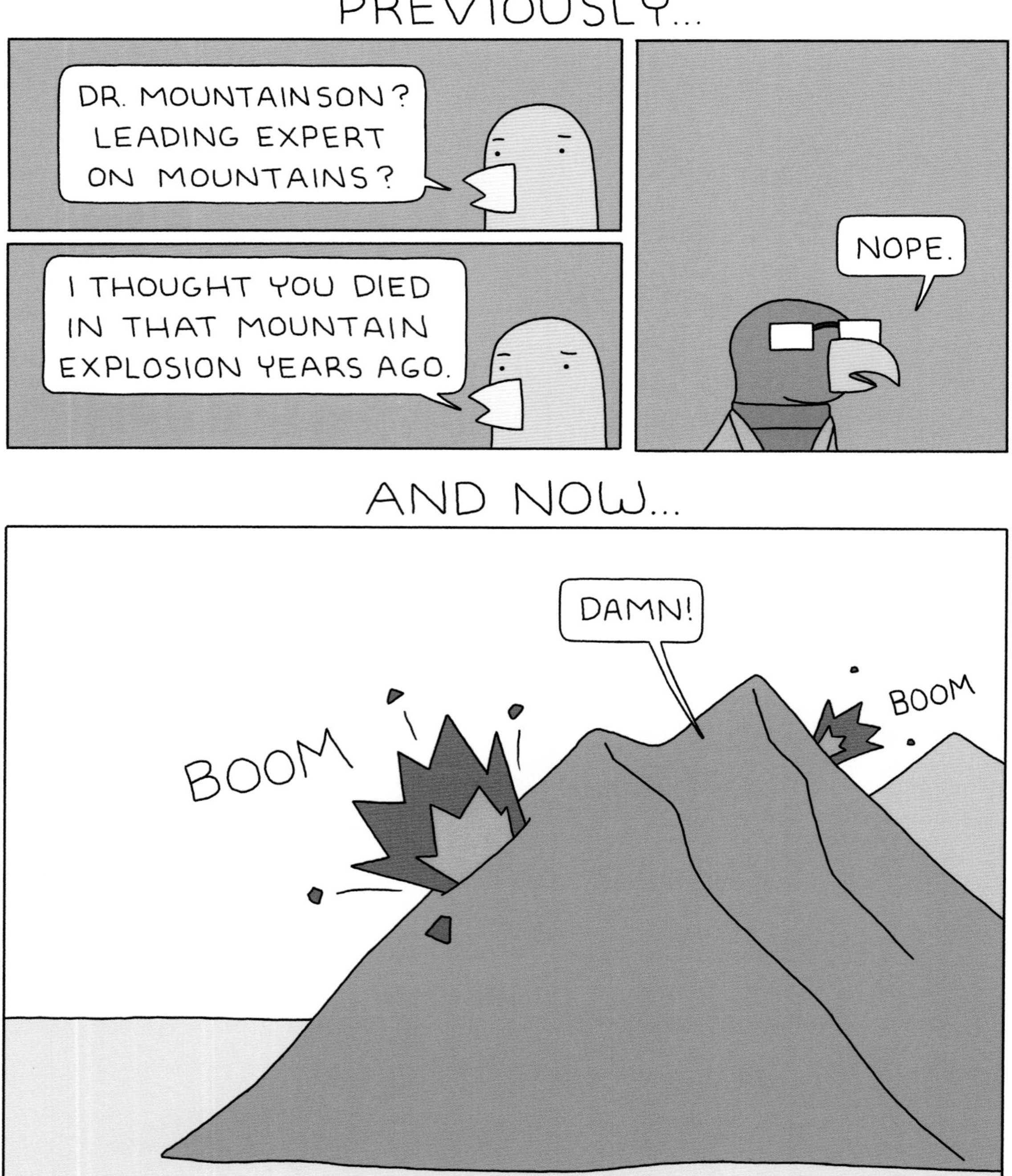
PREVIOUSLY...
DR. MOUNTAINSON? LEADING EXPERT ON MOUNTAINS?
I THOUGHT YOU DIED IN THAT MOUNTAIN EXPLOSION YEARS AGO.
NOPE.
AND NOW...
DAMN!
BOOM
BOOM

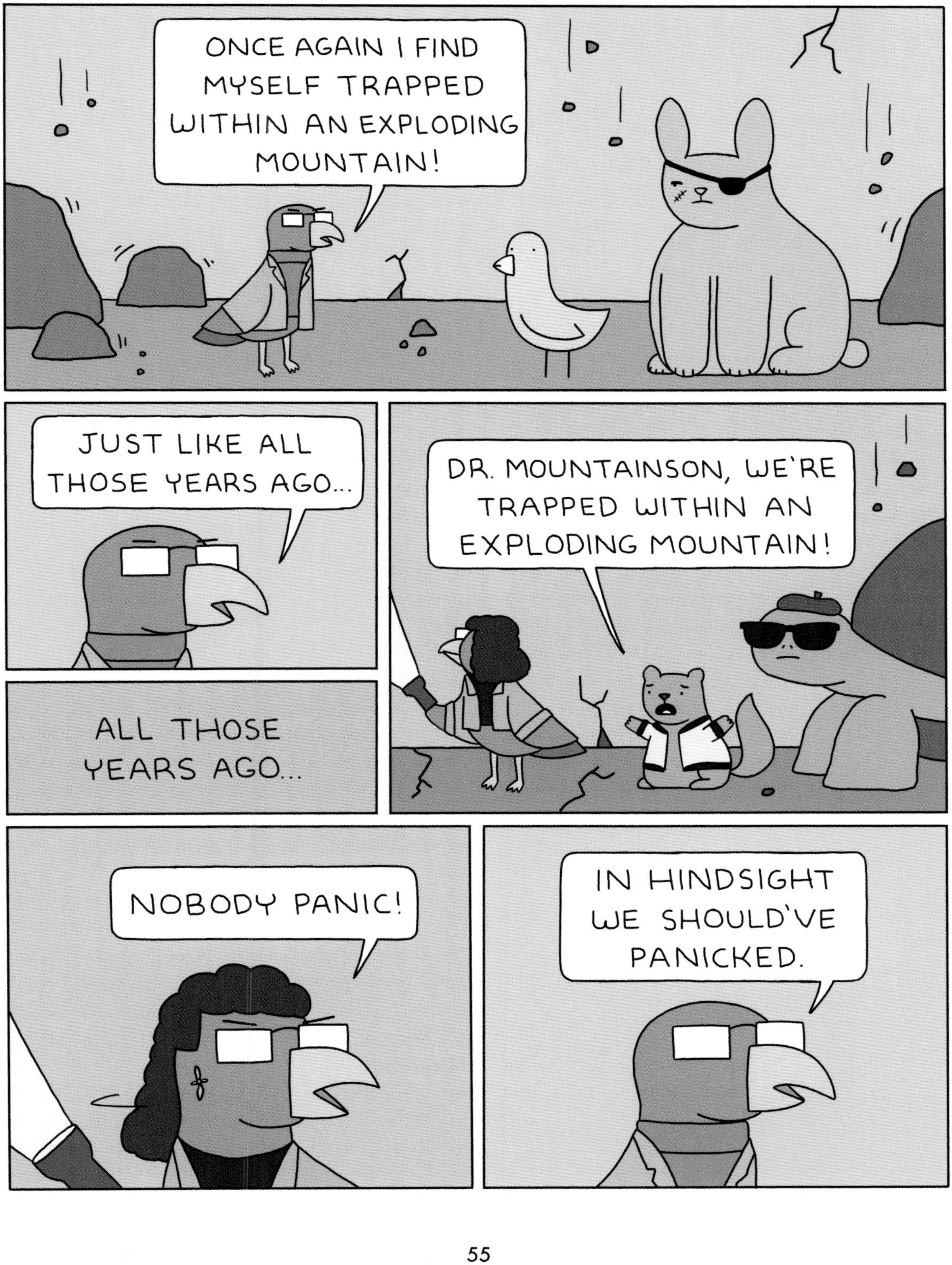
ONCE AGAIN I FIND MYSELF TRAPPED WITHIN AN EXPLODING MOUNTAIN!
JUST LIKE ALL THOSE YEARS AGO...
ALL THOSE YEARS AGO...
DR. MOUNTAINSON, WE'RE TRAPPED WITHIN AN EXPLODING MOUNTAIN!
NOBODY PANIC!
IN HINDSIGHT WE SHOULD'VE PANICKED.

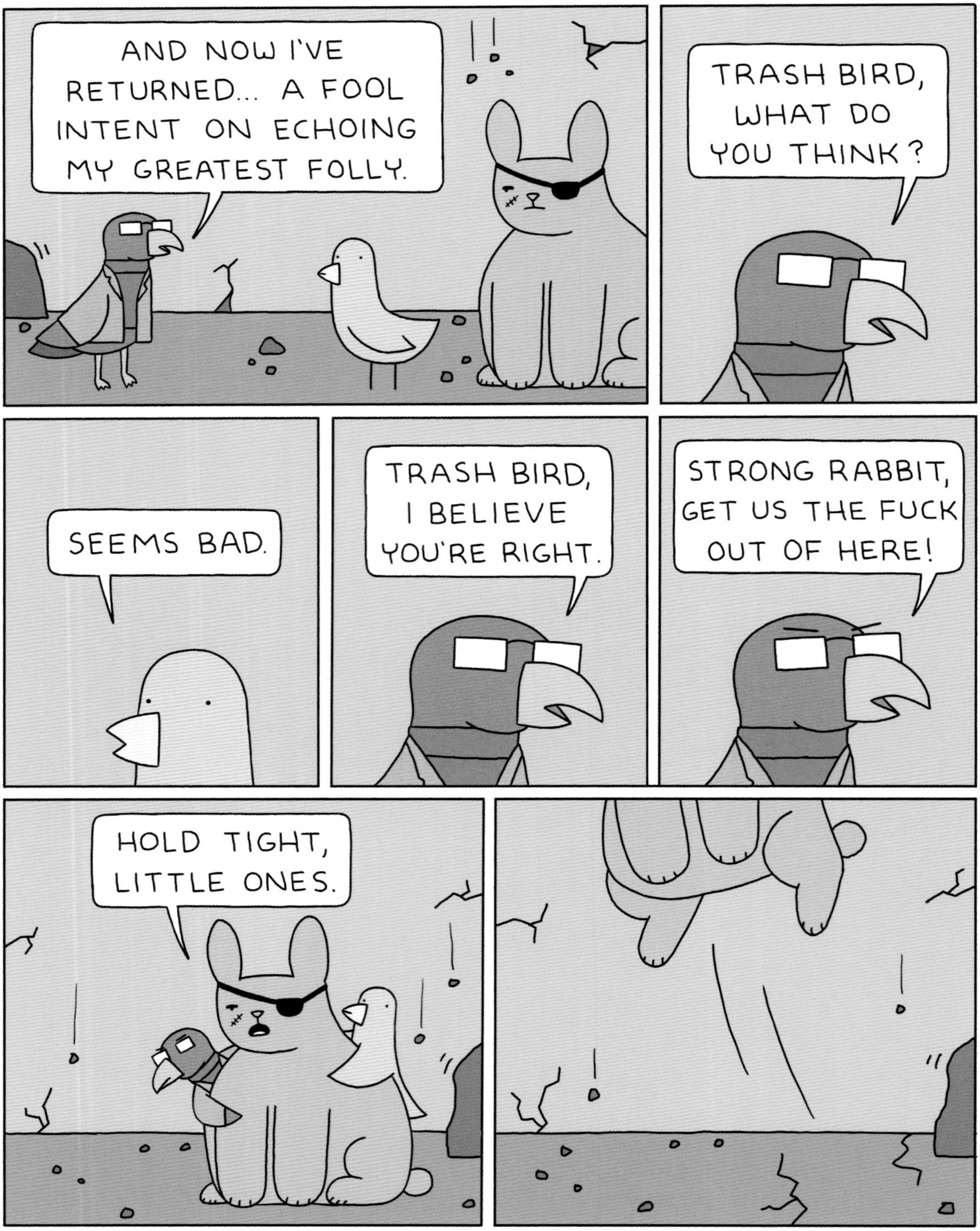
AND NOW I'VE RETURNED... A FOOL INTENT ON ECHOING MY GREATEST FOLLY.
TRASH BIRD, WHAT DO YOU THINK?
SEEMS BAD.
TRASH BIRD, I BELIEVE YOU'RE RIGHT.
STRONG RABBIT, GET US THE FUCK OUT OF HERE!
HOLD TIGHT, LITTLE ONES.

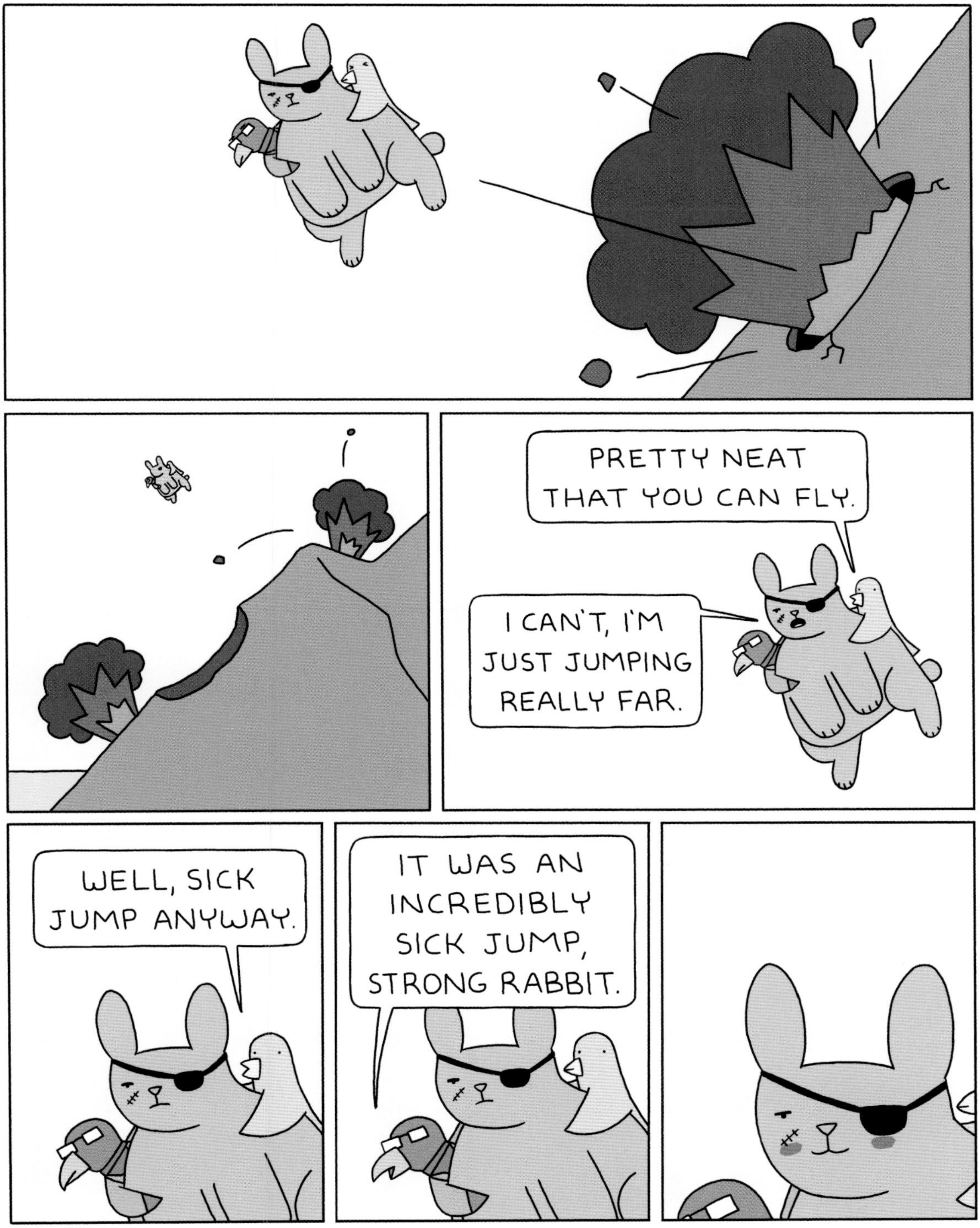
PRETTY NEAT THAT YOU CAN FLY.
I CAN'T, I'M JUST JUMPING REALLY FAR.
WELL, SICK JUMP ANYWAY.
IT WAS AN INCREDIBLY SICK JUMP, STRONG RABBIT.

As a Kid

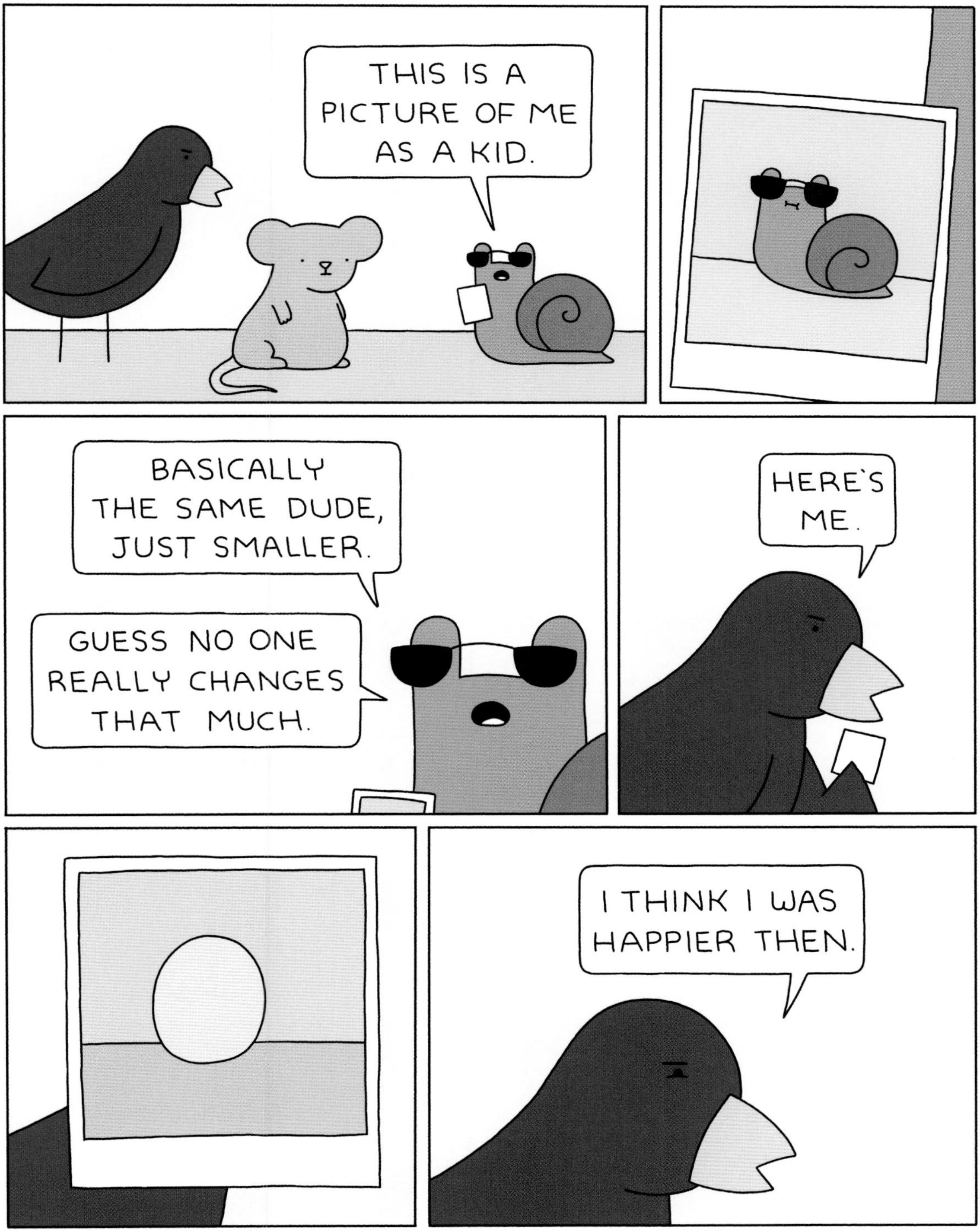
THIS IS A PICTURE OF ME AS A KID.
BASICALLY THE SAME DUDE, JUST SMALLER.
GUESS NO ONE REALLY CHANGES THAT MUCH.
HERE'S ME.
I THINK I WAS HAPPIER THEN.

A Badder Mouse

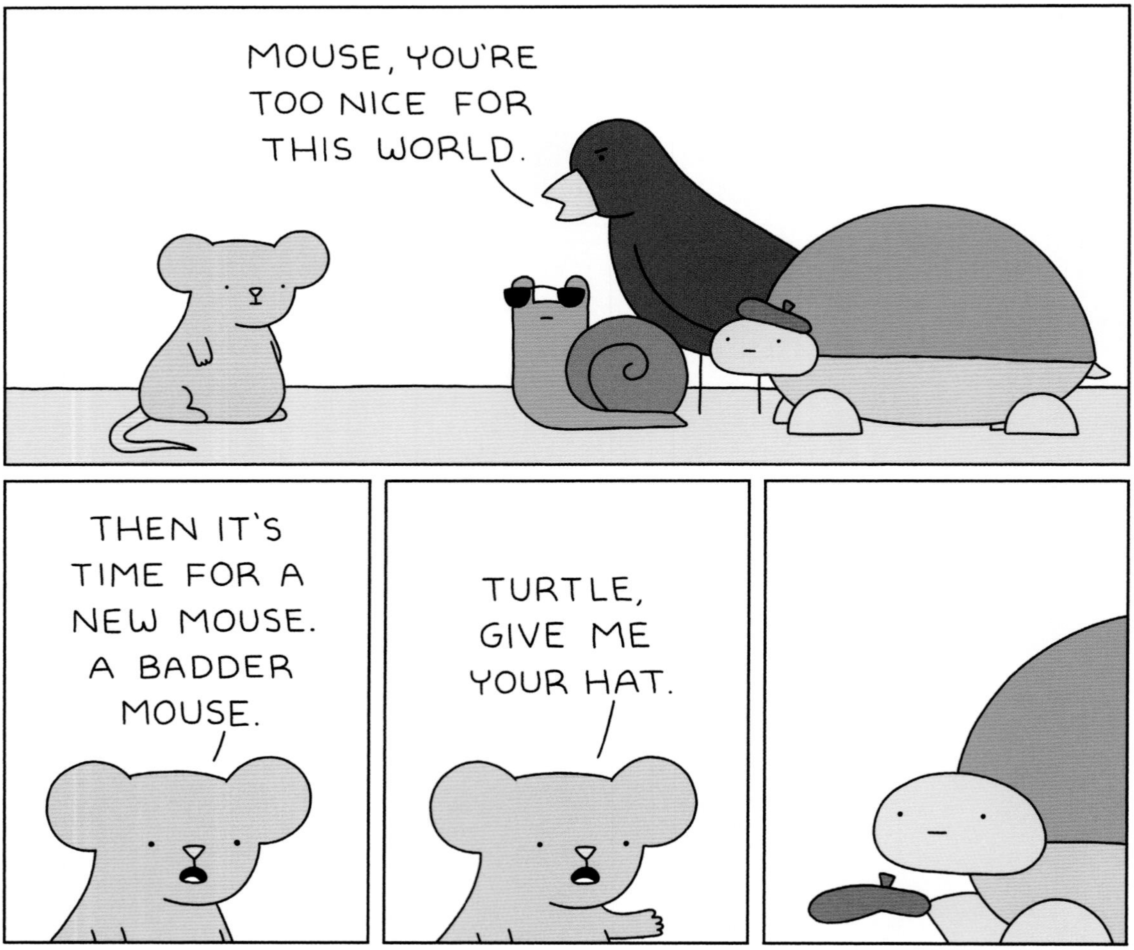
MOUSE, YOU'RE TOO NICE FOR THIS WORLD.
THEN IT'S TIME FOR A NEW MOUSE. A BADDER MOUSE.
TURTLE, GIVE ME YOUR HAT.

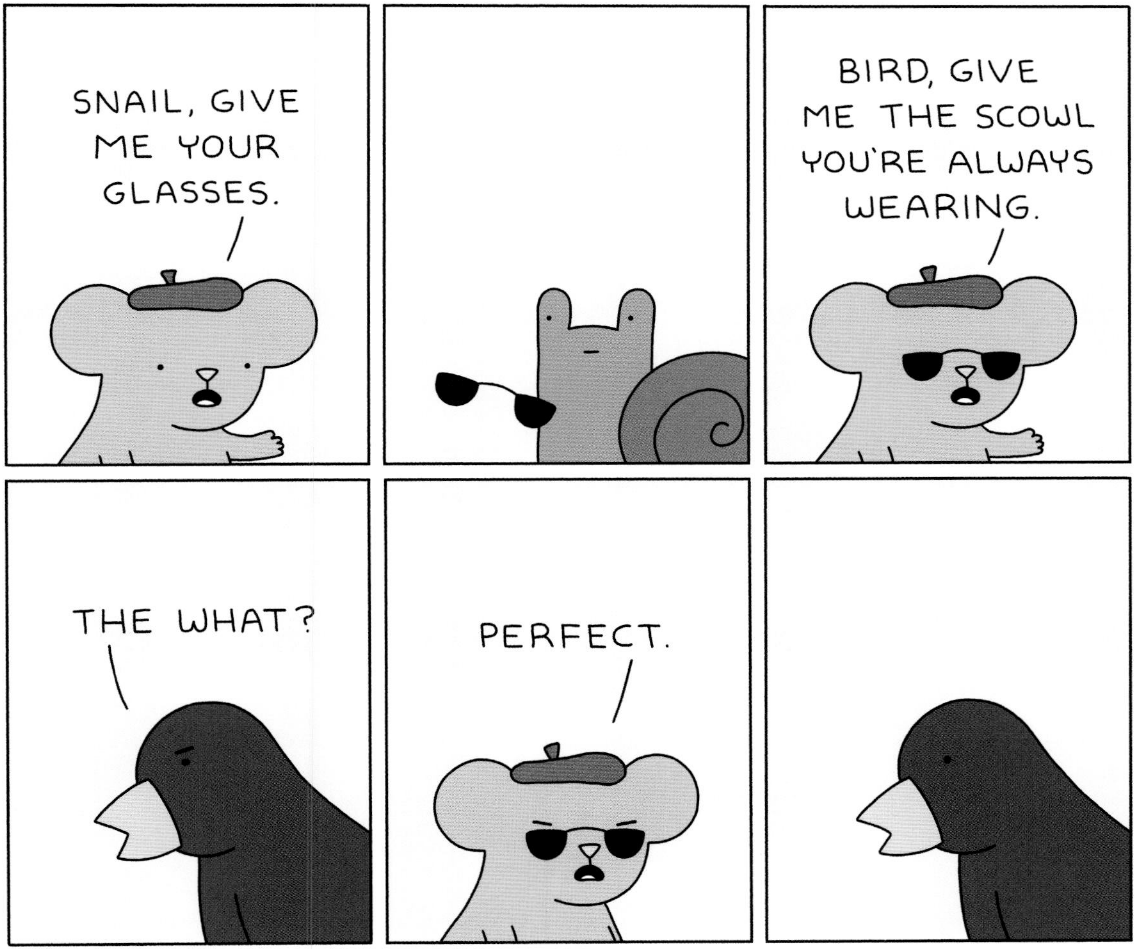
SNAIL, GIVE ME YOUR GLASSES.
BIRD, GIVE ME THE SCOWL YOU'RE ALWAYS WEARING.
THE WHAT?
PERFECT.

Been Real

IT'S BEEN REAL.
...REAL SHITTY.

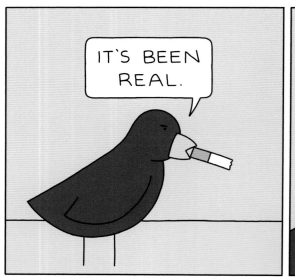

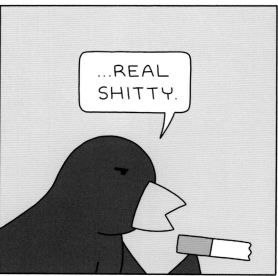

My Best Friends

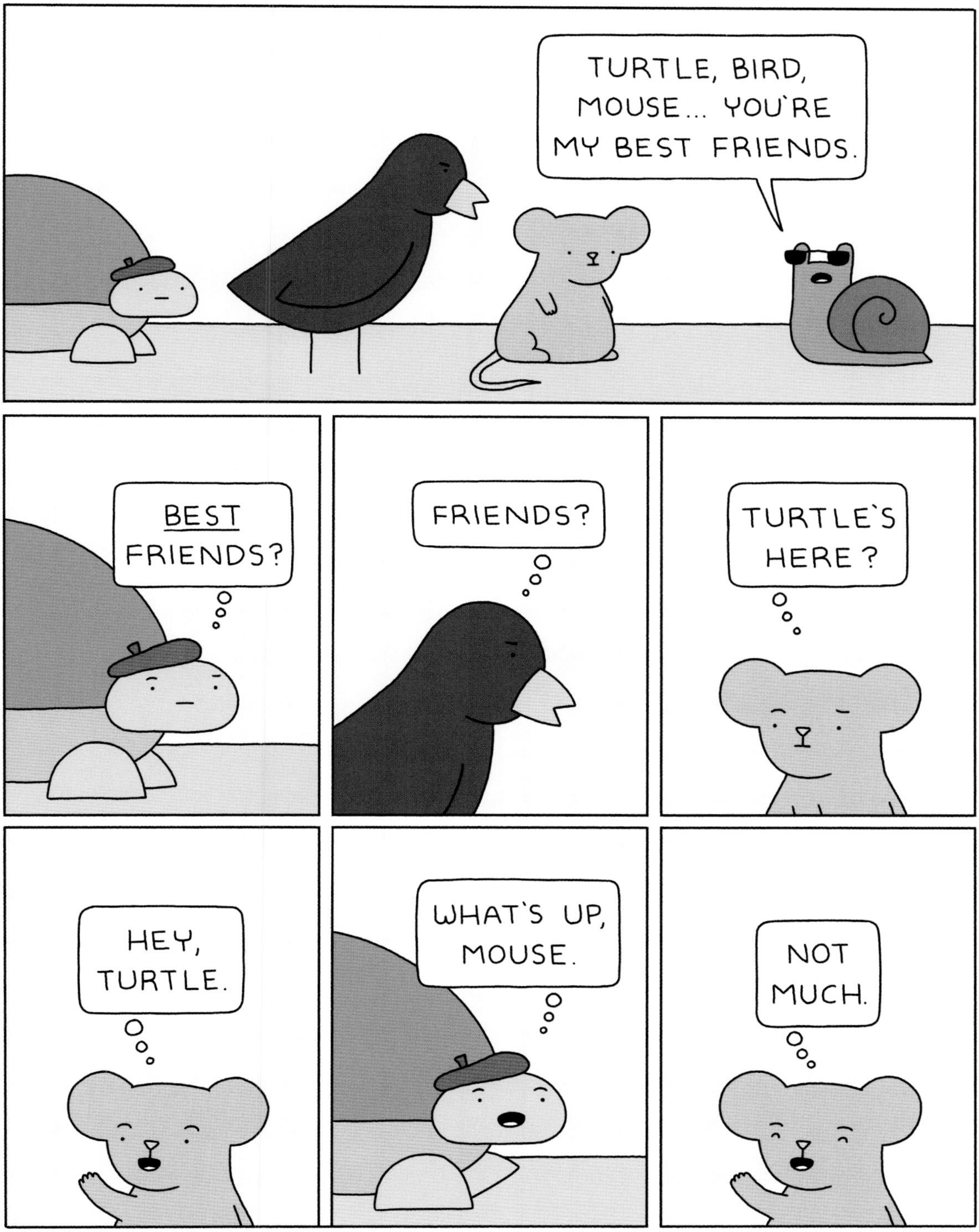
TURTLE, BIRD, MOUSE... YOU'RE MY BEST FRIENDS.
BEST FRIENDS?
FRIENDS?
TURTLE'S HERE?
HEY, TURTLE.
WHAT'S UP, MOUSE.
NOT MUCH.

All the Places

WOW, I'VE BEEN TO ALL THE PLACES ON MY LIST.
MY HOUSE

A Break

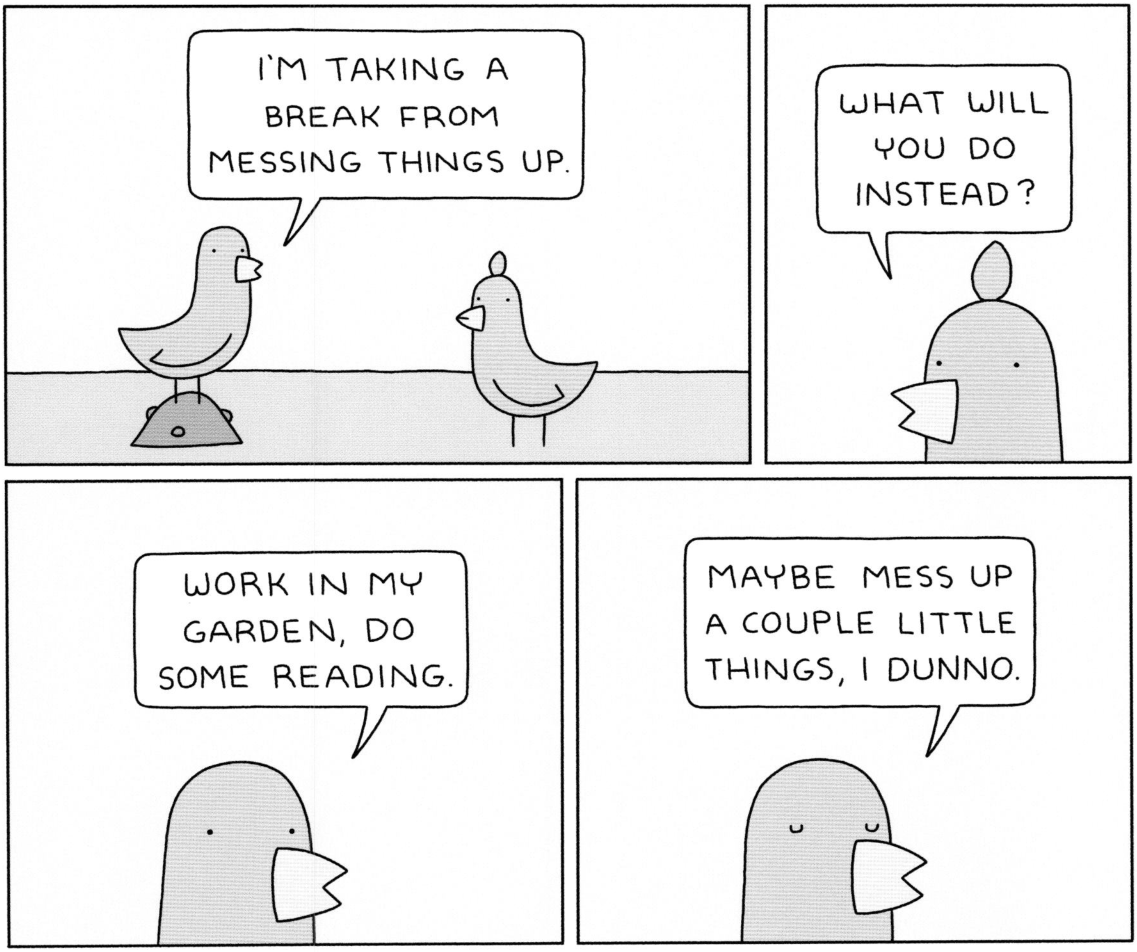
I'M TAKING A BREAK FROM MESSING THINGS UP.
WHAT WILL YOU DO INSTEAD?
WORK IN MY GARDEN, DO SOME READING.
MAYBE MESS UP A COUPLE LITTLE THINGS, I DUNNO.

A Pond

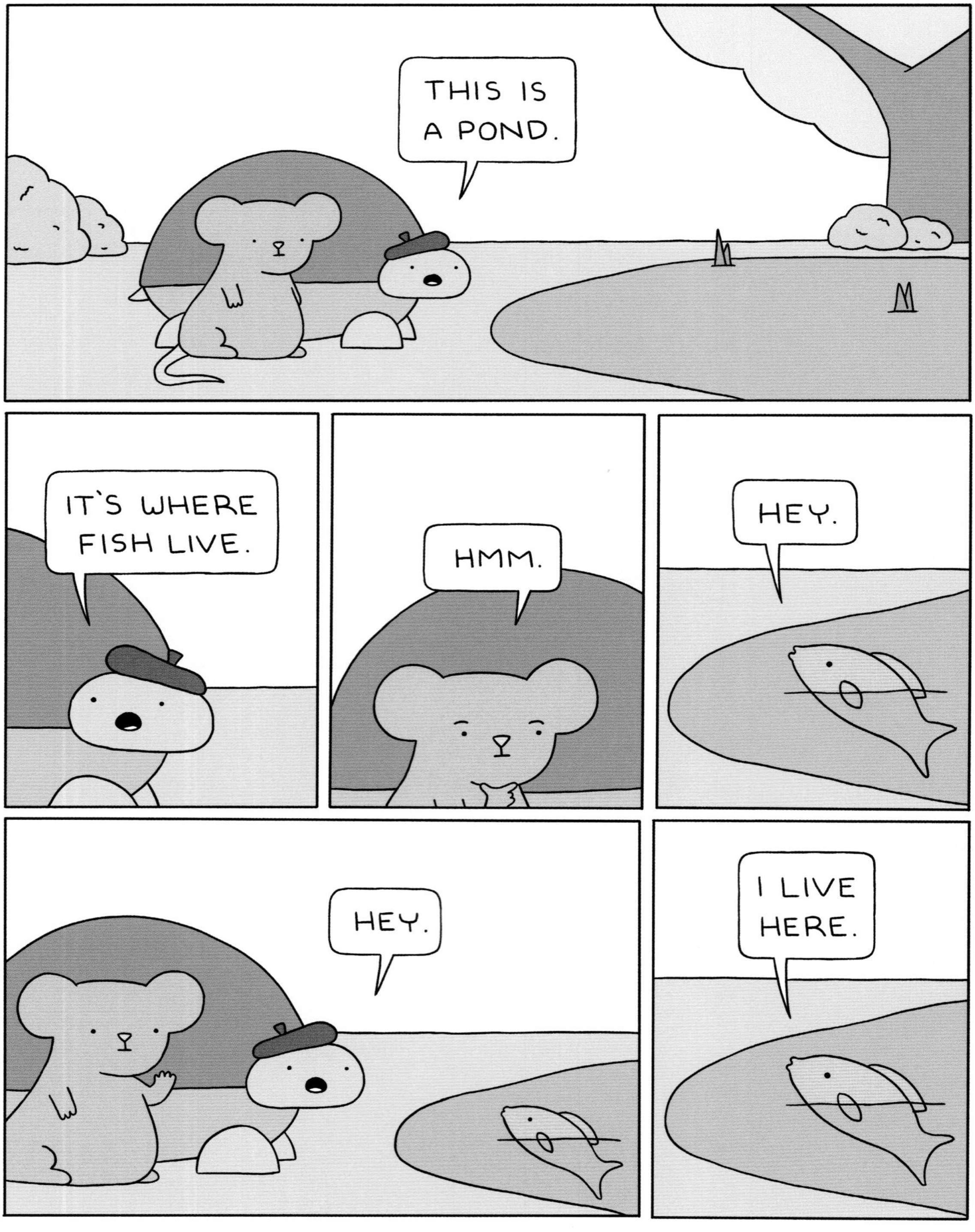
THIS IS A POND.
IT'S WHERE FISH LIVE.
HMM.
HEY.
HEY.
I LIVE HERE.

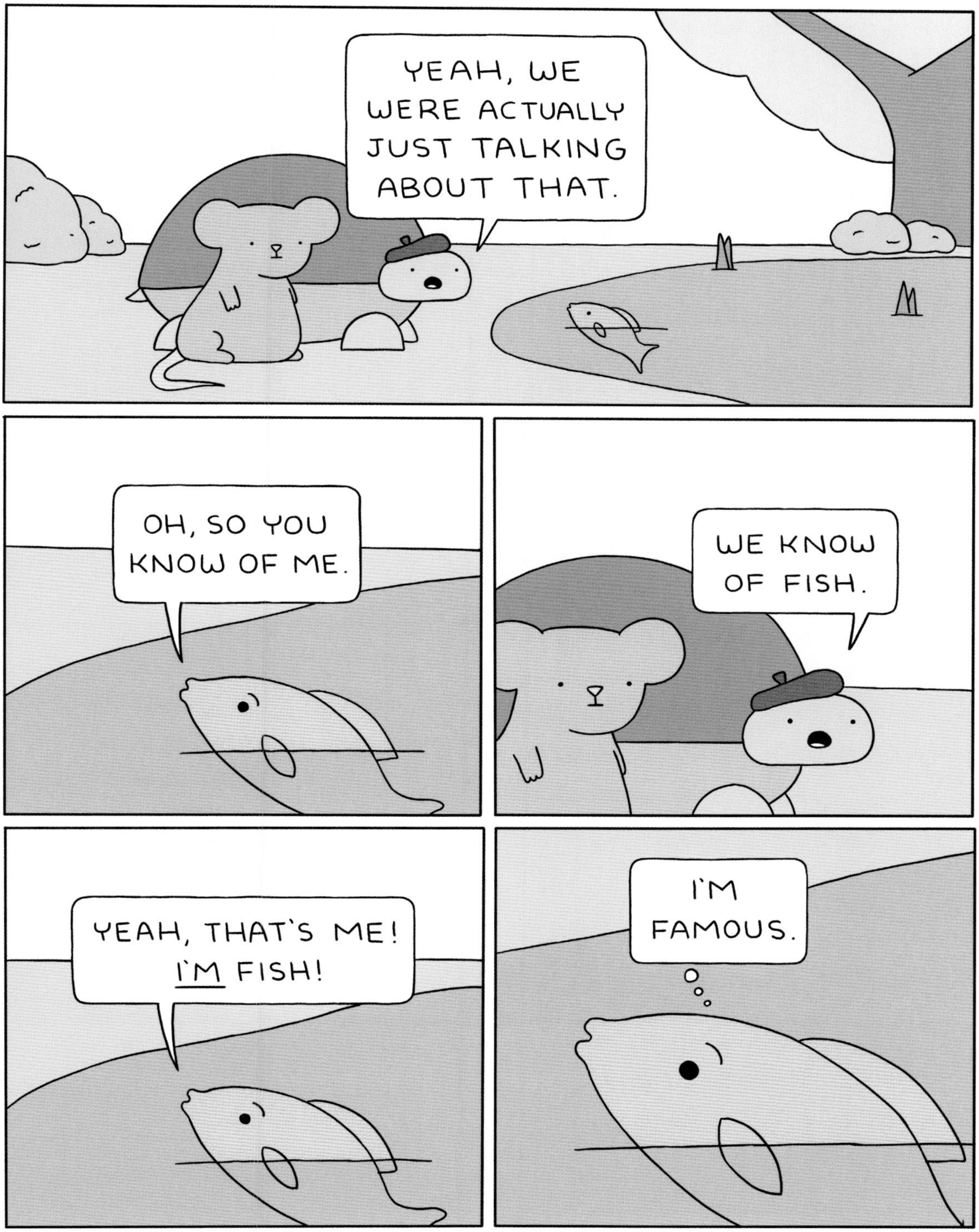
YEAH, WE WERE ACTUALLY JUST TALKING ABOUT THAT.
OH, SO YOU KNOW OF ME.
WE KNOW OF FISH.
YEAH, THAT'S ME! I'M FISH!
I'M FAMOUS.

Changes

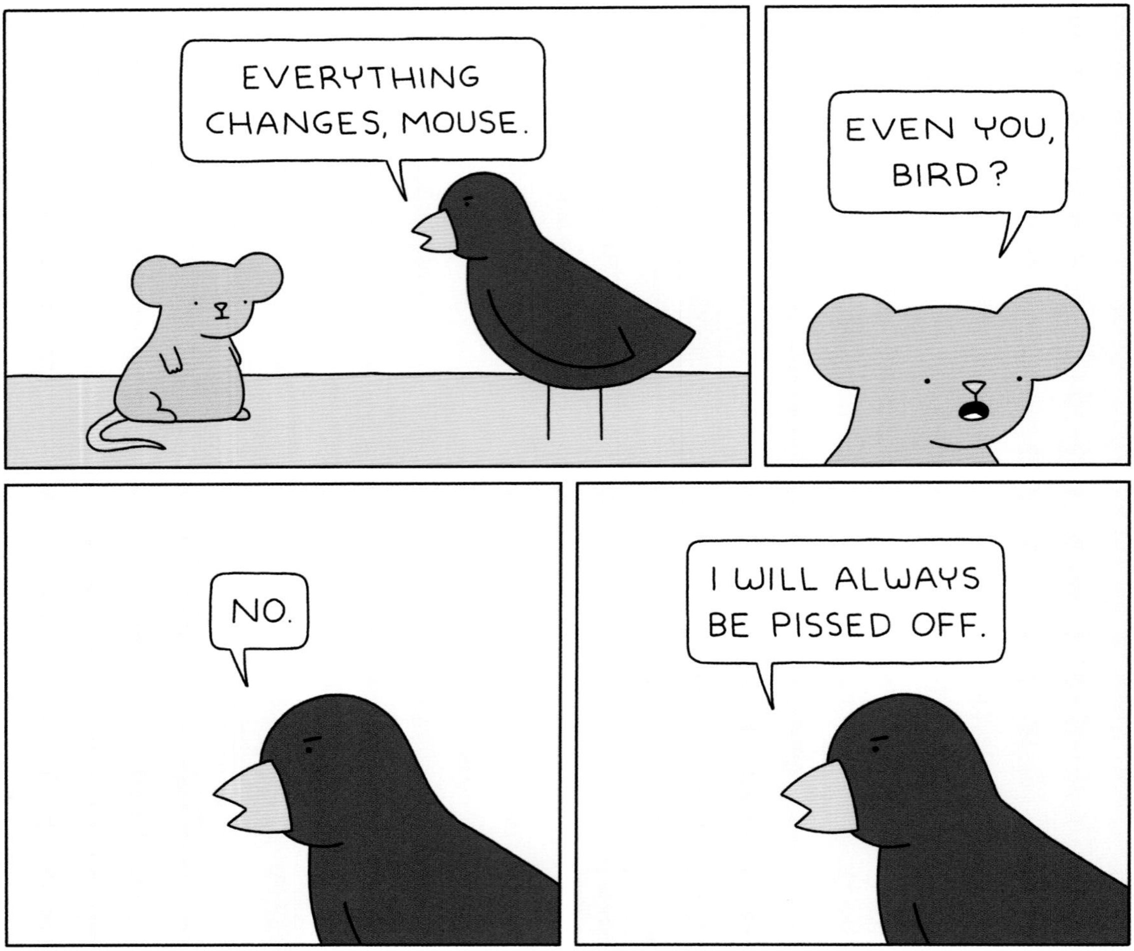
EVERYTHING CHANGES, MOUSE.
EVEN YOU, BIRD?
NO.
I WILL ALWAYS BE PISSED OFF.

Natural Enemies

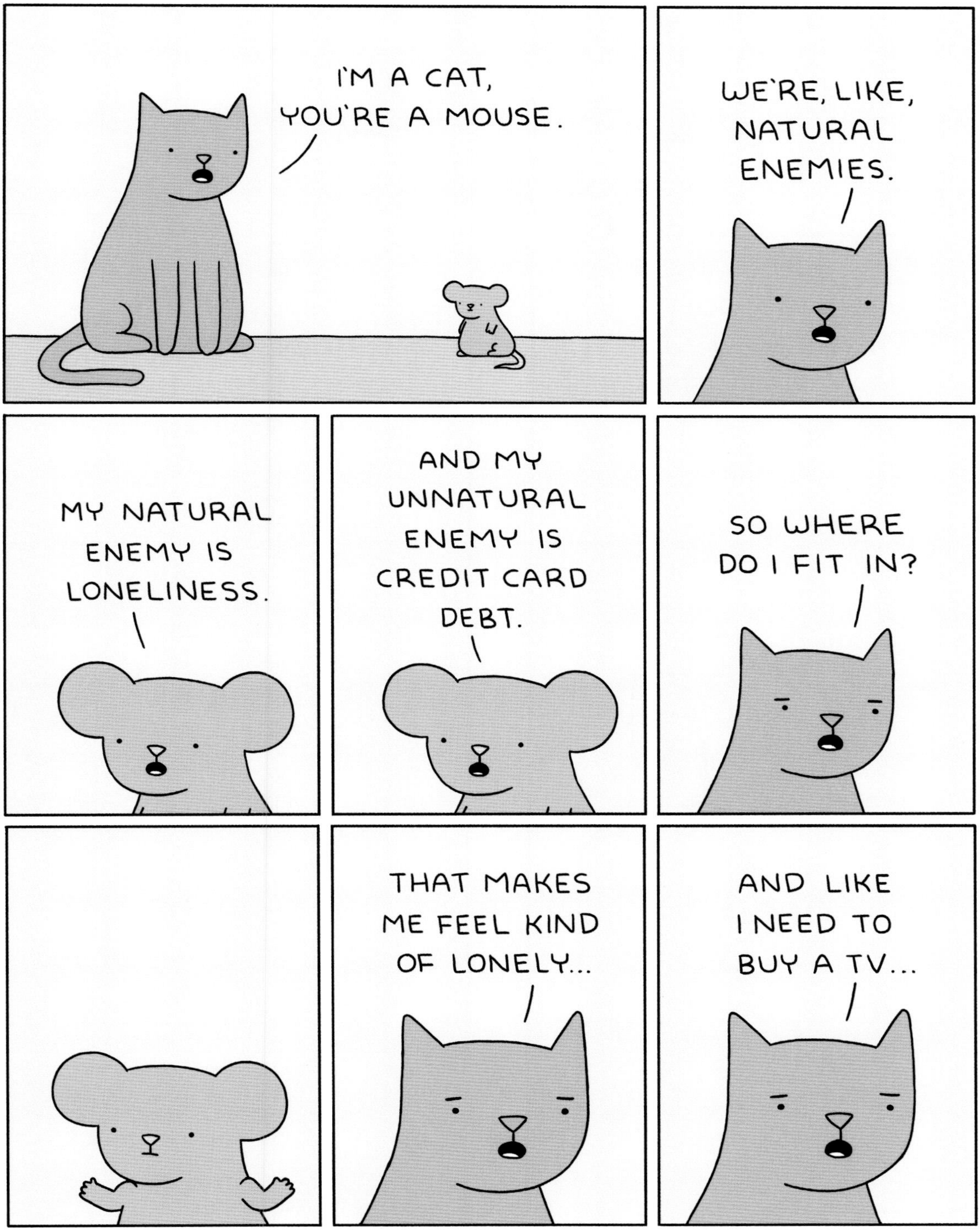
I'M A CAT, YOU'RE A MOUSE.
WE'RE, LIKE, NATURAL ENEMIES.
MY NATURAL ENEMY IS LONELINESS.
AND MY UNNATURAL ENEMY IS CREDIT CARD DEBT.
SO WHERE DO I FIT IN?
THAT MAKES ME FEEL KIND OF LONELY...
AND LIKE I NEED TO BUY A TV...

How You Want

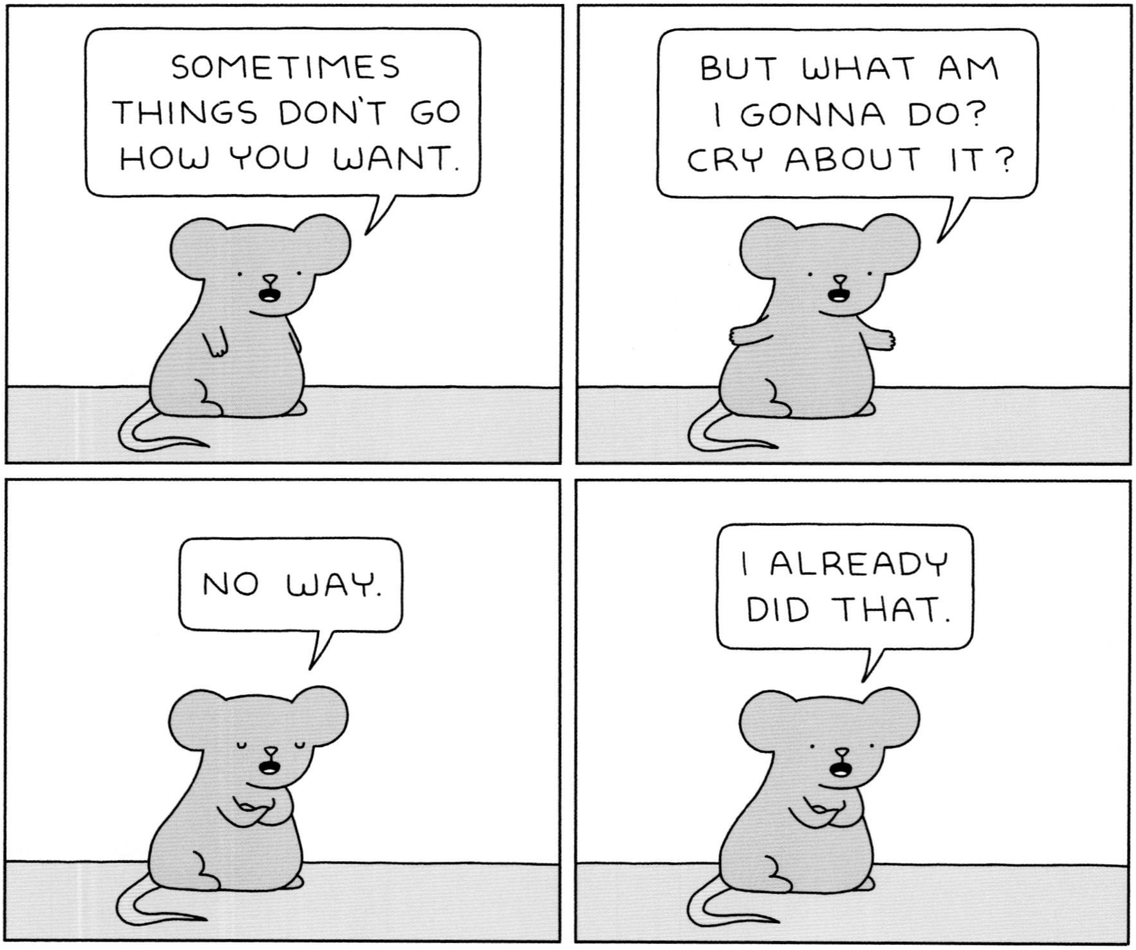
SOMETIMES THINGS DON'T GO HOW YOU WANT.
BUT WHAT AM I GONNA DO? CRY ABOUT IT?
NO WAY.
I ALREADY DID THAT.

Do Something

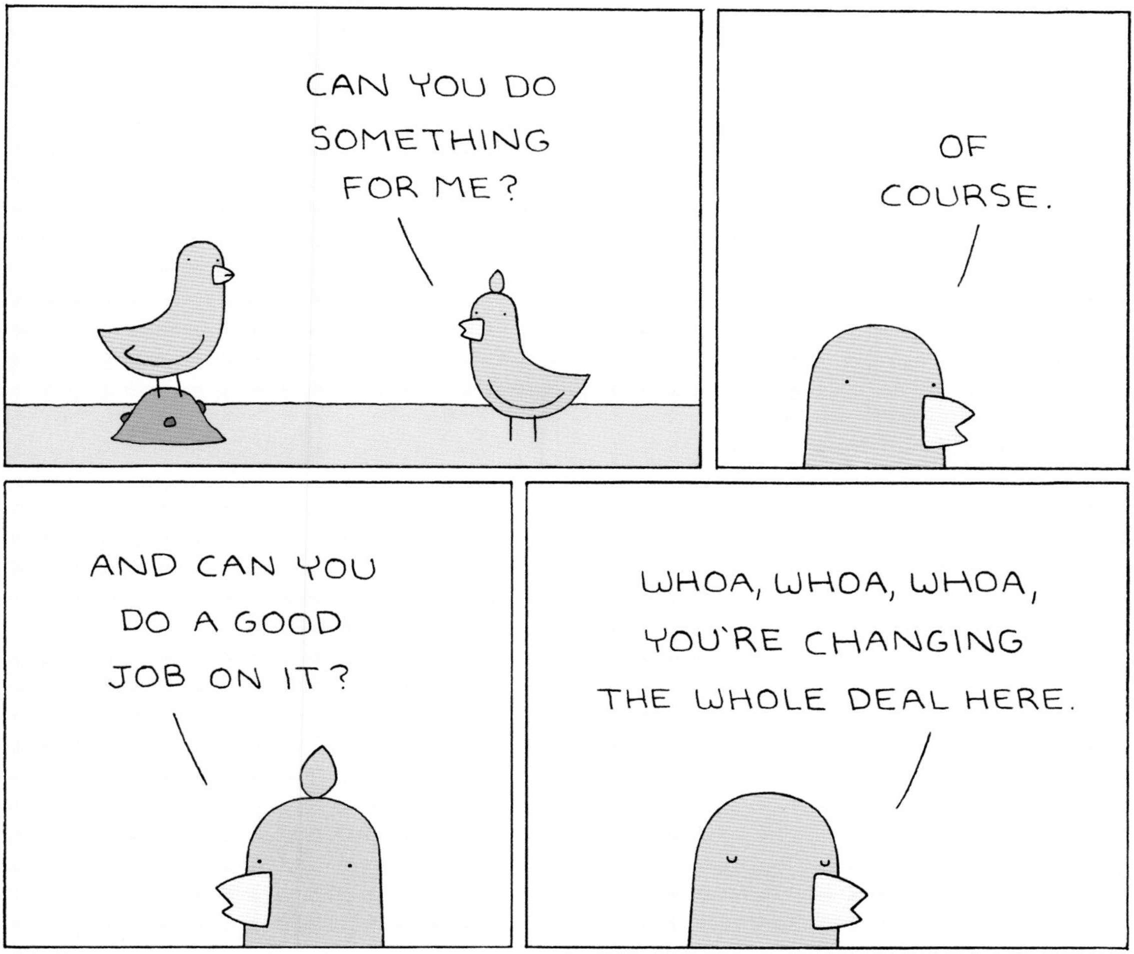
CAN YOU DO SOMETHING FOR ME?
OF COURSE.
AND CAN YOU DO A GOOD JOB ON IT?
WHOA, WHOA, WHOA, YOU'RE CHANGING THE WHOLE DEAL HERE.

Looking

LOOKING FOR LOVE.
OR SOME KIND OF FOOD.

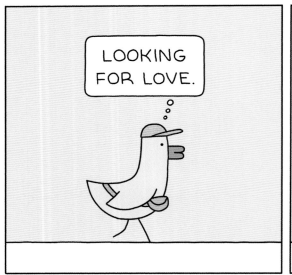

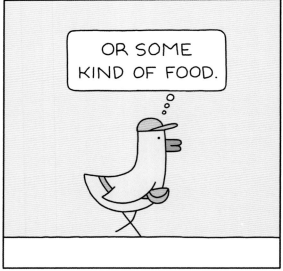

Knows My Name

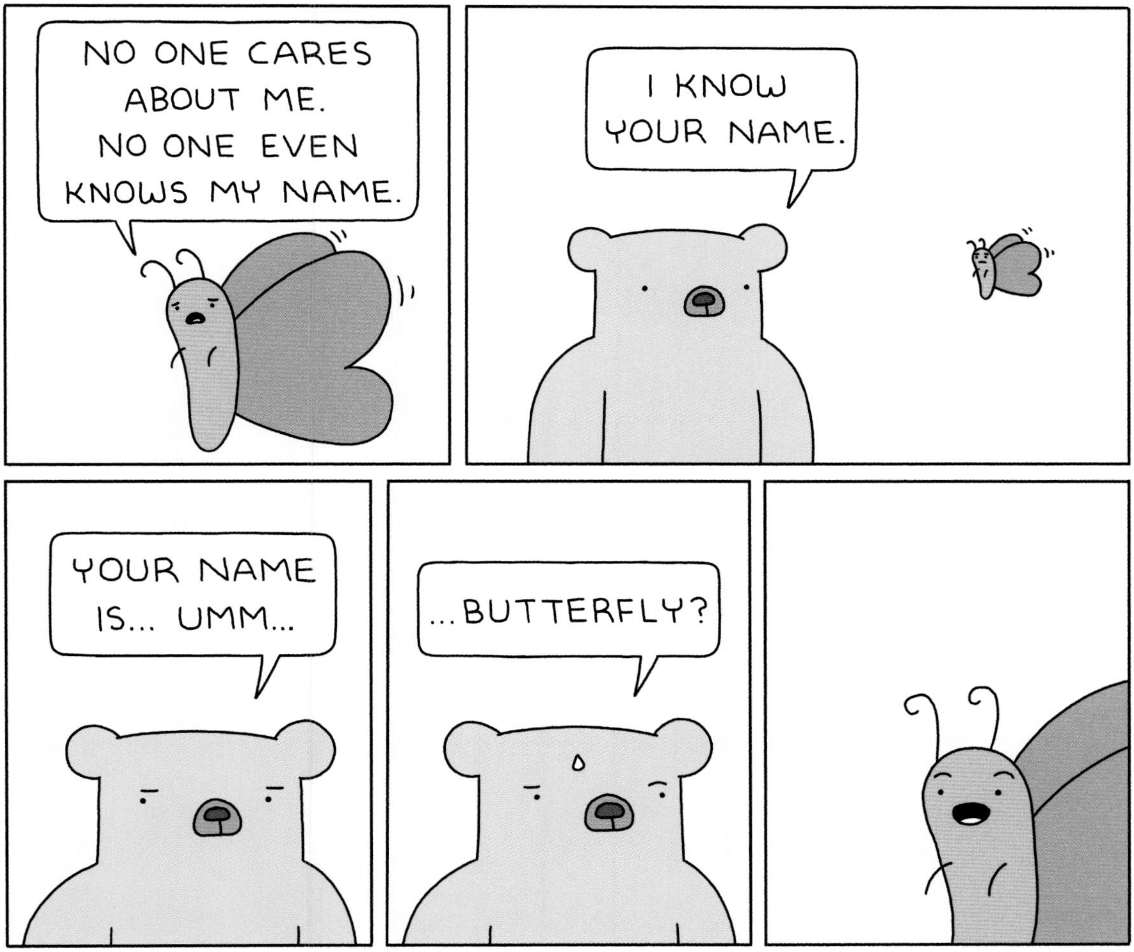
NO ONE CARES ABOUT ME. NO ONE EVEN KNOWS MY NAME.
I KNOW YOUR NAME.
YOUR NAME IS... UMM...
...BUTTERFLY?

One Day

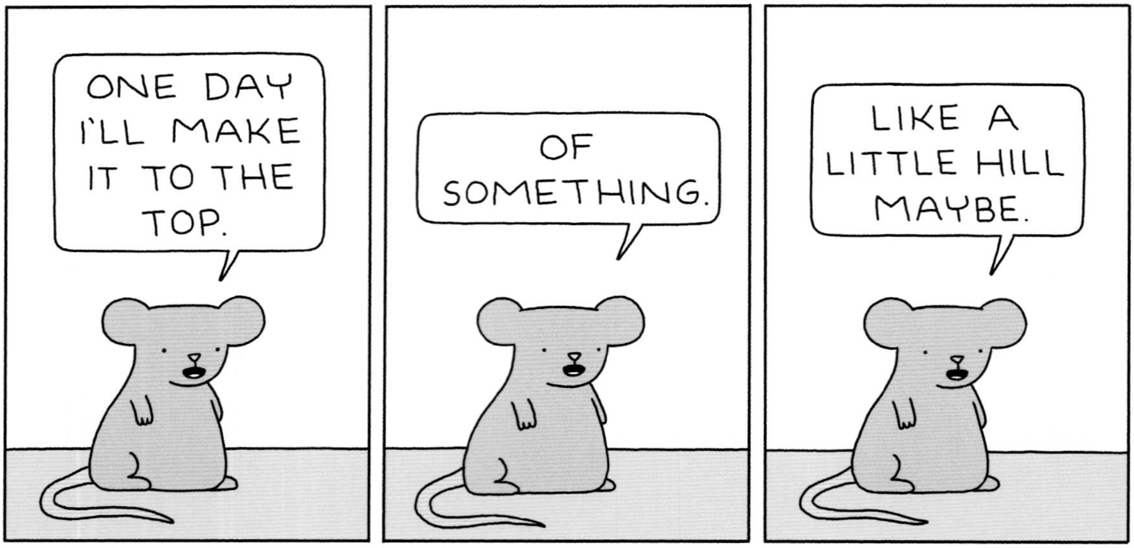
ONE DAY I'LL MAKE IT TO THE TOP.
OF SOMETHING.
LIKE A LITTLE HILL MAYBE.

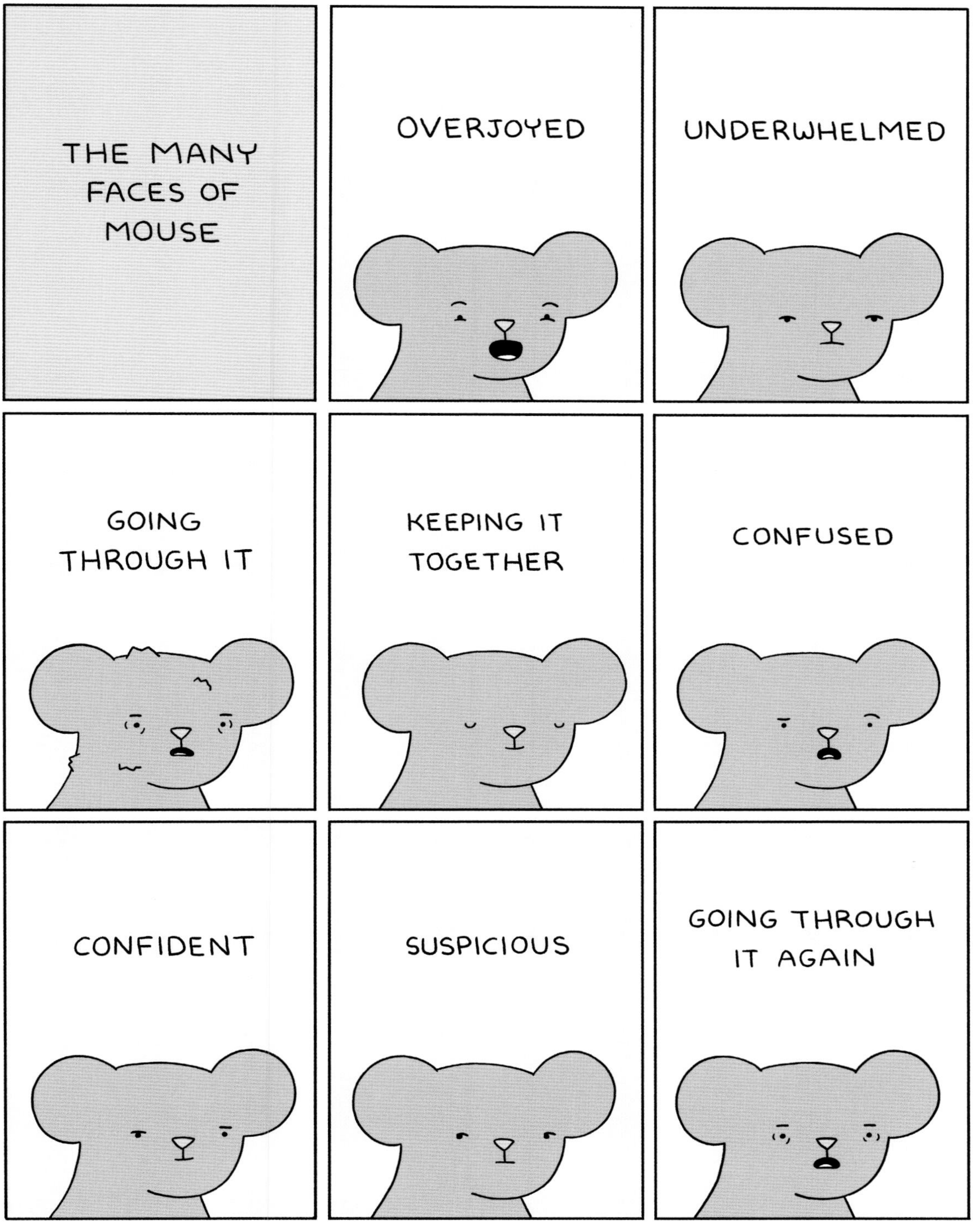
THE MANY FACES OF MOUSE
OVERJOYED
UNDERWHELMED
GOING THROUGH IT
KEEPING IT TOGETHER
CONFUSED
CONFIDENT
SUSPICIOUS
GOING THROUGH IT AGAIN

Just Ask

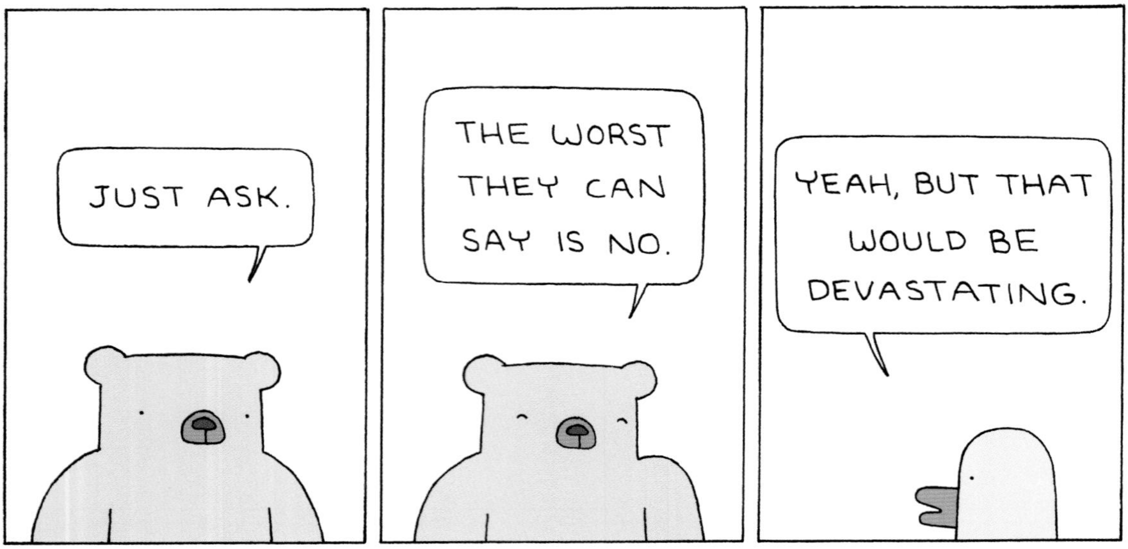
JUST ASK.
THE WORST THEY CAN SAY IS NO.
YEAH, BUT THAT WOULD BE DEVASTATING.

Learn Some Words

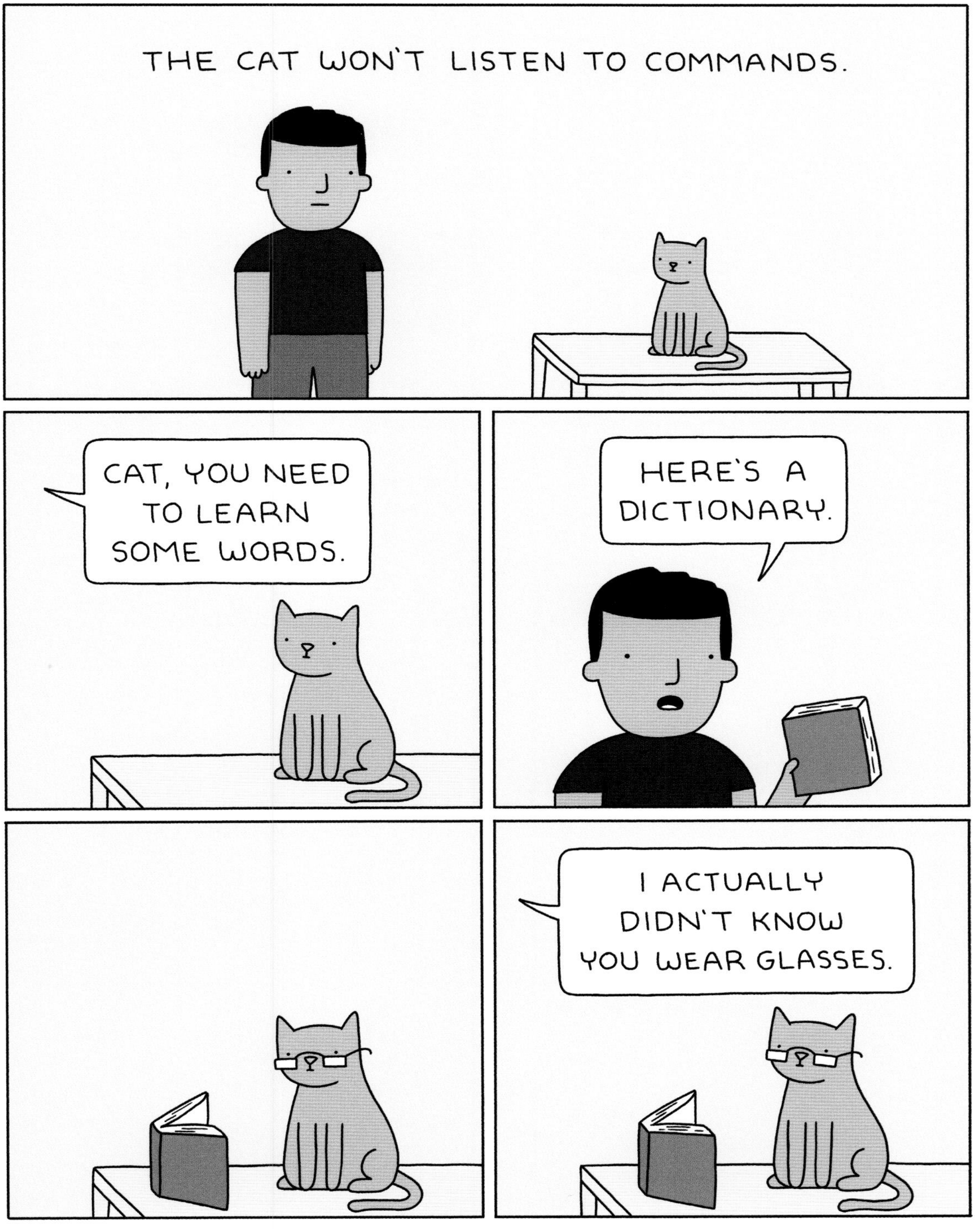
THE CAT WON'T LISTEN TO COMMANDS.
CAT, YOU NEED TO LEARN SOME WORDS.
HERE'S A DICTIONARY.
I ACTUALLY DIDN'T KNOW YOU WEAR GLASSES.

A Snake

A SNAKE!
I HEARD SNAKES HAVE POISON MOUTHS AND CAN KILL WITH A KISS!
IT'S ALL TRUE.
AND WE'RE GOOD AT SPORTS AND GUITAR AS WELL.

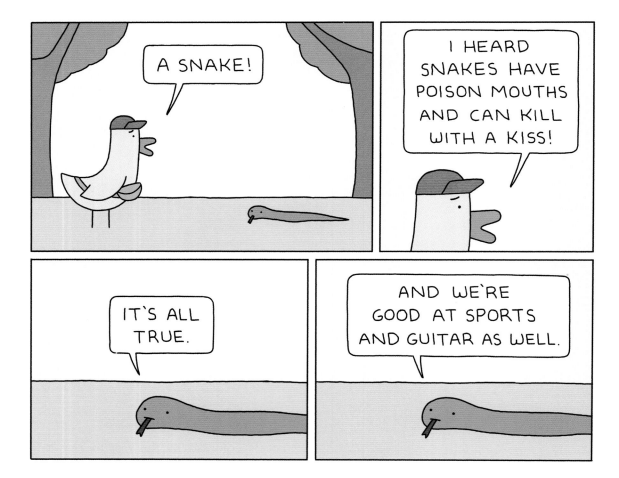

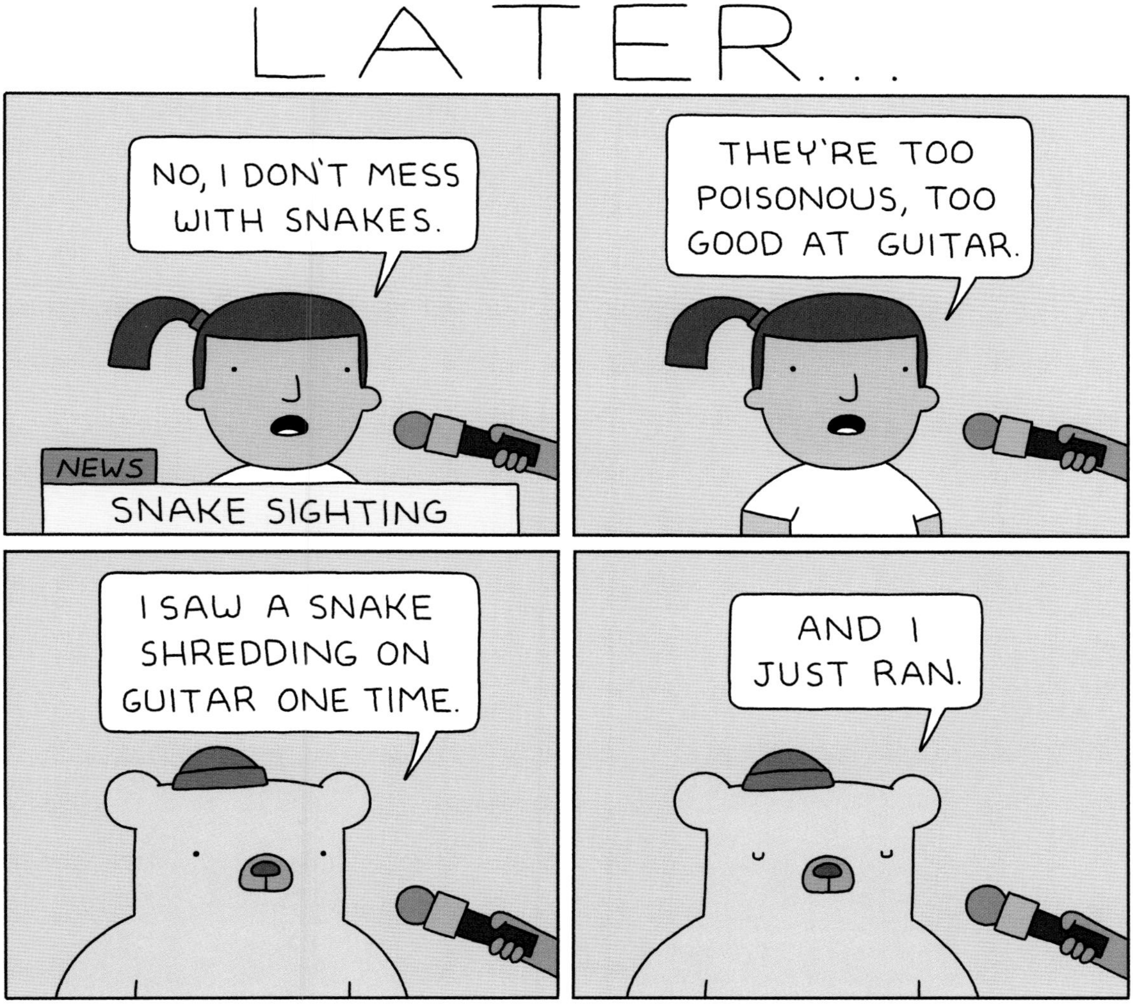
LATER...
NO, I DON'T MESS WITH SNAKES.
NEWS
SNAKE SIGHTING
THEY'RE TOO POISONOUS, TOO GOOD AT GUITAR.
I SAW A SNAKE SHREDDING ON GUITAR ONE TIME.
AND I JUST RAN.

Chef

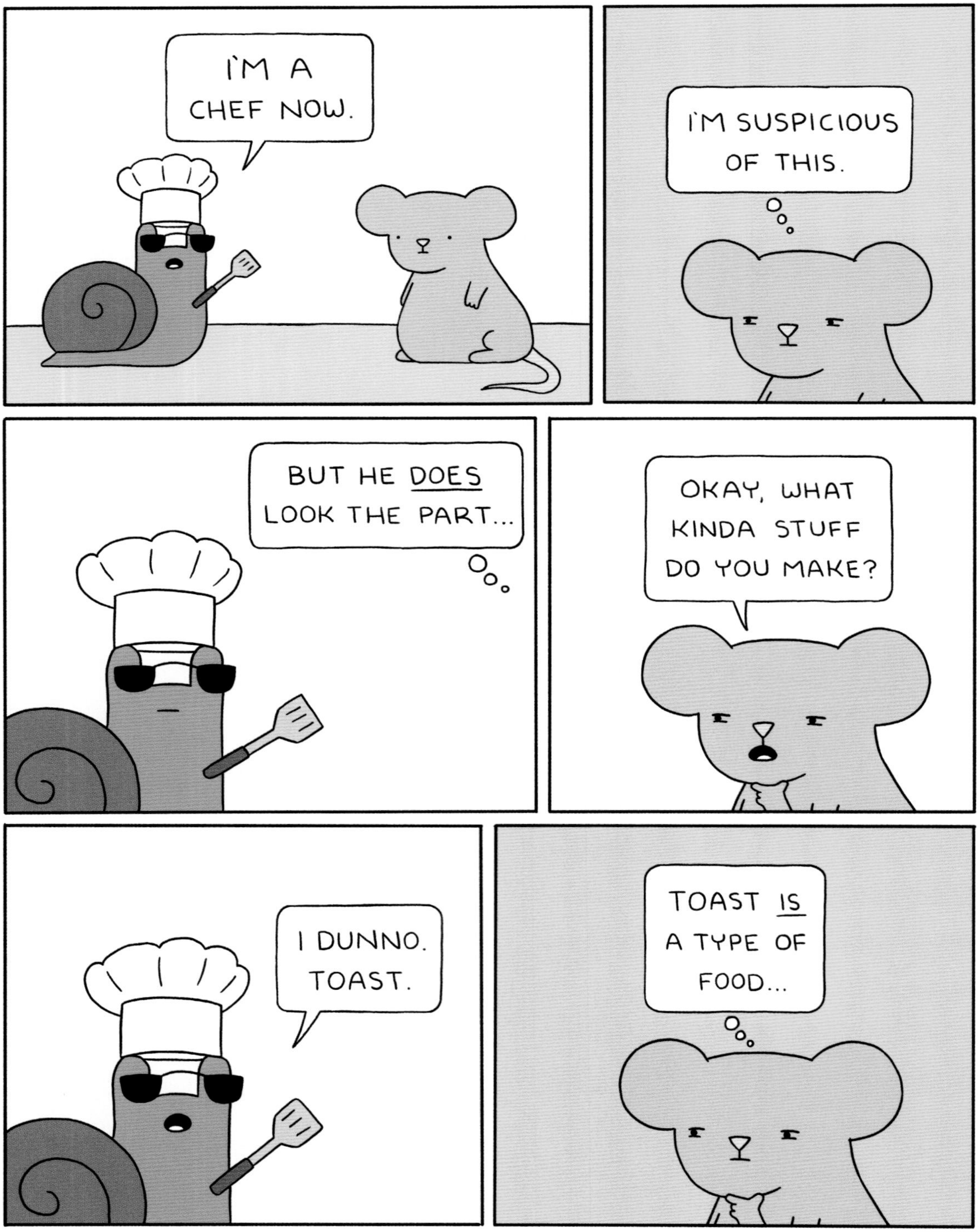
I'M A CHEF NOW.
I'M SUSPICIOUS OF THIS.
BUT HE DOES LOOK THE PART...
OKAY, WHAT KINDA STUFF DO YOU MAKE?
I DUNNO. TOAST.
TOAST IS A TYPE OF FOOD...

Little Bird

LITTLE BIRD, HOW ARE YOU TODAY?
FURIOUS!

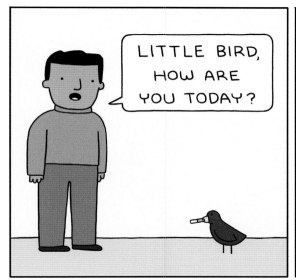

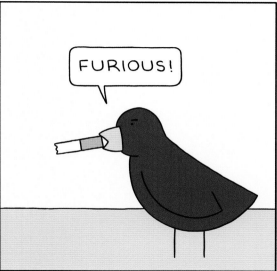

Hoops

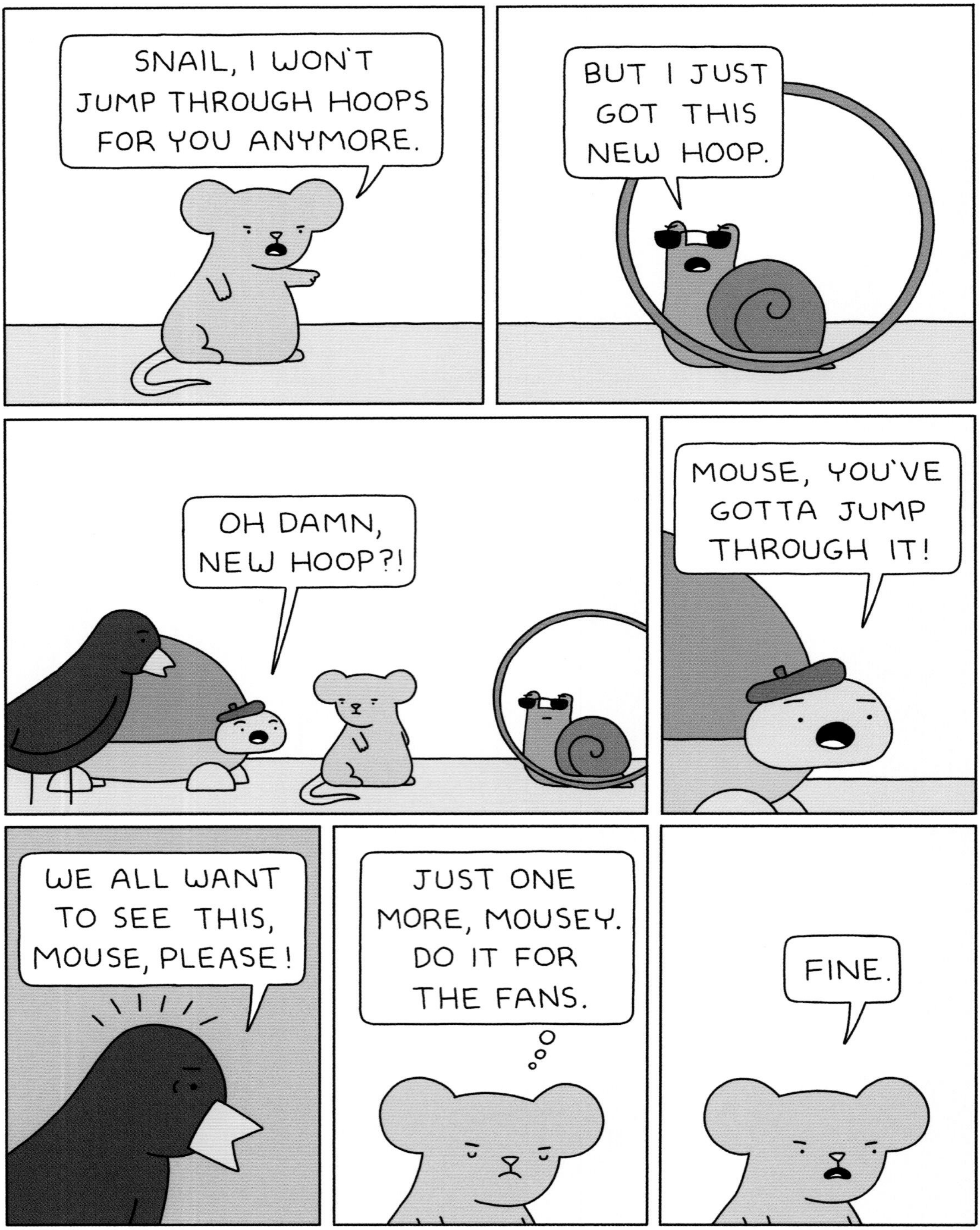
SNAIL, I WON'T JUMP THROUGH HOOPS FOR YOU ANYMORE.
BUT I JUST GOT THIS NEW HOOP.
OH DAMN, NEW HOOP?!
MOUSE, YOU'VE GOTTA JUMP THROUGH IT!
WE ALL WANT TO SEE THIS, MOUSE, PLEASE!
JUST ONE MORE, MOUSEY. DO IT FOR THE FANS.
FINE.

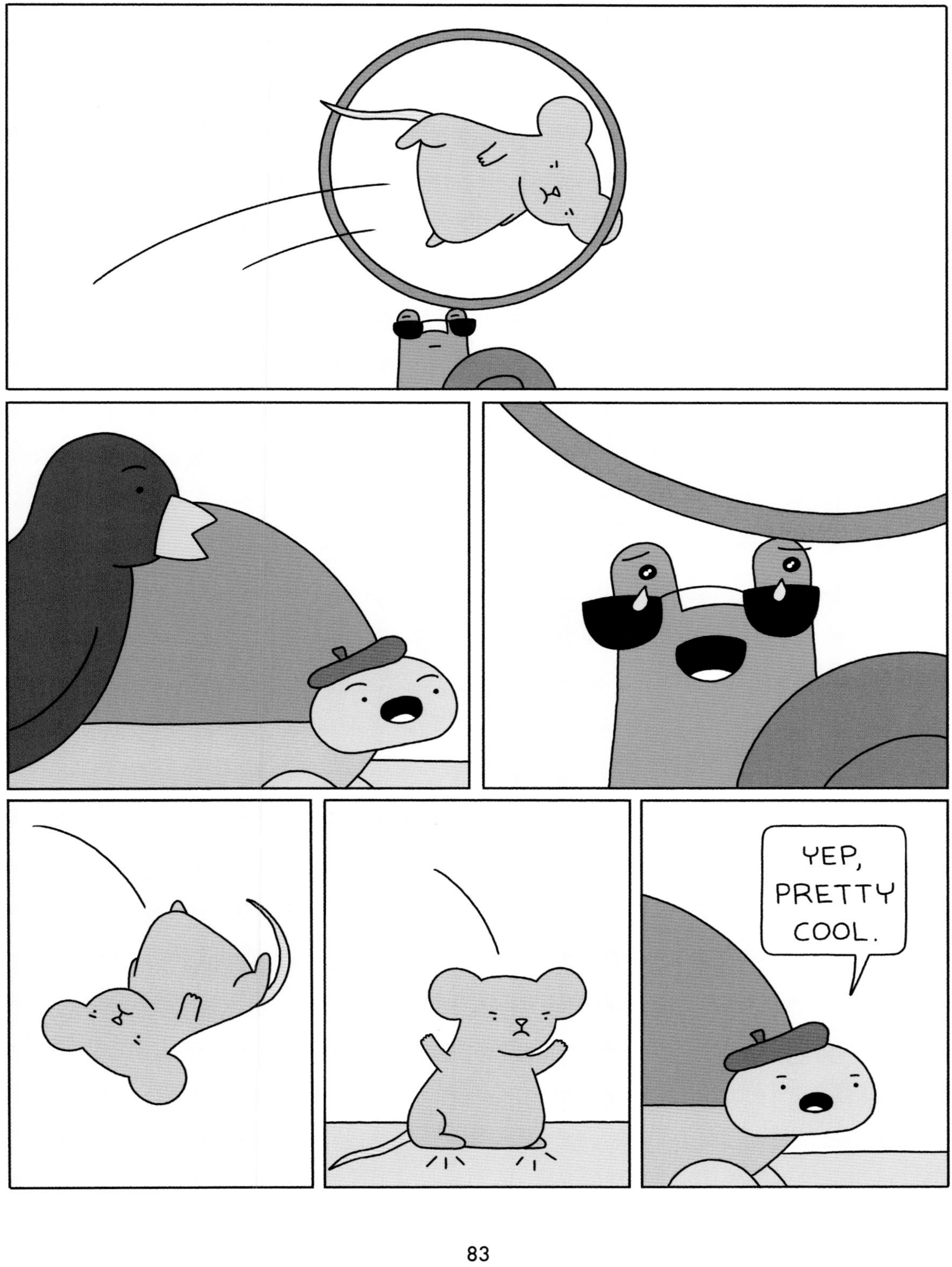
YEP, PRETTY COOL.

Dog-tor

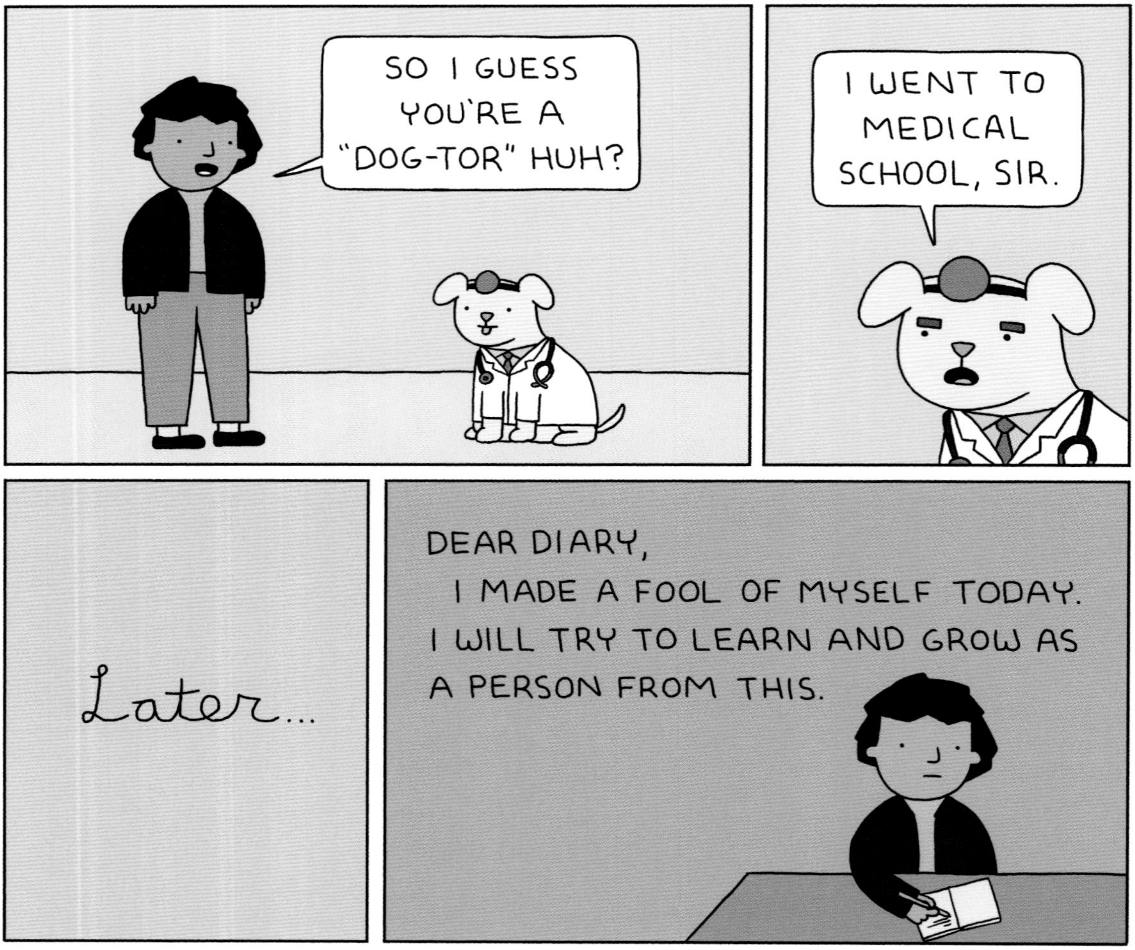
SO I GUESS YOU'RE A "DOG-TOR" HUH?
I WENT TO MEDICAL SCHOOL, SIR.
Later...
DEAR DIARY,
I MADE A FOOL OF MYSELF TODAY. I WILL TRY TO LEARN AND GROW AS A PERSON FROM THIS.

Nineties Called

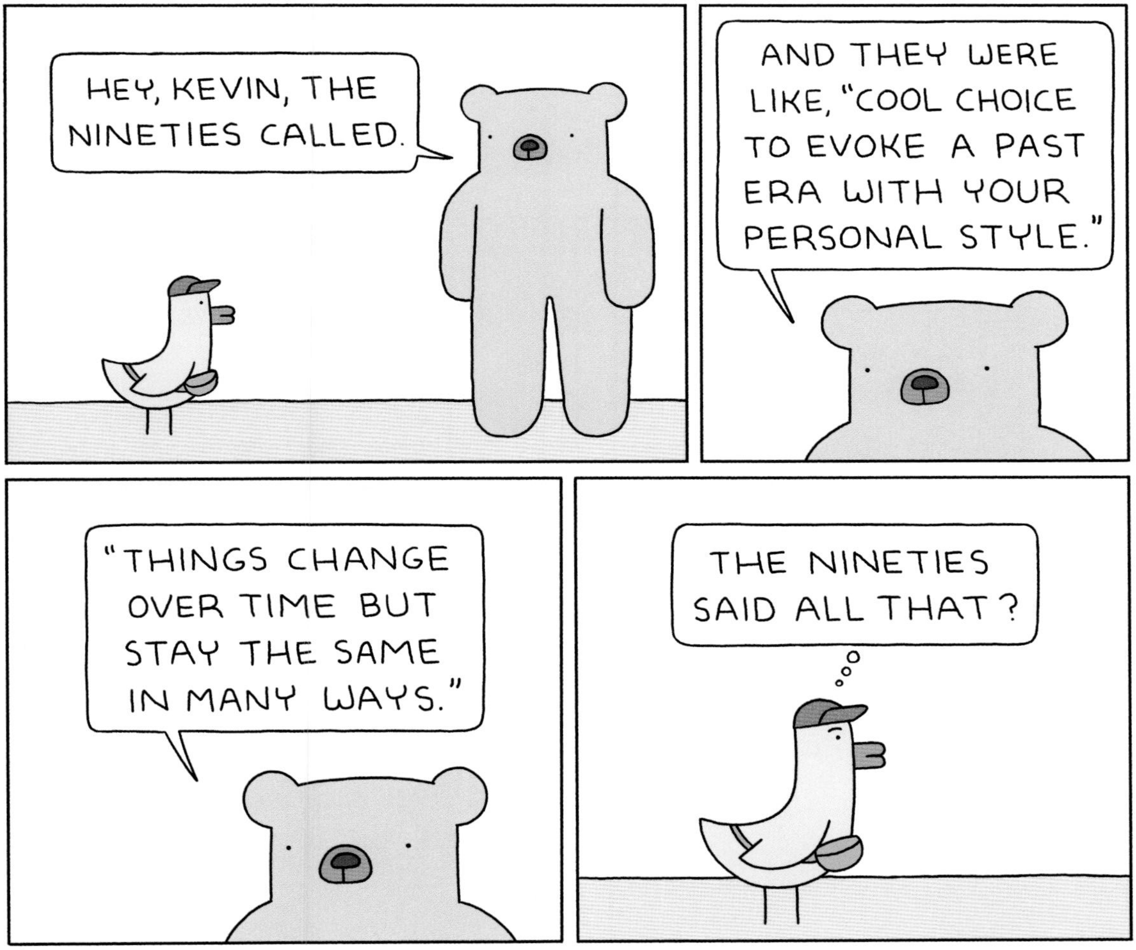
HEY, KEVIN, THE NINETIES CALLED.
AND THEY WERE LIKE, "COOL CHOICE TO EVOKE A PAST ERA WITH YOUR PERSONAL STYLE."
"THINGS CHANGE OVER TIME BUT STAY THE SAME IN MANY WAYS."
THE NINETIES SAID ALL THAT?

Think

DO YOU EVER THINK—
NOT IF I CAN HELP IT.

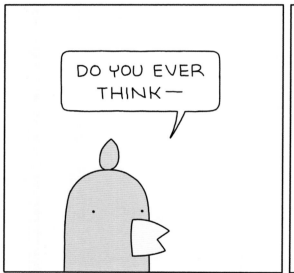

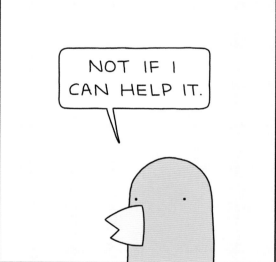

Everything Cool

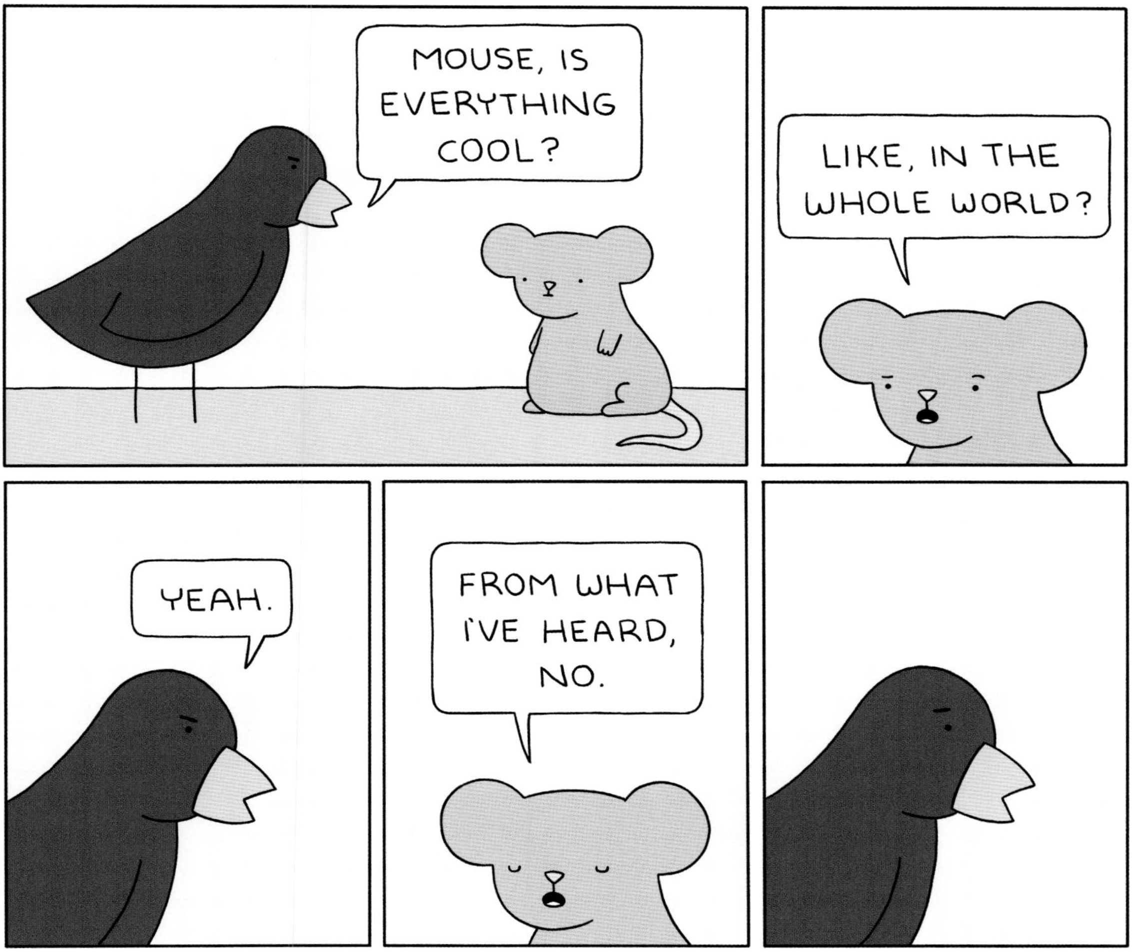

MOUSE, IS EVERYTHING COOL?
LIKE, IN THE WHOLE WORLD?
YEAH.
FROM WHAT I'VE HEARD, NO.

The Smartest

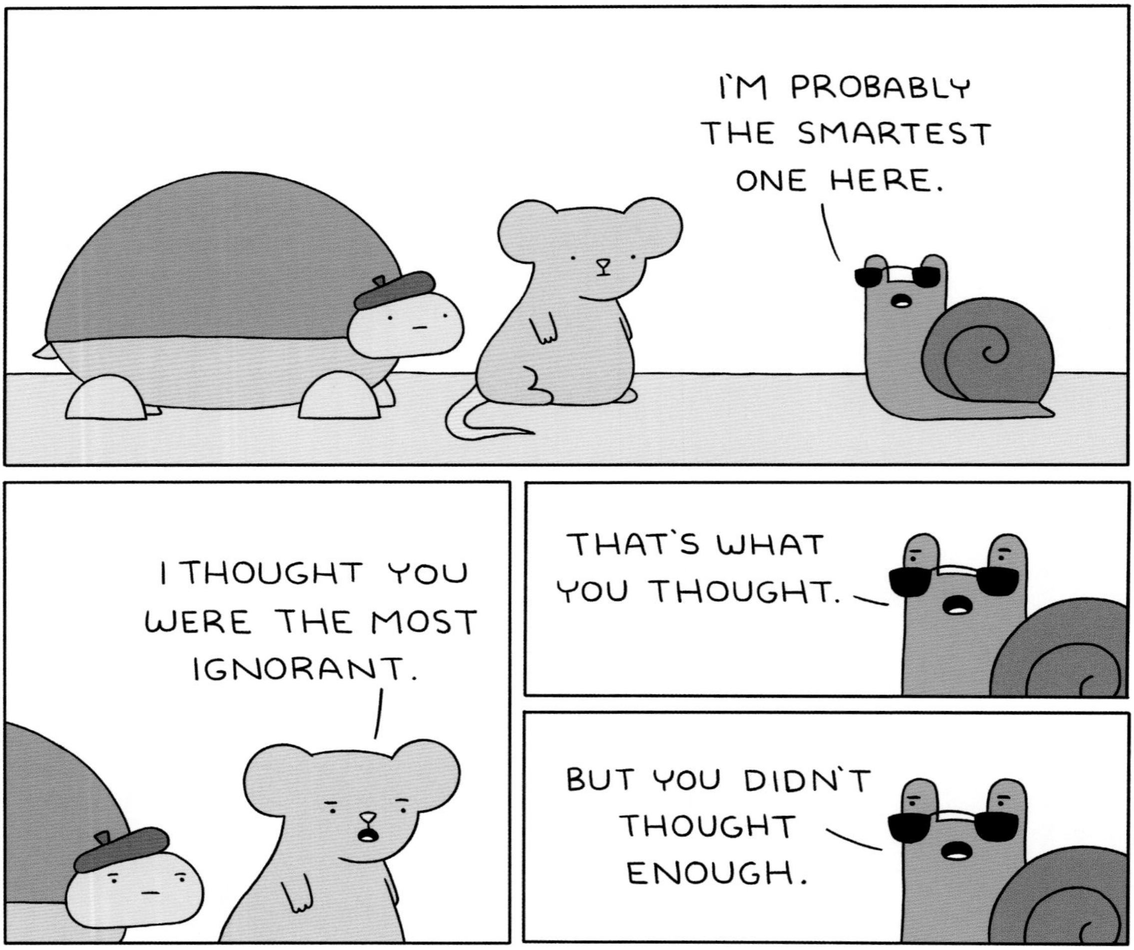
I'M PROBABLY THE SMARTEST ONE HERE.
I THOUGHT YOU WERE THE MOST IGNORANT.
THAT'S WHAT YOU THOUGHT.
BUT YOU DIDN'T THOUGHT ENOUGH.

Grumpy

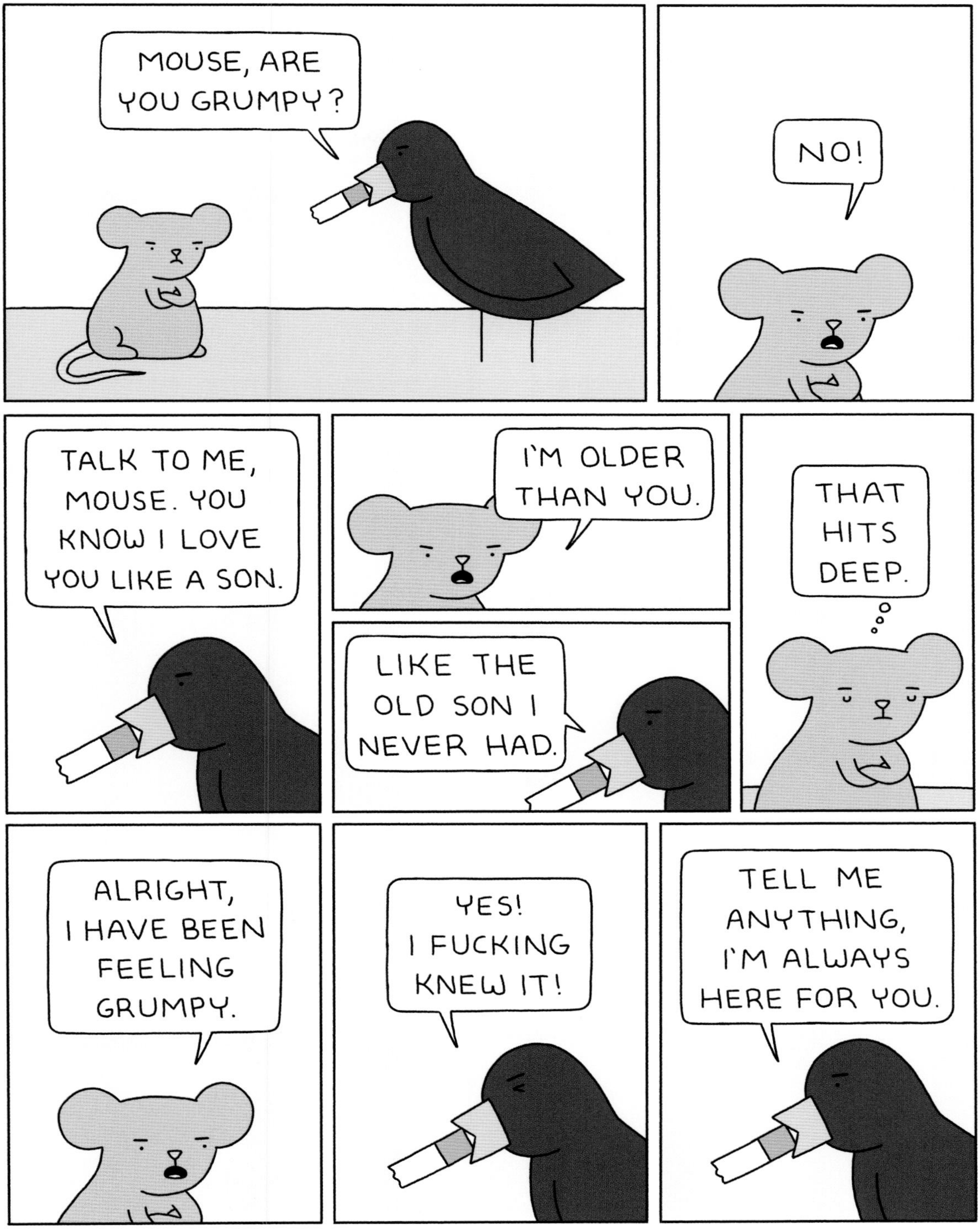
MOUSE, ARE YOU GRUMPY?
NO!
TALK TO ME, MOUSE. YOU KNOW I LOVE YOU LIKE A SON.
I'M OLDER THAN YOU.
LIKE THE OLD SON I NEVER HAD.
THAT HITS DEEP.
ALRIGHT, I HAVE BEEN FEELING GRUMPY.
YES! I FUCKING KNEW IT!
TELL ME ANYTHING, I'M ALWAYS HERE FOR YOU.

Made Mistakes

IN MY PAST I'VE MADE MISTAKES.
BUT IN MY FUTURE...
I WILL MAKE DIFFERENT MISTAKES.

Eat Cheese

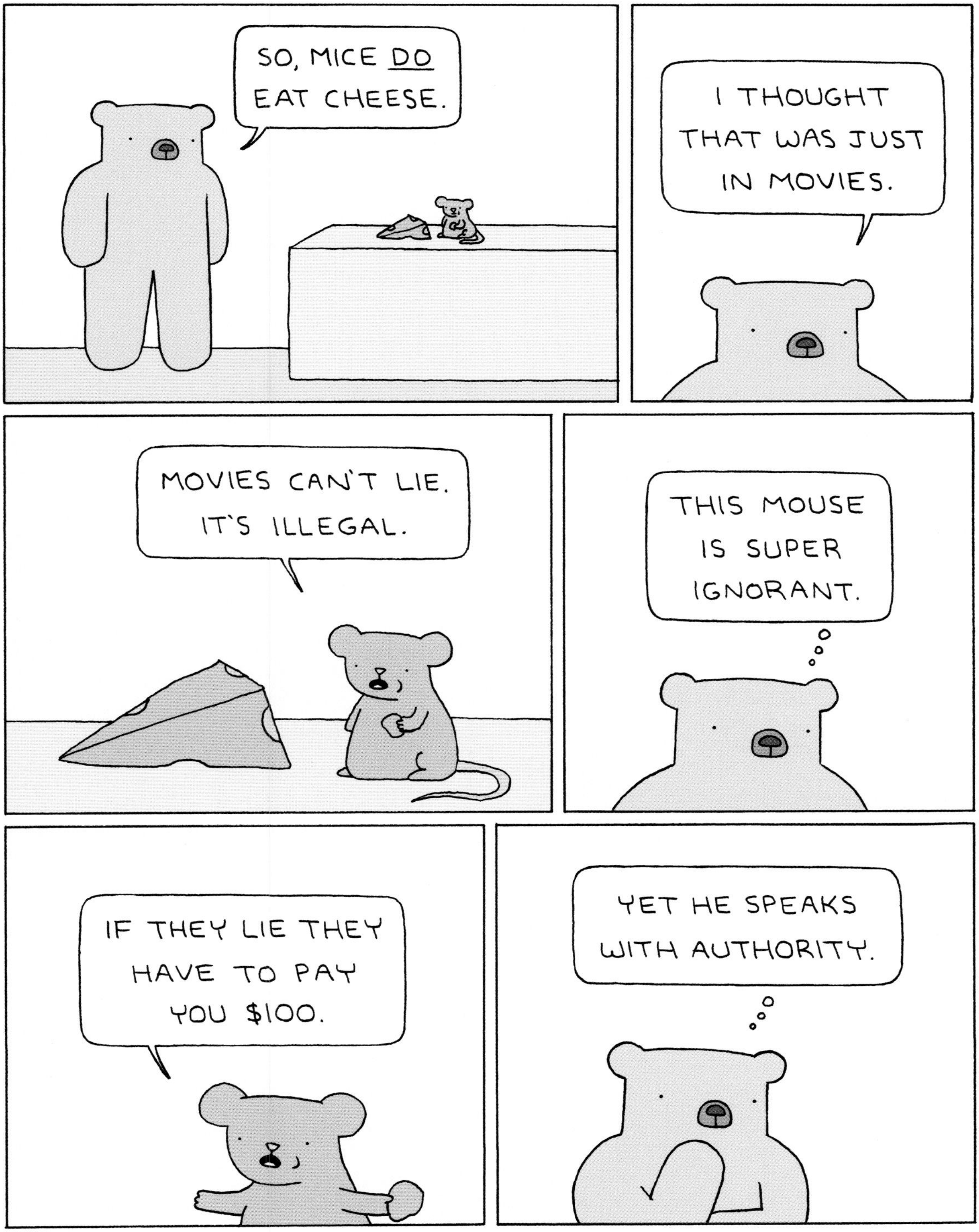
SO, MICE DO EAT CHEESE.
I THOUGHT THAT WAS JUST IN MOVIES.
MOVIES CAN'T LIE. IT'S ILLEGAL.
THIS MOUSE IS SUPER IGNORANT.
IF THEY LIE THEY HAVE TO PAY YOU $100.
YET HE SPEAKS WITH AUTHORITY.

Here's Where

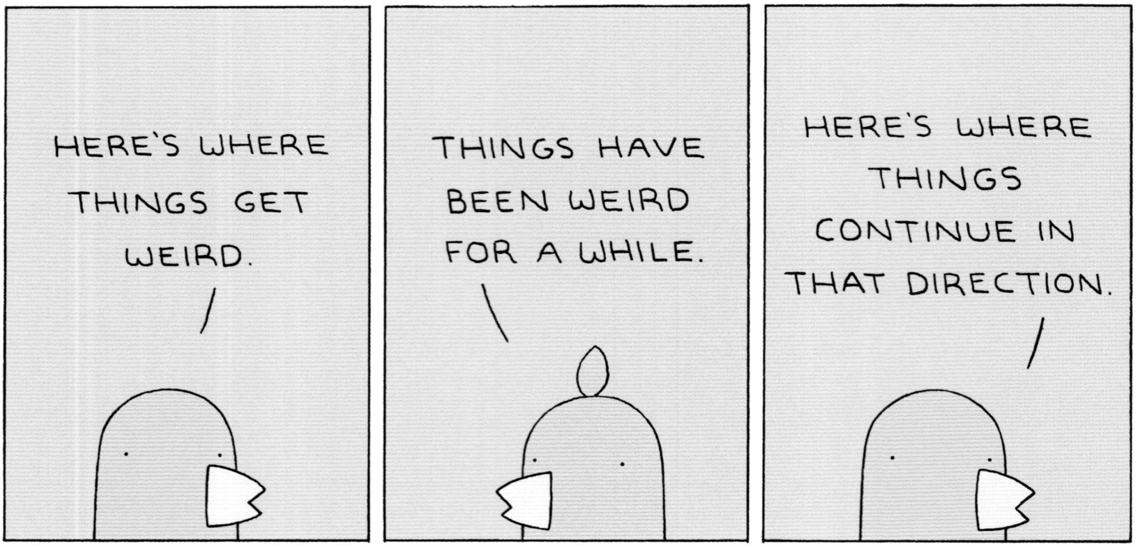
HERE'S WHERE THINGS GET WEIRD.
THINGS HAVE BEEN WEIRD FOR A WHILE.
HERE'S WHERE THINGS CONTINUE IN THAT DIRECTION.

Nothing Scares Me

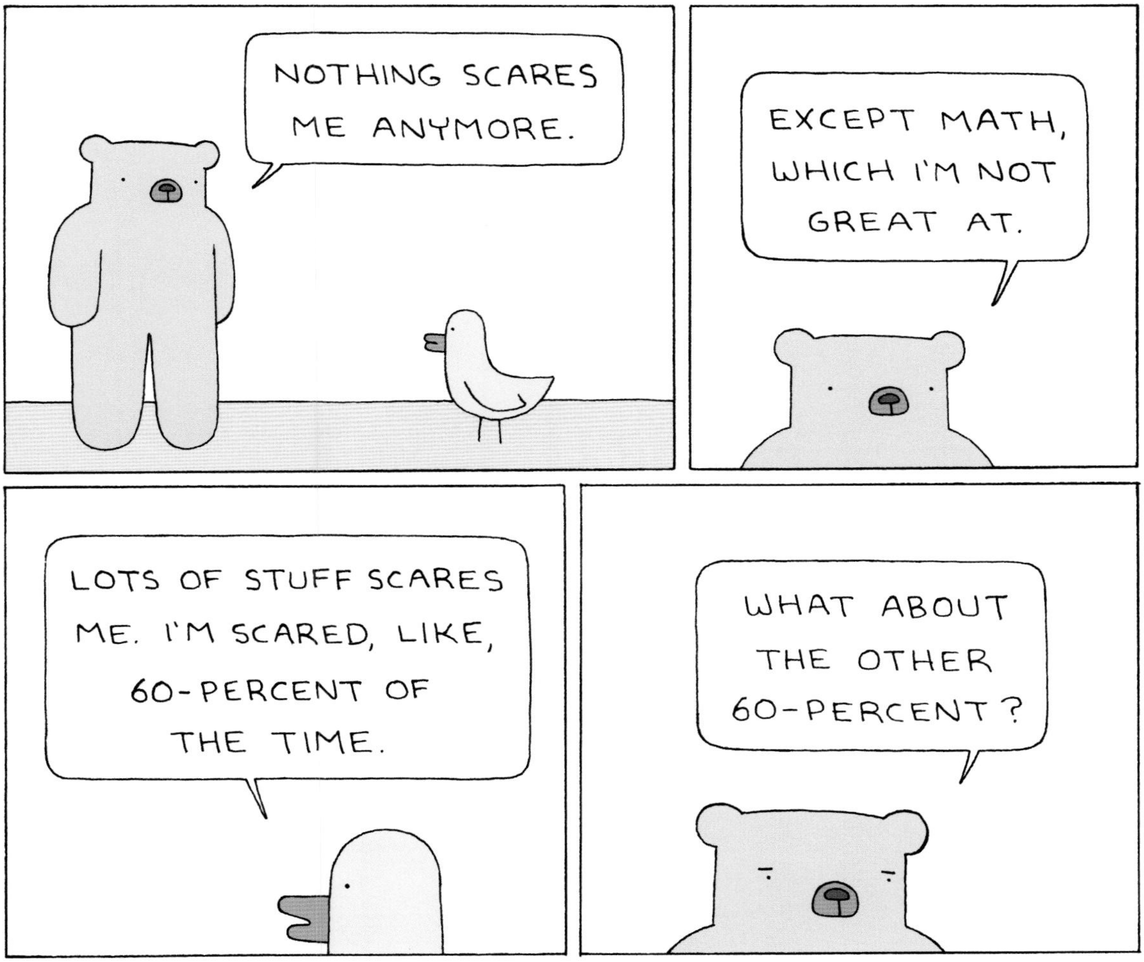
NOTHING SCARES ME ANYMORE.
EXCEPT MATH, WHICH I'M NOT GREAT AT.
LOTS OF STUFF SCARES ME. I'M SCARED, LIKE, 60-PERCENT OF THE TIME.
WHAT ABOUT THE OTHER 60-PERCENT?

Please Rate

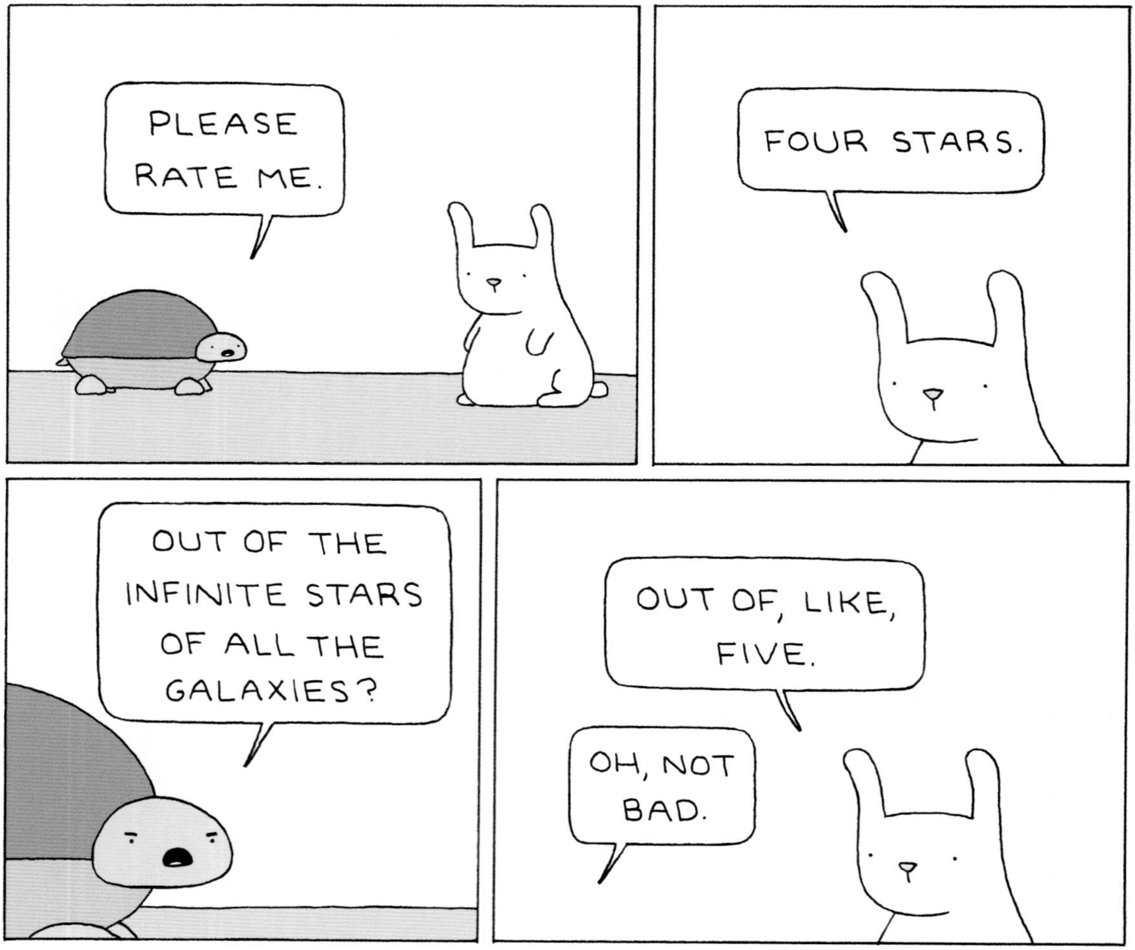
PLEASE RATE ME.
FOUR STARS.
OUT OF THE INFINITE STARS OF ALL THE GALAXIES?
OUT OF, LIKE, FIVE.
OH, NOT BAD.

Keeps You Going

MA'AM, WHAT IS IT THAT KEEPS YOU GOING?
MY DESIRE TO CRUSH MY ENEMIES.
AND MY SENSE OF WONDER.

Everything

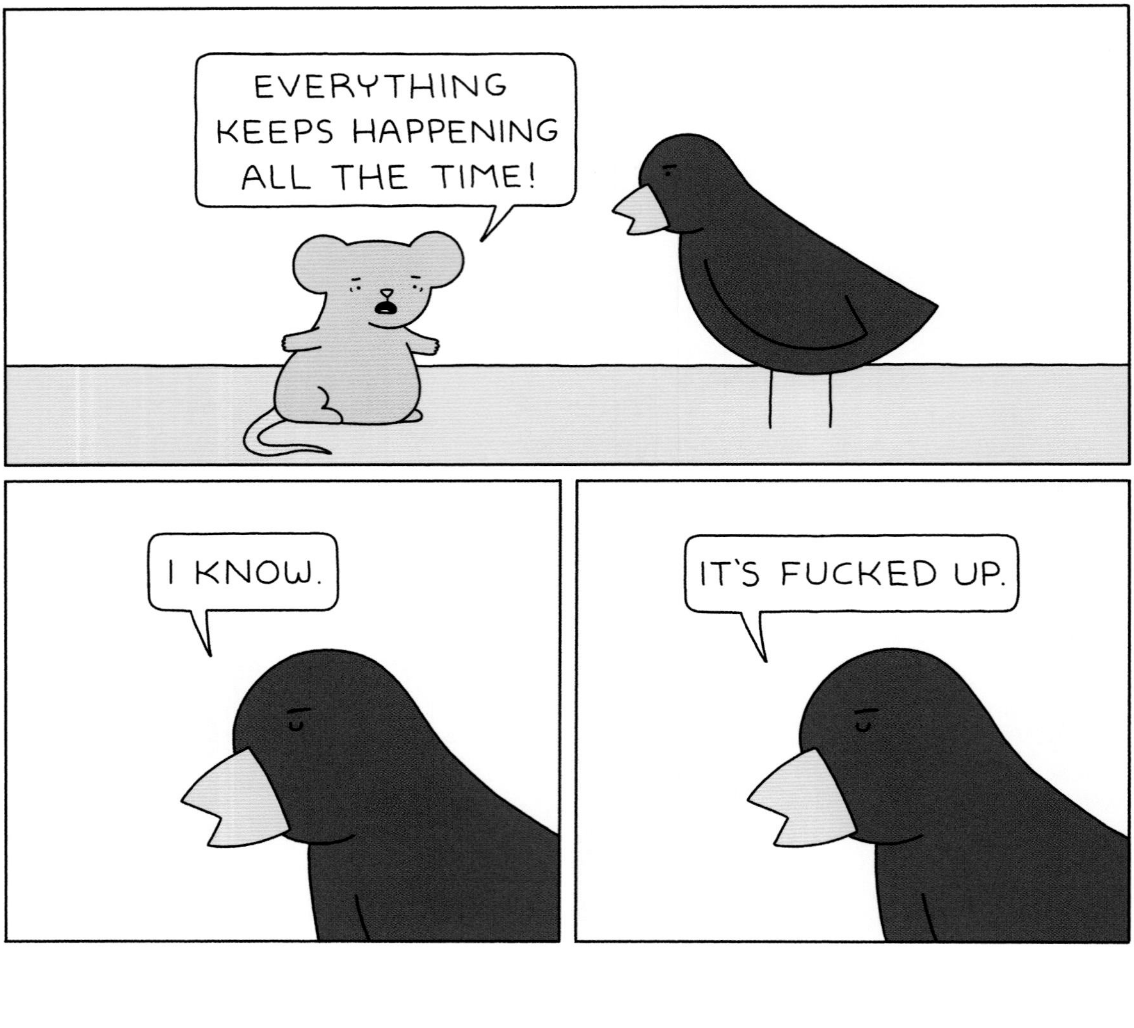
EVERYTHING KEEPS HAPPENING ALL THE TIME!
I KNOW.
IT'S FUCKED UP.

Fly

PRETTY COOL I CAN FLY I GUESS.
I NEVER THINK ABOUT THAT ANYMORE.
IT'S WILD THE STUFF YOU CAN NORMALIZE.
I REMEMBER THE FIRST TIME...
PRETTY COOL I CAN FLY I GUESS.

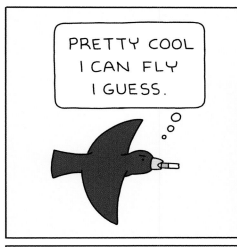

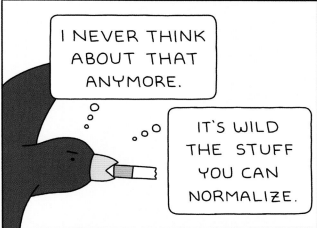

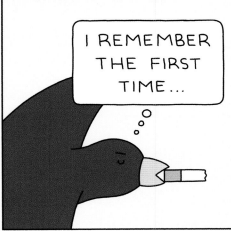

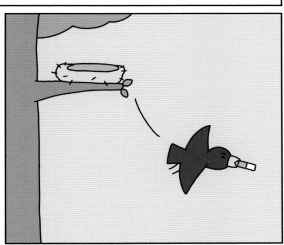

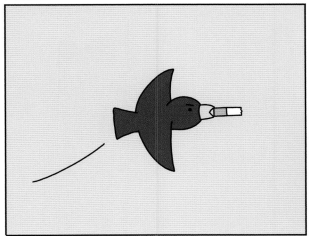

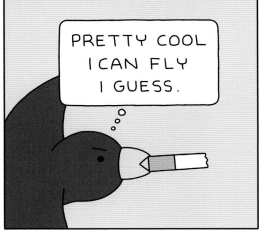

Get Serious

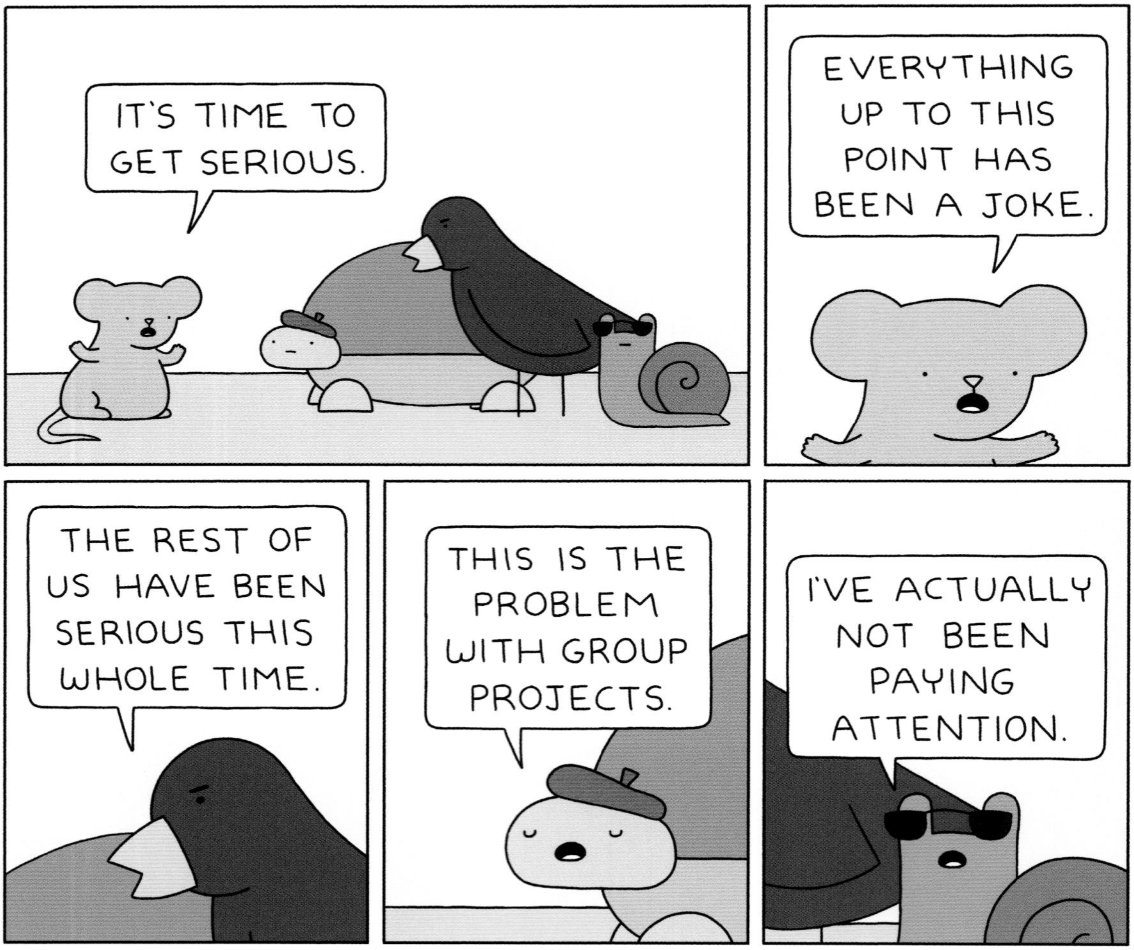
IT'S TIME TO GET SERIOUS.
EVERYTHING UP TO THIS POINT HAS BEEN A JOKE.
THE REST OF US HAVE BEEN SERIOUS THIS WHOLE TIME.
THIS IS THE PROBLEM WITH GROUP PROJECTS.
I'VE ACTUALLY NOT BEEN PAYING ATTENTION.

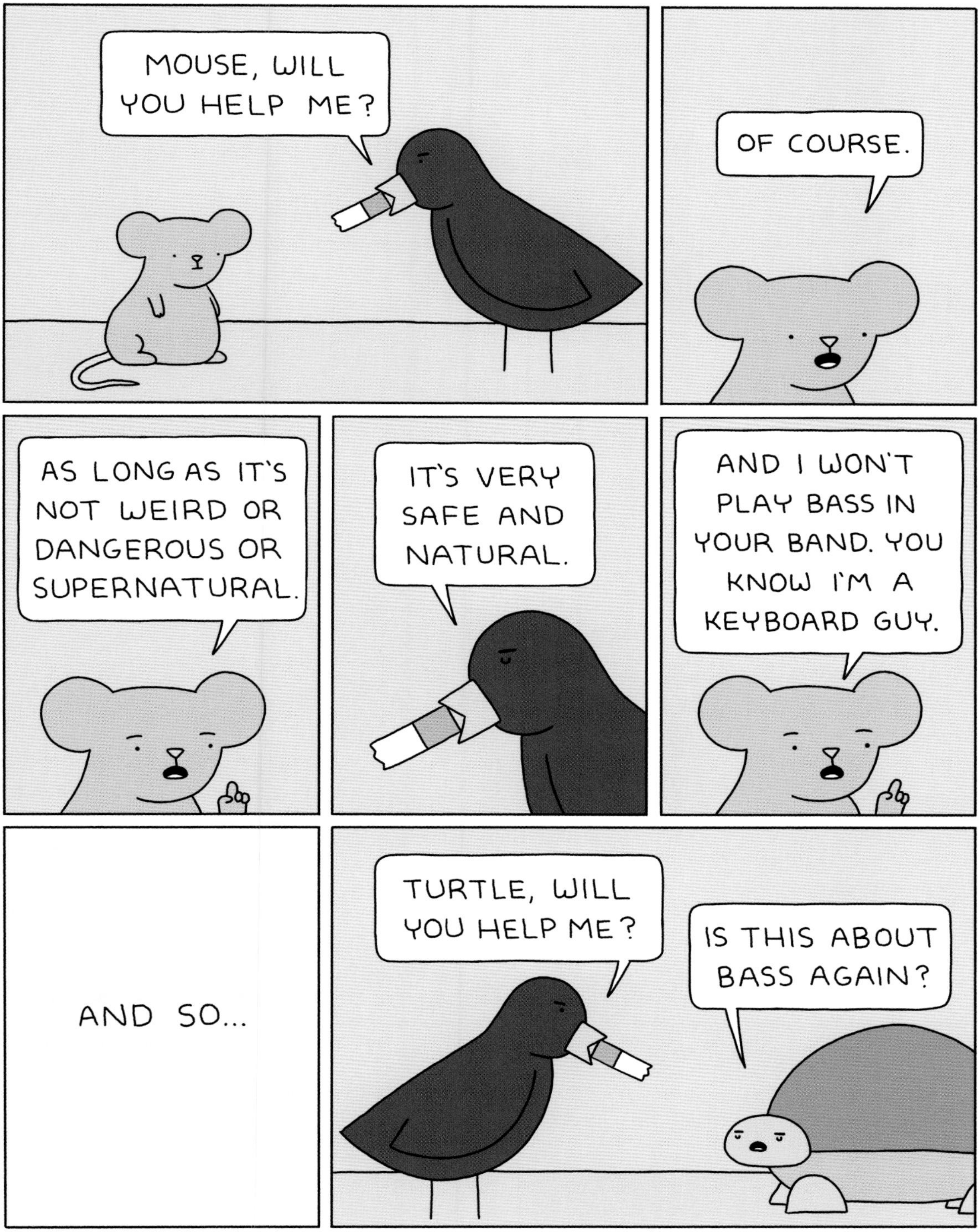
MOUSE, WILL YOU HELP ME?
OF COURSE.
AS LONG AS IT'S NOT WEIRD OR DANGEROUS OR SUPERNATURAL.
IT'S VERY SAFE AND NATURAL.
AND I WON'T PLAY BASS IN YOUR BAND. YOU KNOW I'M A KEYBOARD GUY.
AND SO...
TURTLE, WILL YOU HELP ME?
IS THIS ABOUT BASS AGAIN?

Get Out of Town

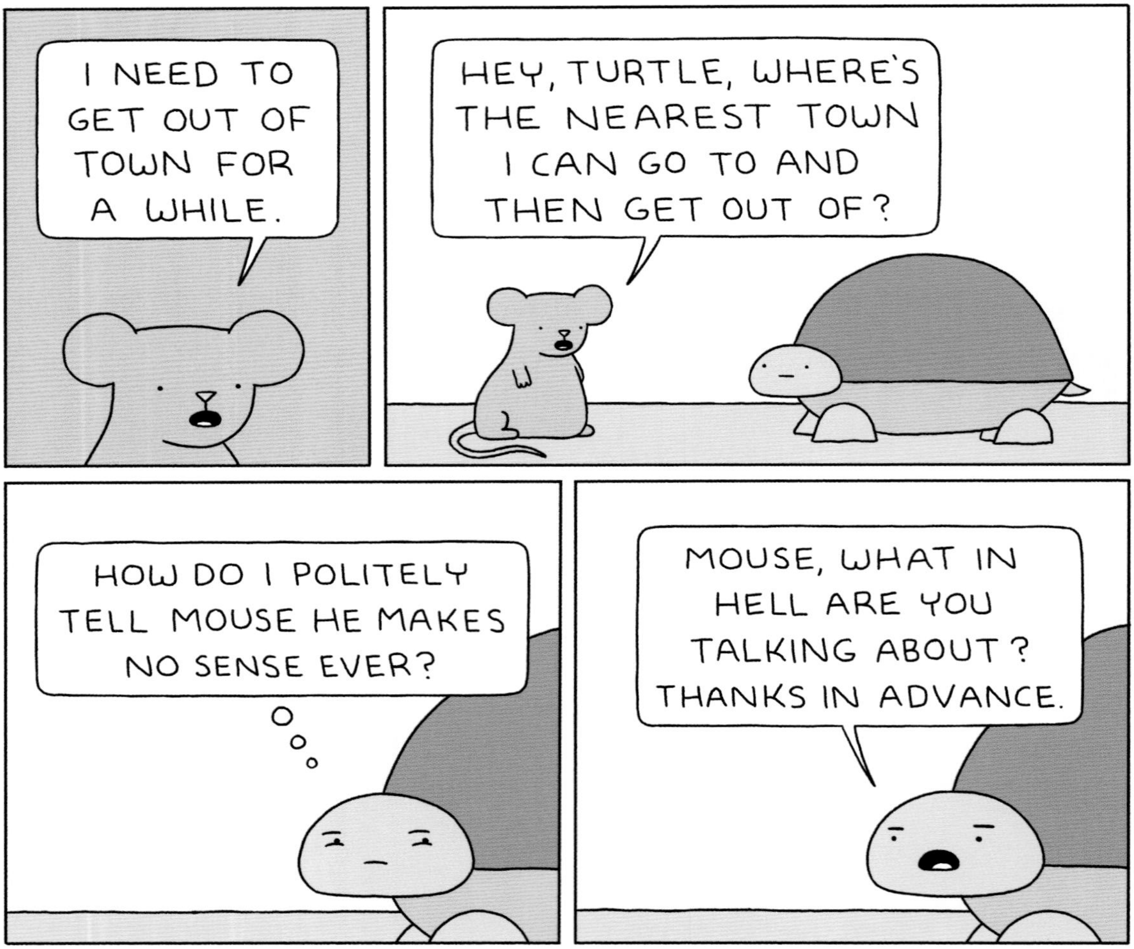
I NEED TO GET OUT OF TOWN FOR A WHILE.
HEY, TURTLE, WHERE'S THE NEAREST TOWN I CAN GO TO AND THEN GET OUT OF?
HOW DO I POLITELY TELL MOUSE HE MAKES NO SENSE EVER?
MOUSE, WHAT IN HELL ARE YOU TALKING ABOUT? THANKS IN ADVANCE.

Like Me

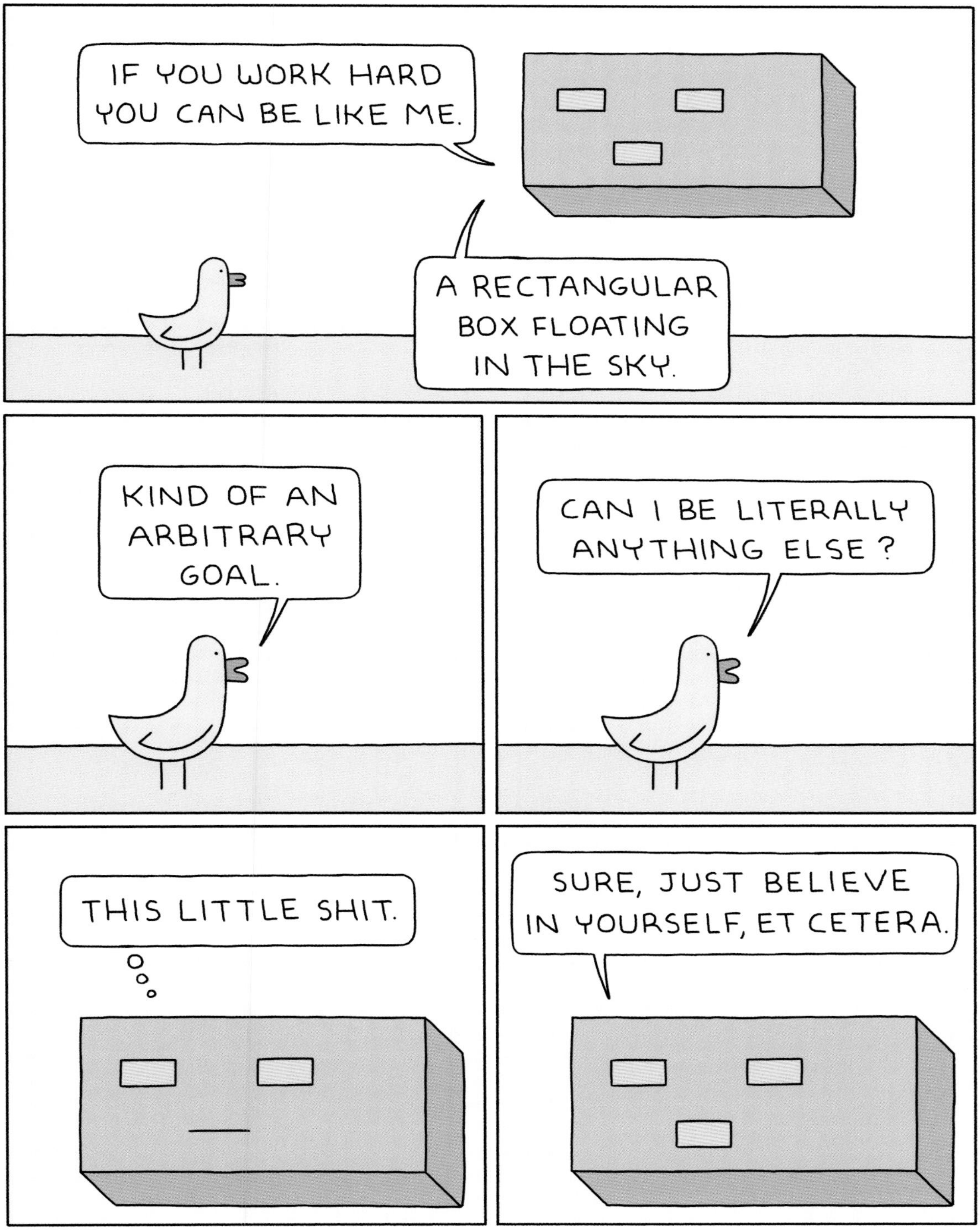
IF YOU WORK HARD YOU CAN BE LIKE ME.
A RECTANGULAR BOX FLOATING IN THE SKY.
KIND OF AN ARBITRARY GOAL.
CAN I BE LITERALLY ANYTHING ELSE?
THIS LITTLE SHIT.
SURE, JUST BELIEVE IN YOURSELF, ET CETERA.

Nothing Done

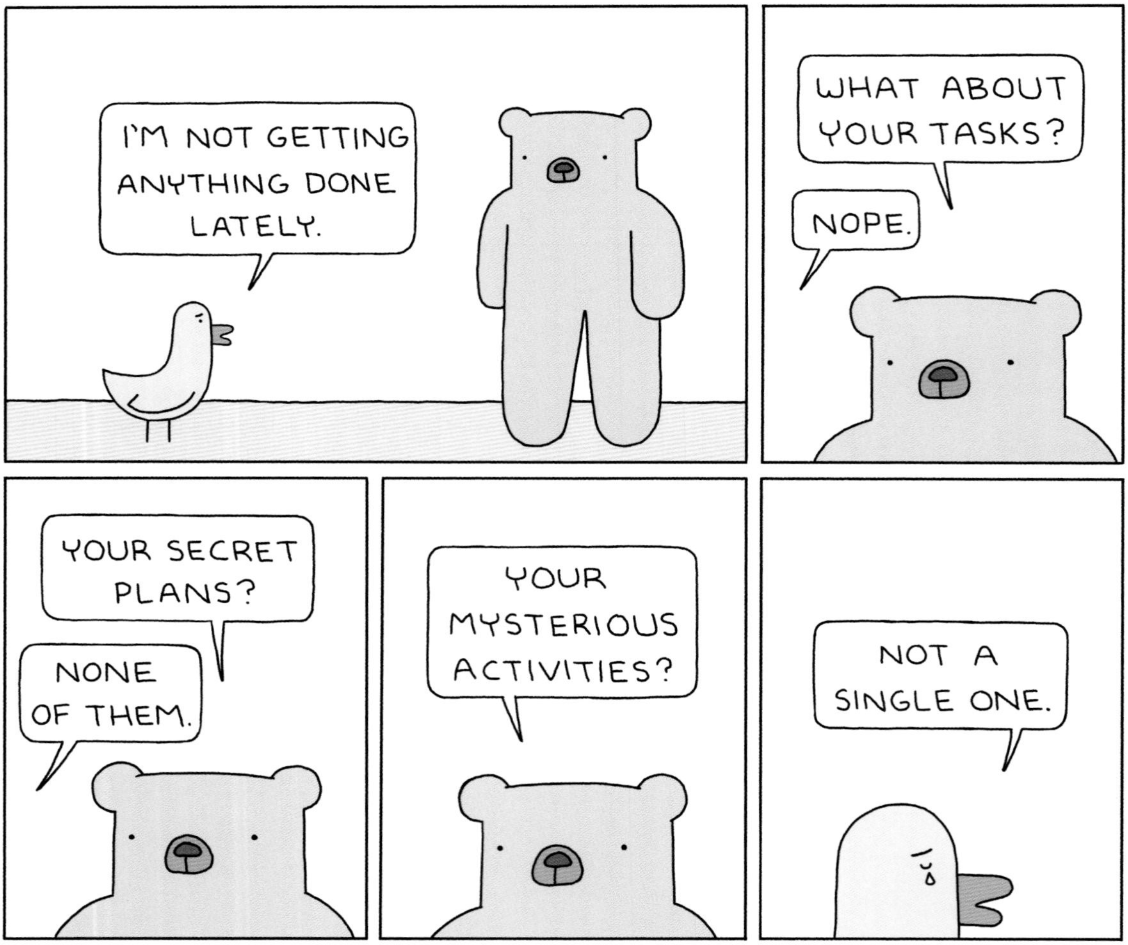
I'M NOT GETTING ANYTHING DONE LATELY.
WHAT ABOUT YOUR TASKS?
NOPE.
YOUR SECRET PLANS?
NONE OF THEM.
YOUR MYSTERIOUS ACTIVITIES?
NOT A SINGLE ONE.

Unusual

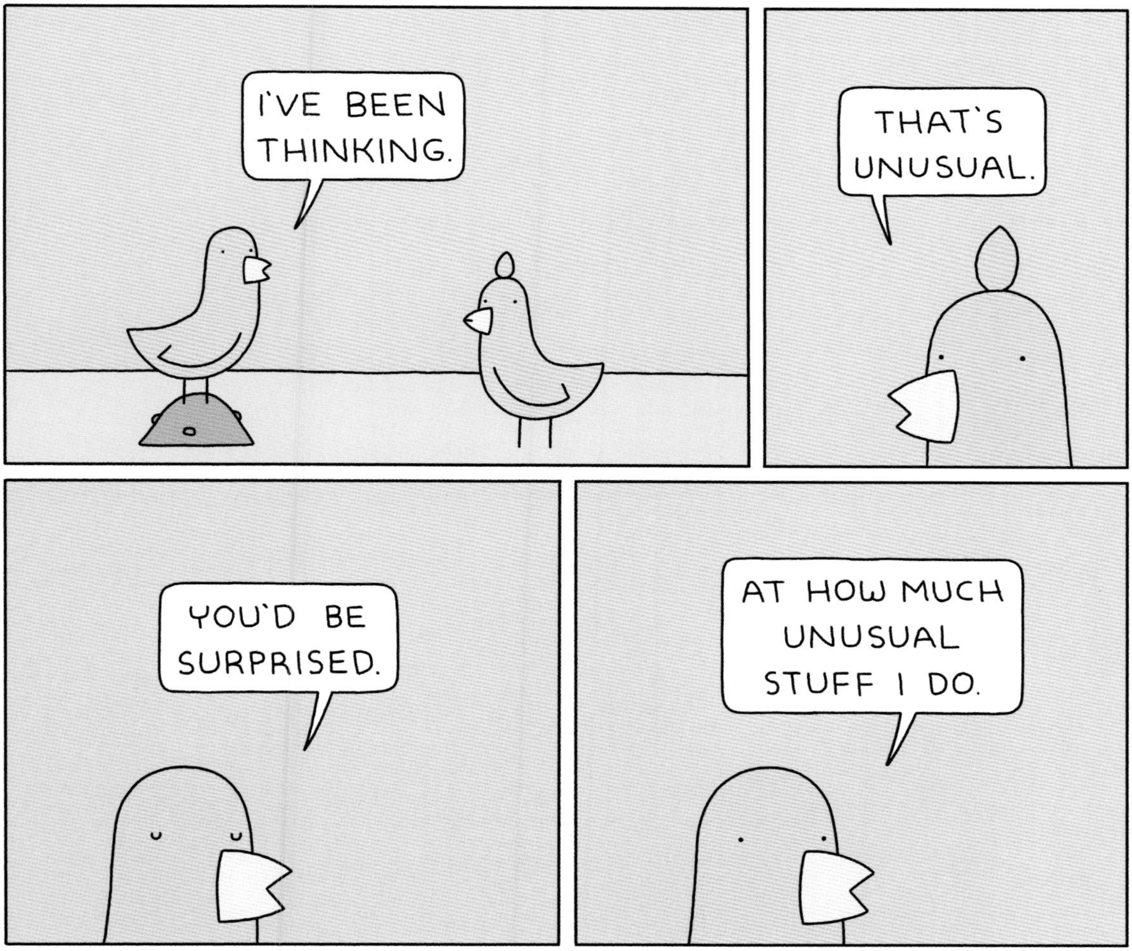
I'VE BEEN THINKING.
THAT'S UNUSUAL.
YOU'D BE SURPRISED.
AT HOW MUCH UNUSUAL STUFF I DO.

A Compliment

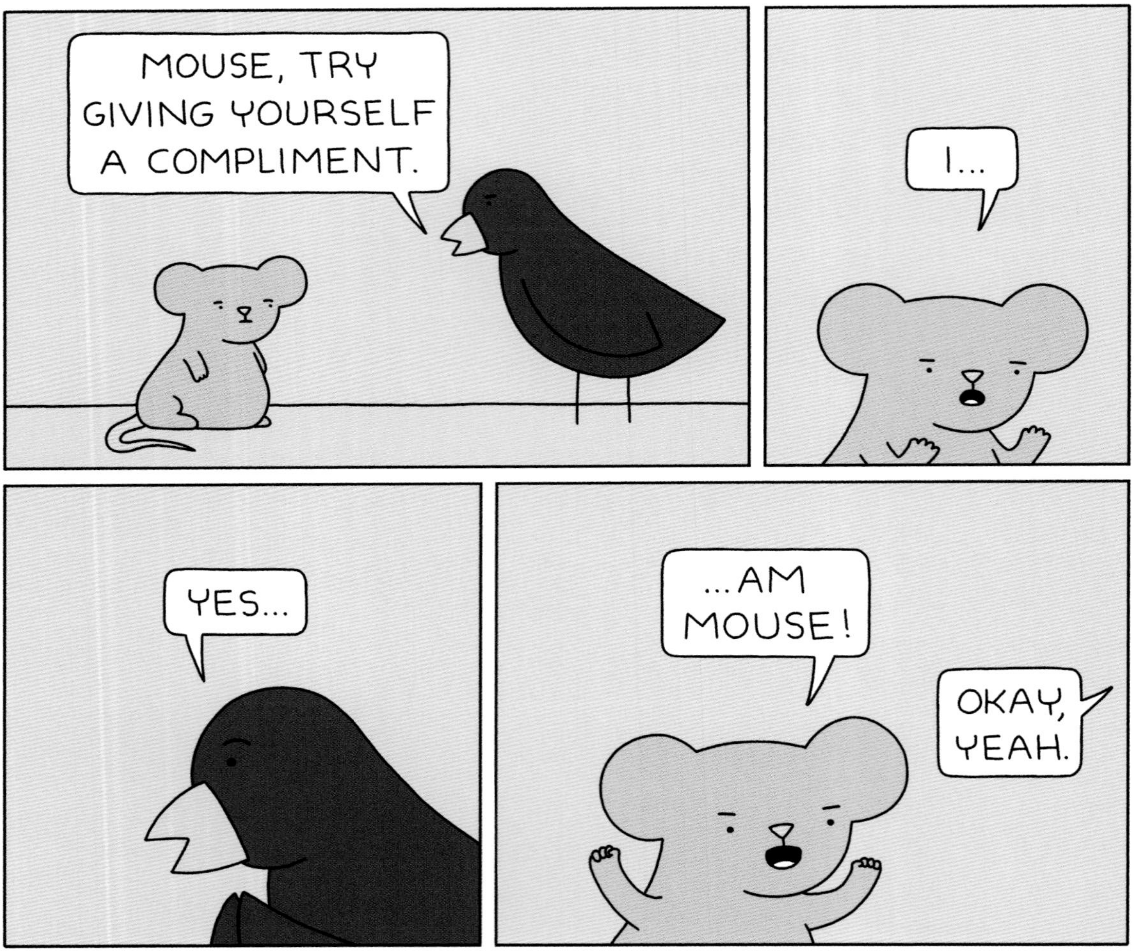
MOUSE, TRY GIVING YOURSELF A COMPLIMENT.
I...
YES...
...AM MOUSE!
OKAY, YEAH.

Learn a Lot

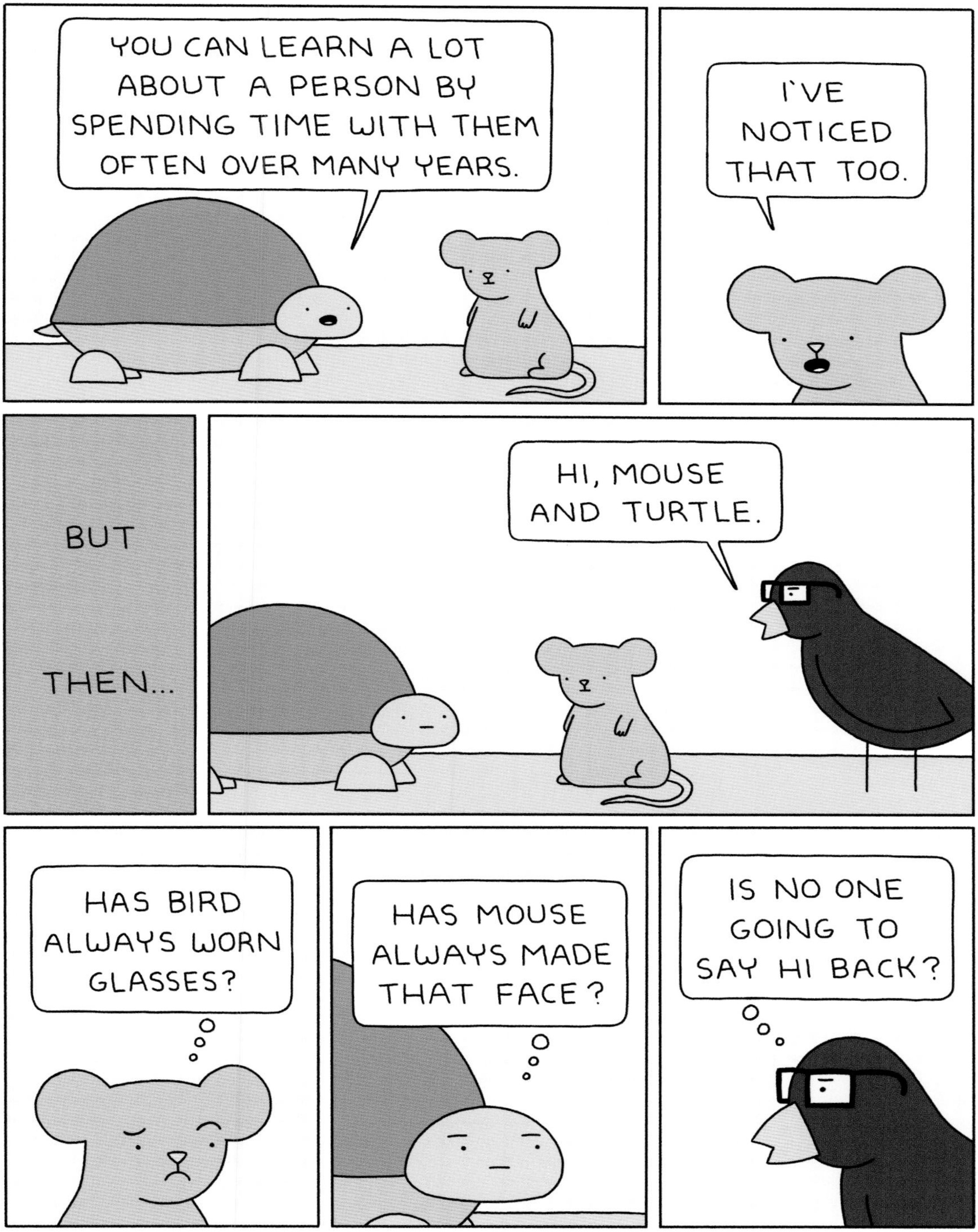
YOU CAN LEARN A LOT ABOUT A PERSON BY SPENDING TIME WITH THEM OFTEN OVER MANY YEARS.
I'VE NOTICED THAT TOO.
BUT
THEN...
HI, MOUSE AND TURTLE.
HAS BIRD ALWAYS WORN GLASSES?
HAS MOUSE ALWAYS MADE THAT FACE?
IS NO ONE GOING TO SAY HI BACK?

Can't Believe

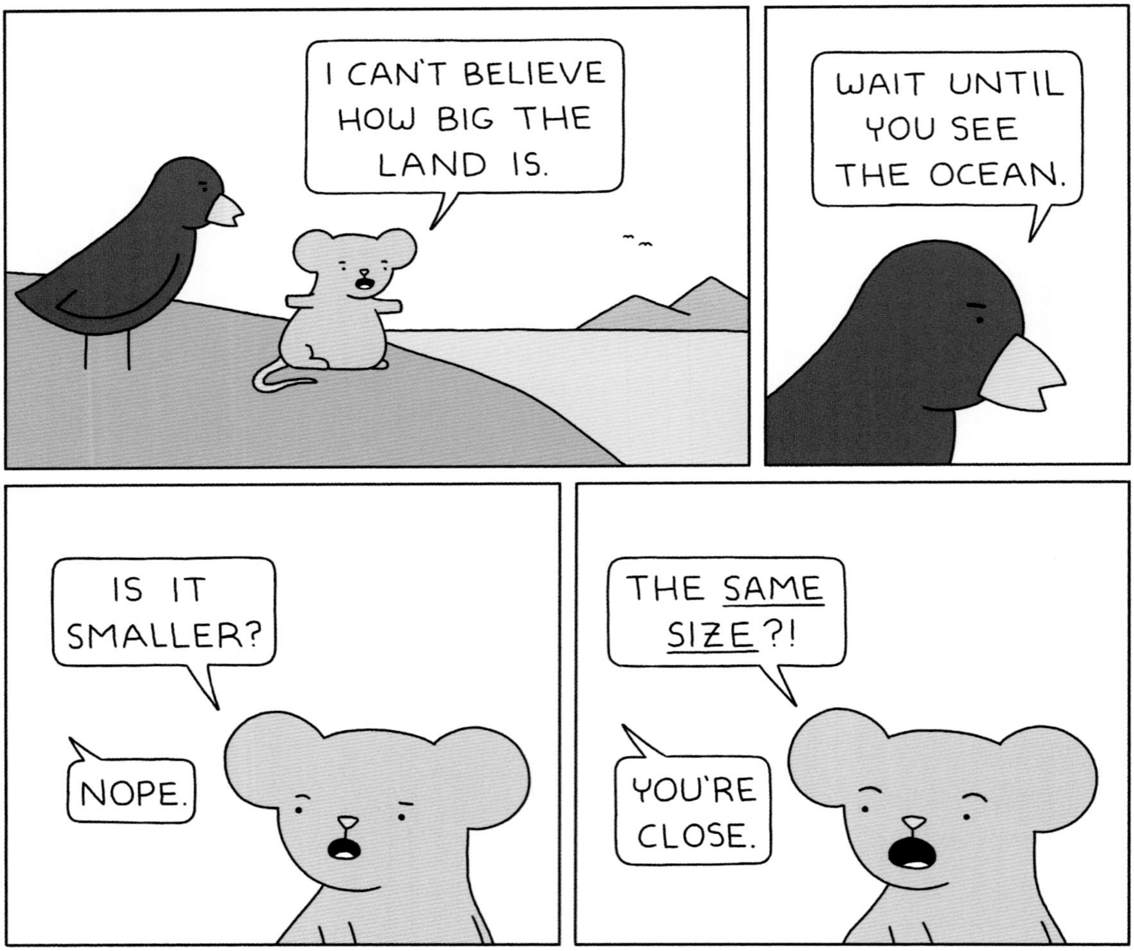
I CAN'T BELIEVE HOW BIG THE LAND IS.
WAIT UNTIL YOU SEE THE OCEAN.
IS IT SMALLER?
NOPE.
THE SAME SIZE?!
YOU'RE CLOSE.

Nothing Ever Happens

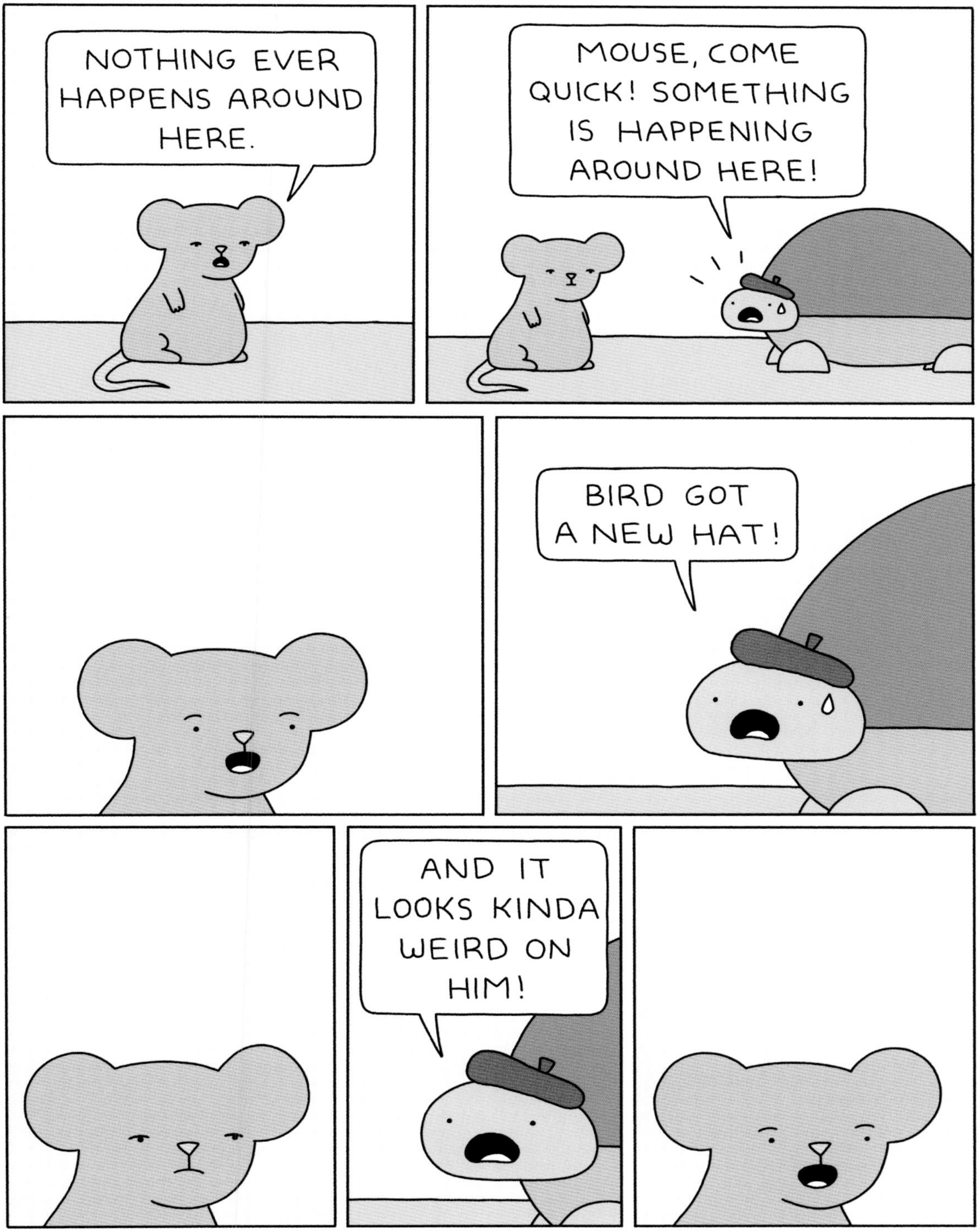
NOTHING EVER HAPPENS AROUND HERE.
MOUSE, COME QUICK! SOMETHING IS HAPPENING AROUND HERE!
BIRD GOT A NEW HAT!
AND IT LOOKS KINDA WEIRD ON HIM!

Let Go

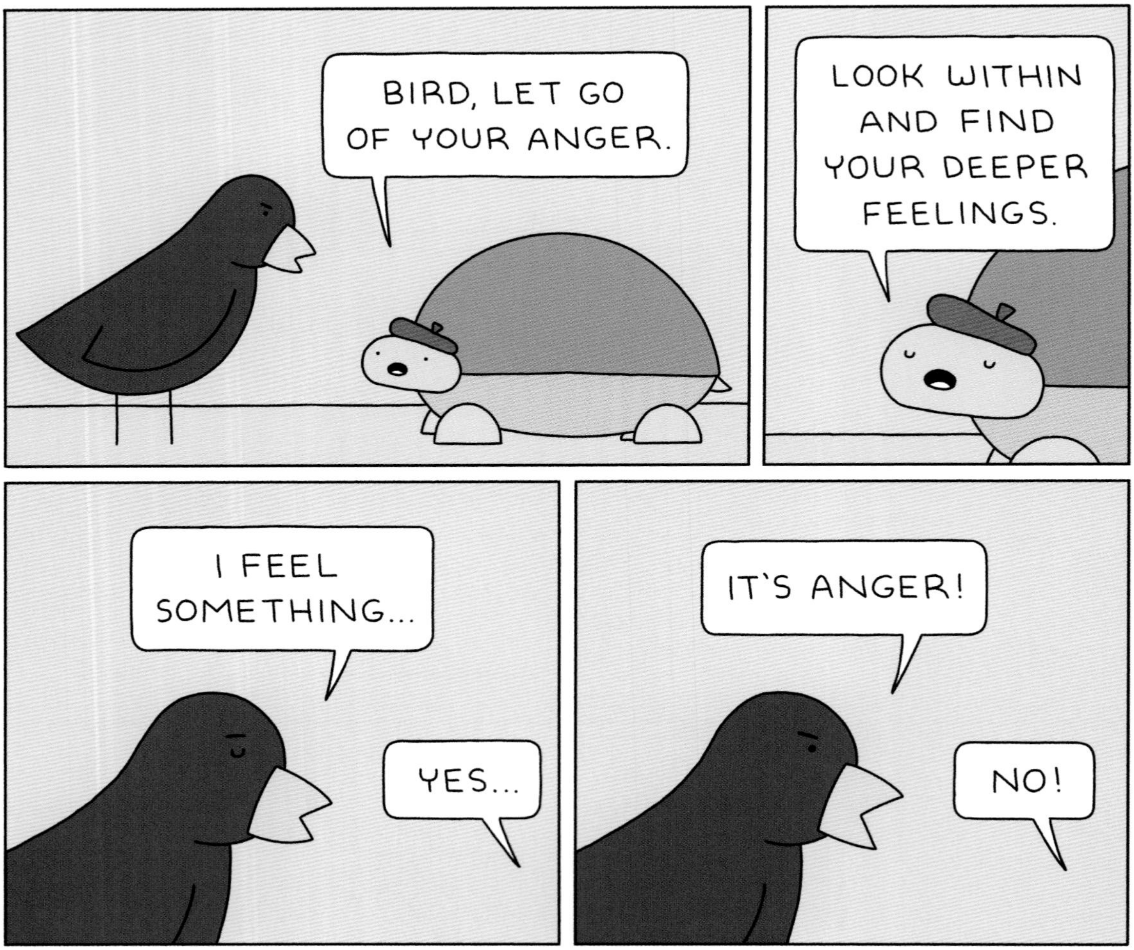
BIRD, LET GO OF YOUR ANGER.
LOOK WITHIN AND FIND YOUR DEEPER FEELINGS.
I FEEL SOMETHING...
YES...
IT'S ANGER!
NO!

Life Crisis

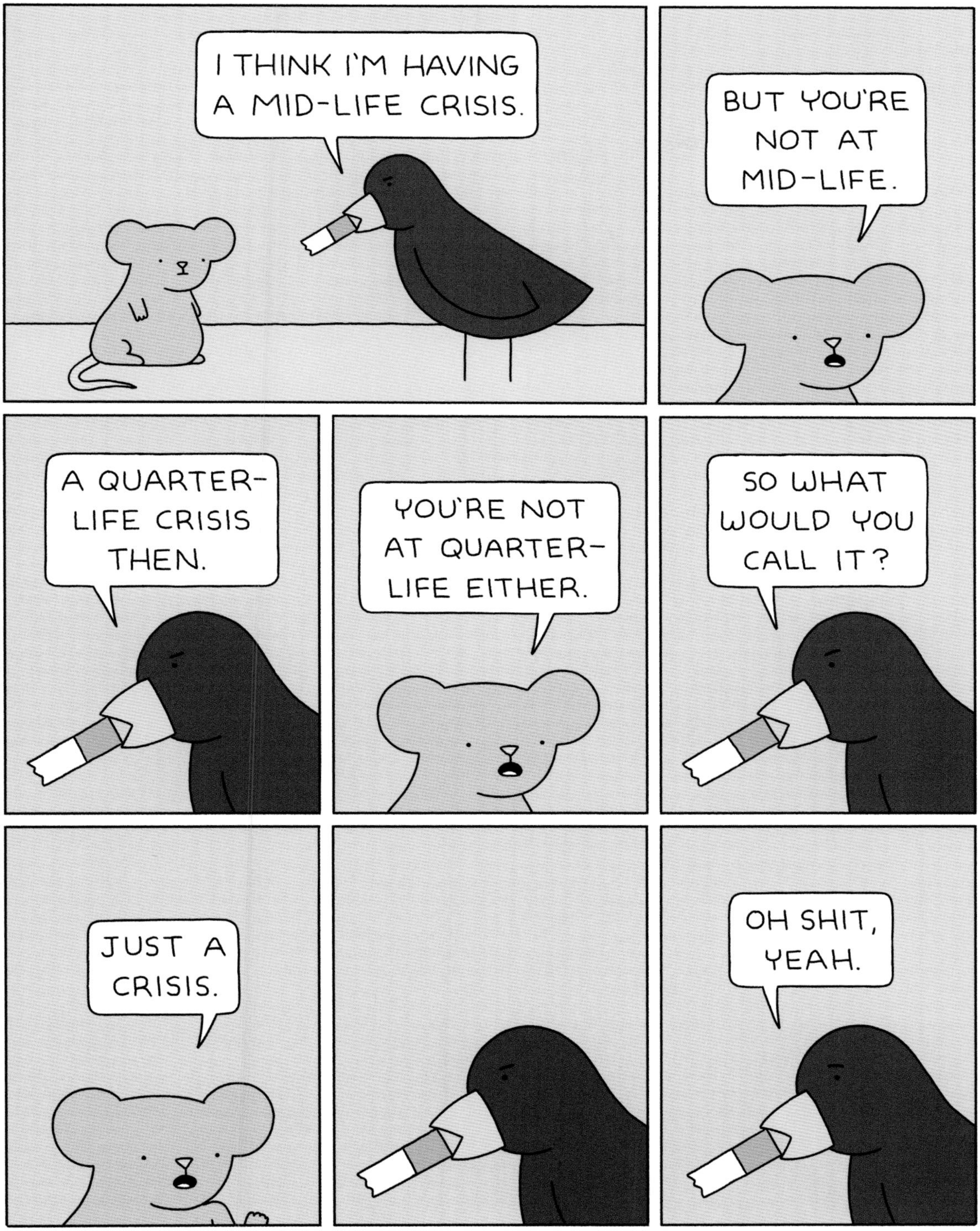

I THINK I'M HAVING A MID-LIFE CRISIS.
BUT YOU'RE NOT AT MID-LIFE.
A QUARTER-LIFE CRISIS THEN.
YOU'RE NOT AT QUARTER-LIFE EITHER.
SO WHAT WOULD YOU CALL IT?
JUST A CRISIS.
OH SHIT, YEAH.

Leaving

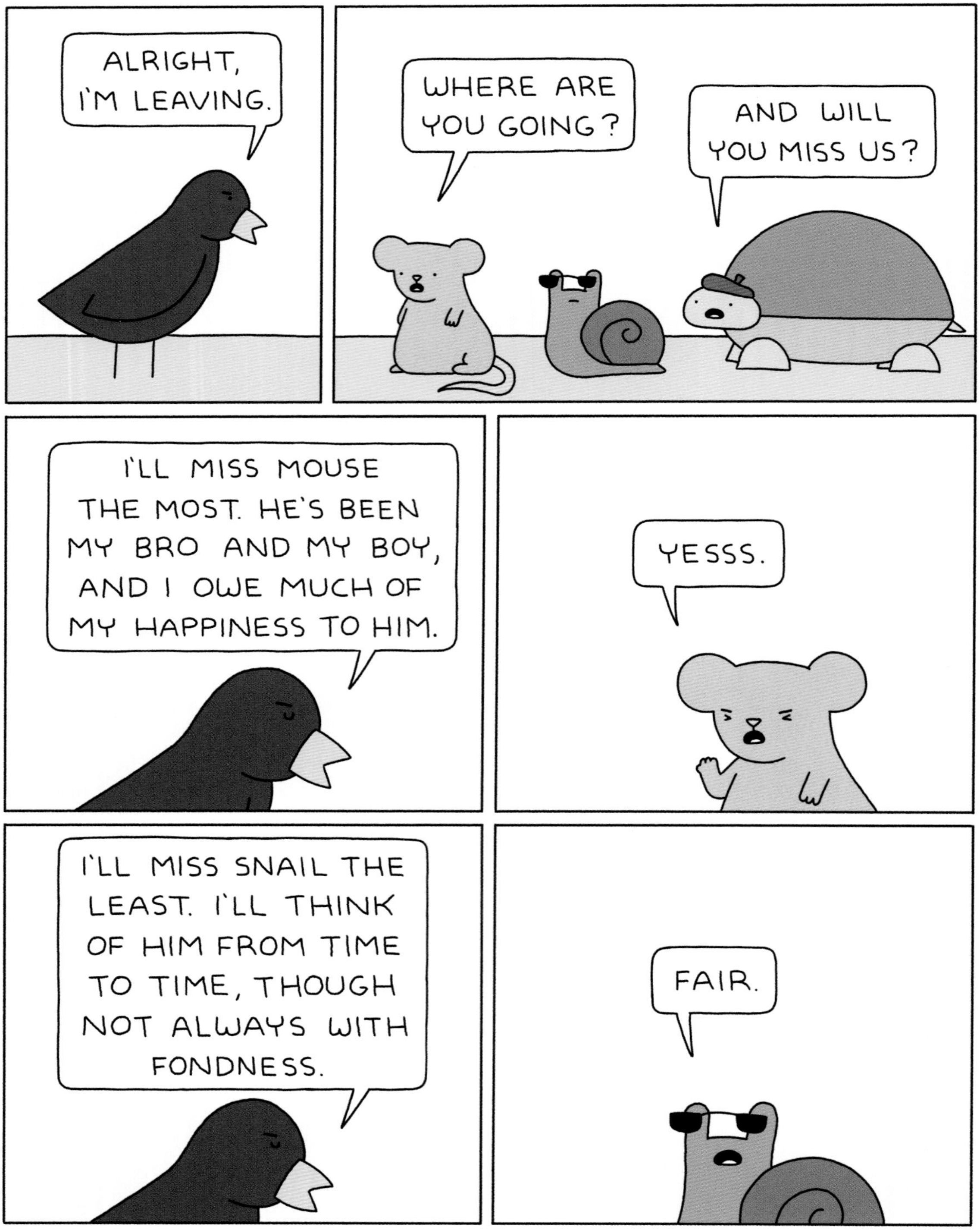
ALRIGHT, I'M LEAVING.
WHERE ARE YOU GOING?
AND WILL YOU MISS US?
I'LL MISS MOUSE THE MOST. HE'S BEEN MY BRO AND MY BOY, AND I OWE MUCH OF MY HAPPINESS TO HIM.
YESSS.
I'LL MISS SNAIL THE LEAST. I'LL THINK OF HIM FROM TIME TO TIME, THOUGH NOT ALWAYS WITH FONDNESS.
FAIR.

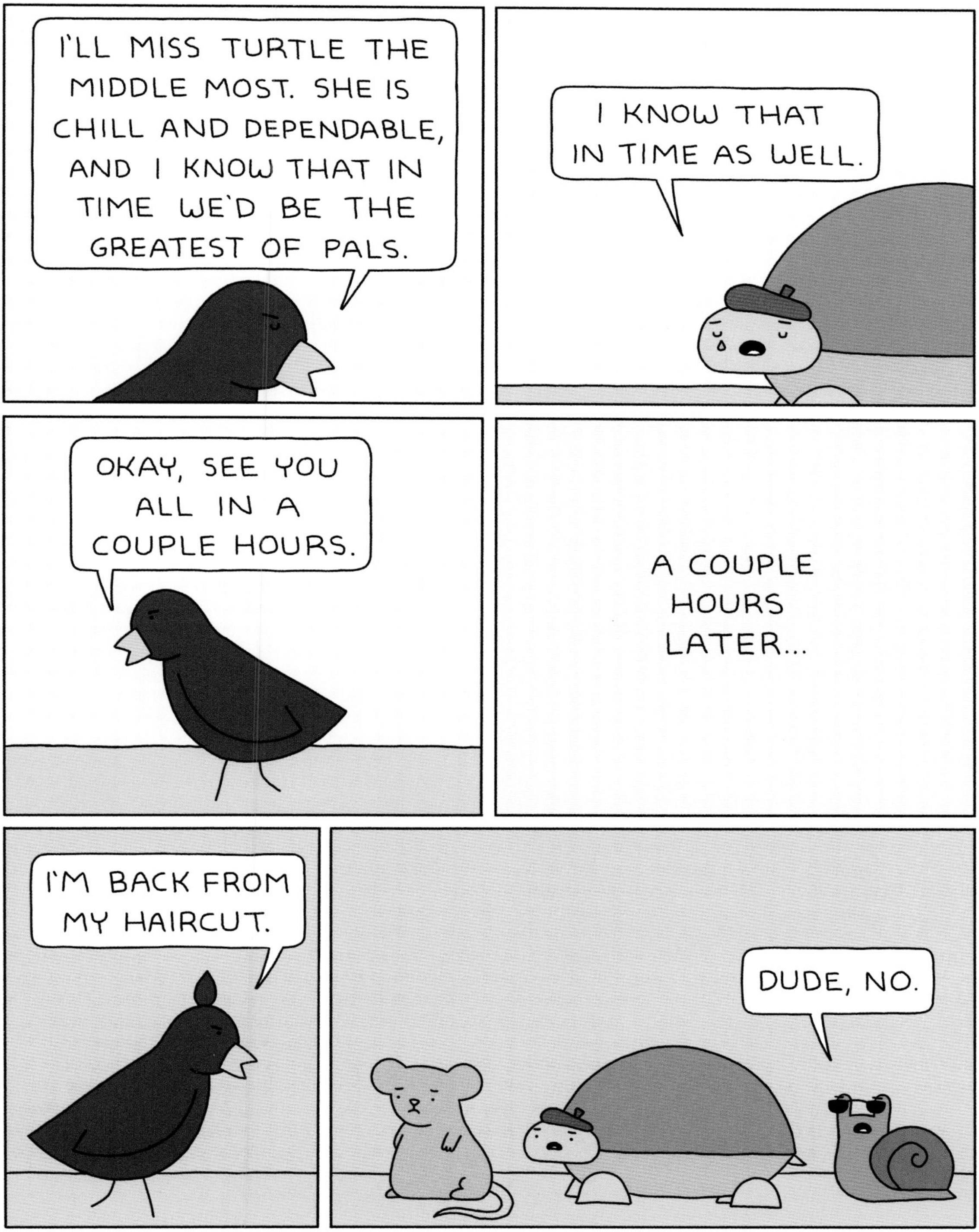
I'LL MISS TURTLE THE MIDDLE MOST. SHE IS CHILL AND DEPENDABLE, AND I KNOW THAT IN TIME WE'D BE THE GREATEST OF PALS.
I KNOW THAT IN TIME AS WELL.
OKAY, SEE YOU ALL IN A COUPLE HOURS.
A COUPLE HOURS LATER...
I'M BACK FROM MY HAIRCUT.
DUDE, NO.

My Shit Together

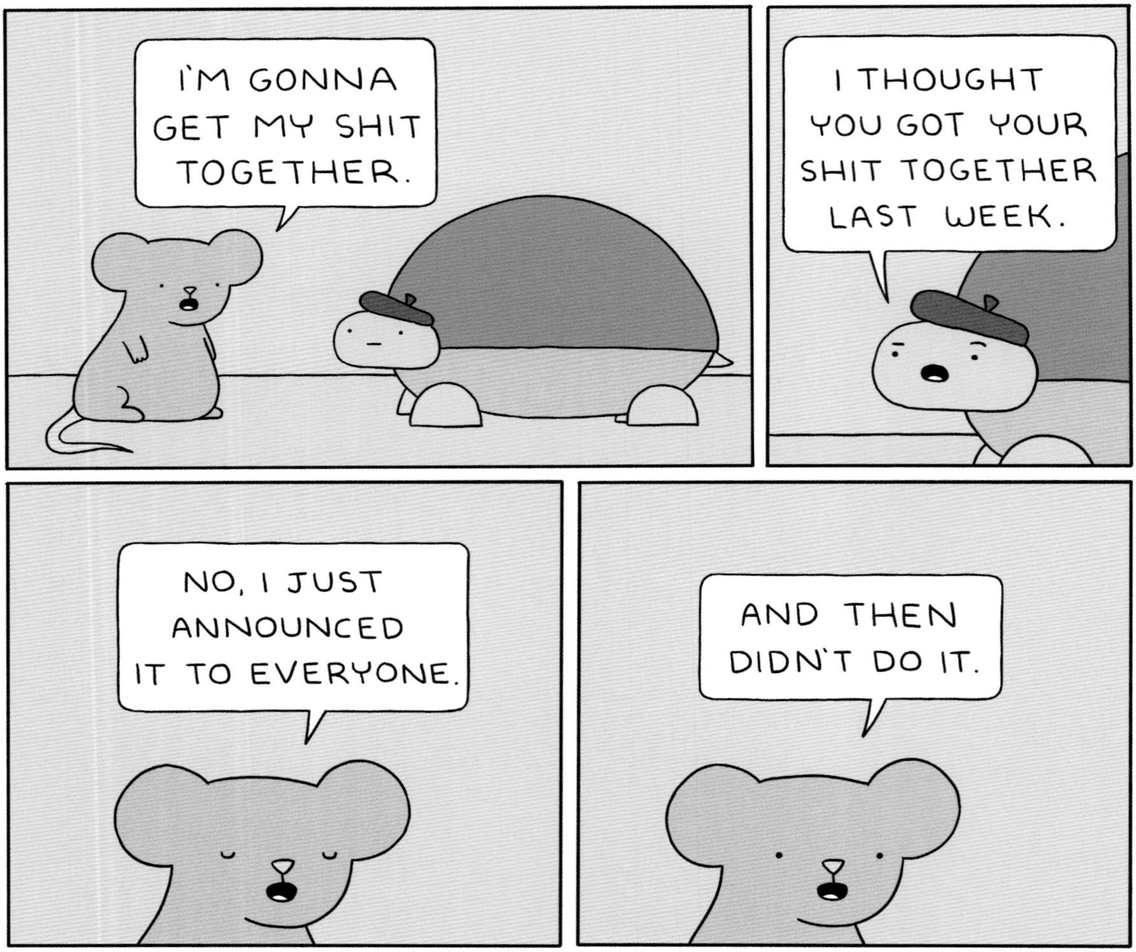
I'M GONNA GET MY SHIT TOGETHER.
I THOUGHT YOU GOT YOUR SHIT TOGETHER LAST WEEK.
NO, I JUST ANNOUNCED IT TO EVERYONE.
AND THEN DIDN'T DO IT.

SEAHORSE

I SAW A LAND HORSE SWIMMING ONCE.

AND I WAS LIKE, "WHO THE FUCK DO YOU THINK YOU ARE?"

Ghosts

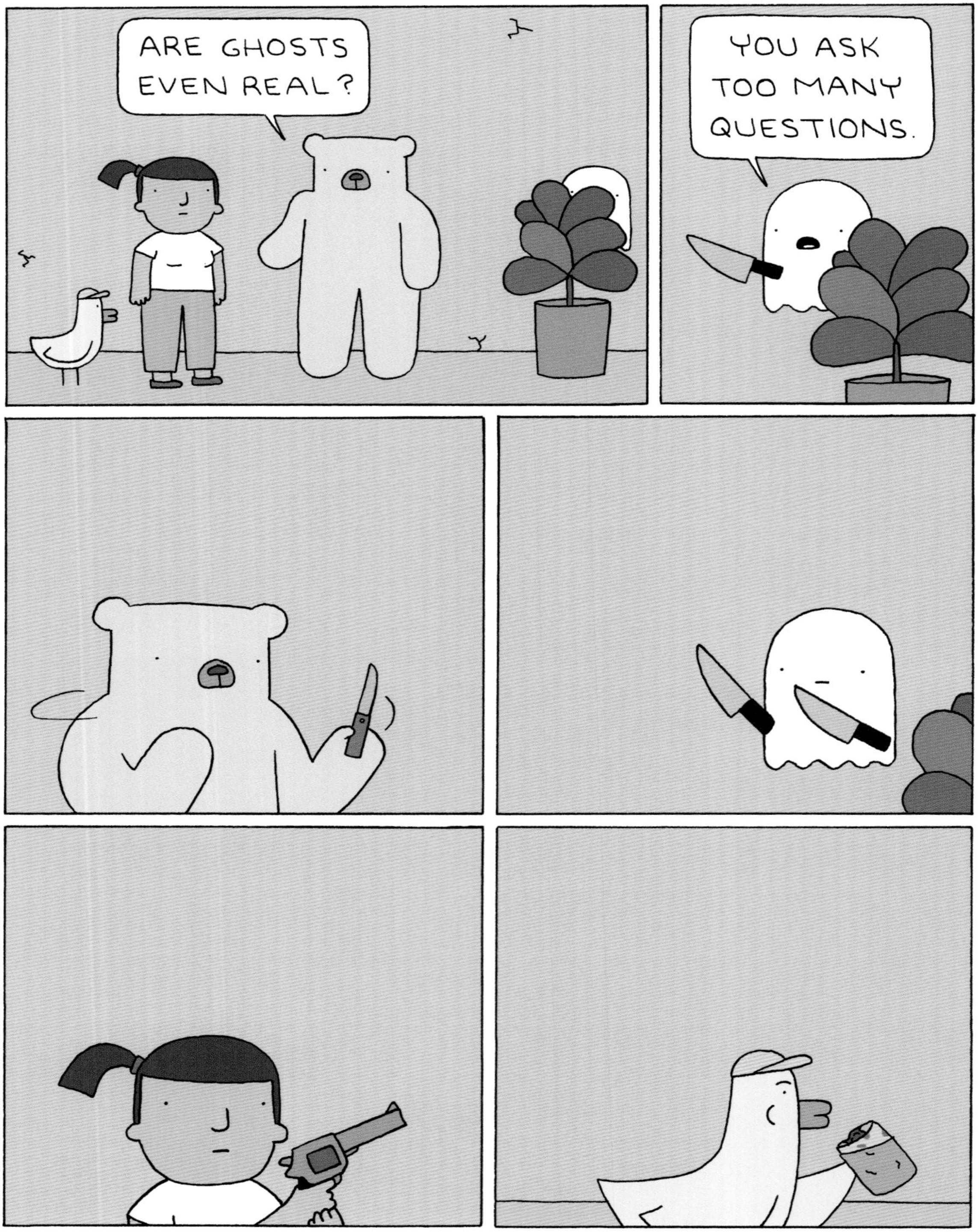
ARE GHOSTS EVEN REAL?
YOU ASK TOO MANY QUESTIONS.

Getting Mad

I'VE BEEN GETTING MAD AT PEOPLE FOR NO REASON.
HUH.

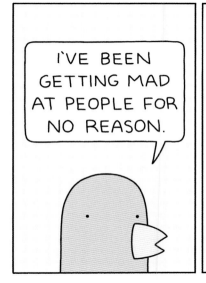

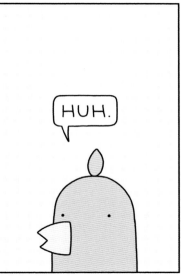

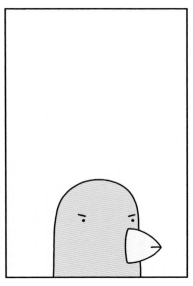

In Thought

AGAIN WE FIND MOUSE DEEP IN THOUGHT, HIS MIND TRAINED ON QUESTIONS OF SELF AND EXISTENCE.

AM I A FUCKING IDIOT?

The Perfect Bird

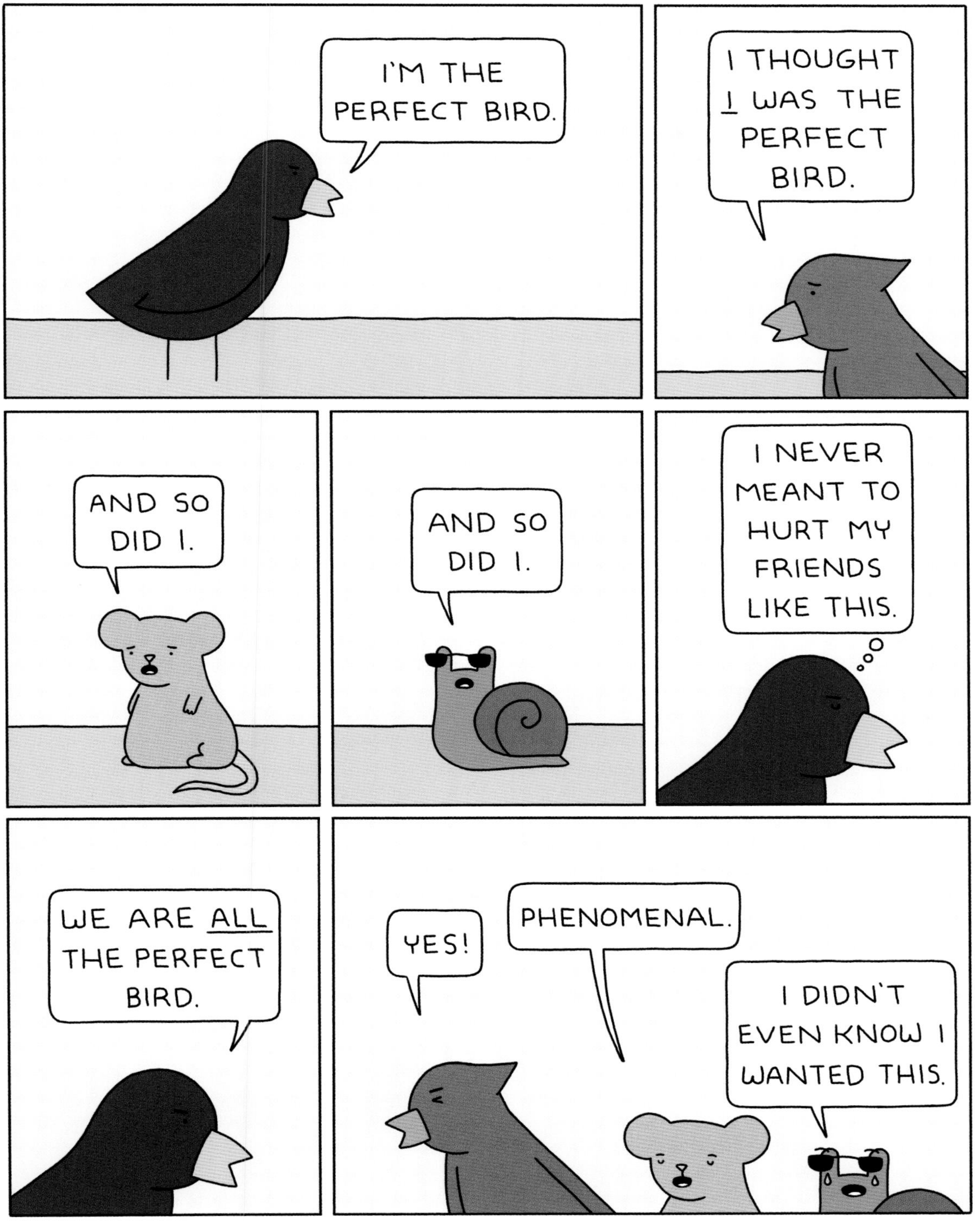
I'M THE PERFECT BIRD.
I THOUGHT I WAS THE PERFECT BIRD.
AND SO DID I.
AND SO DID I.
I NEVER MEANT TO HURT MY FRIENDS LIKE THIS.
WE ARE ALL THE PERFECT BIRD.
YES!
PHENOMENAL.
I DIDN'T EVEN KNOW I WANTED THIS.

Get to Work

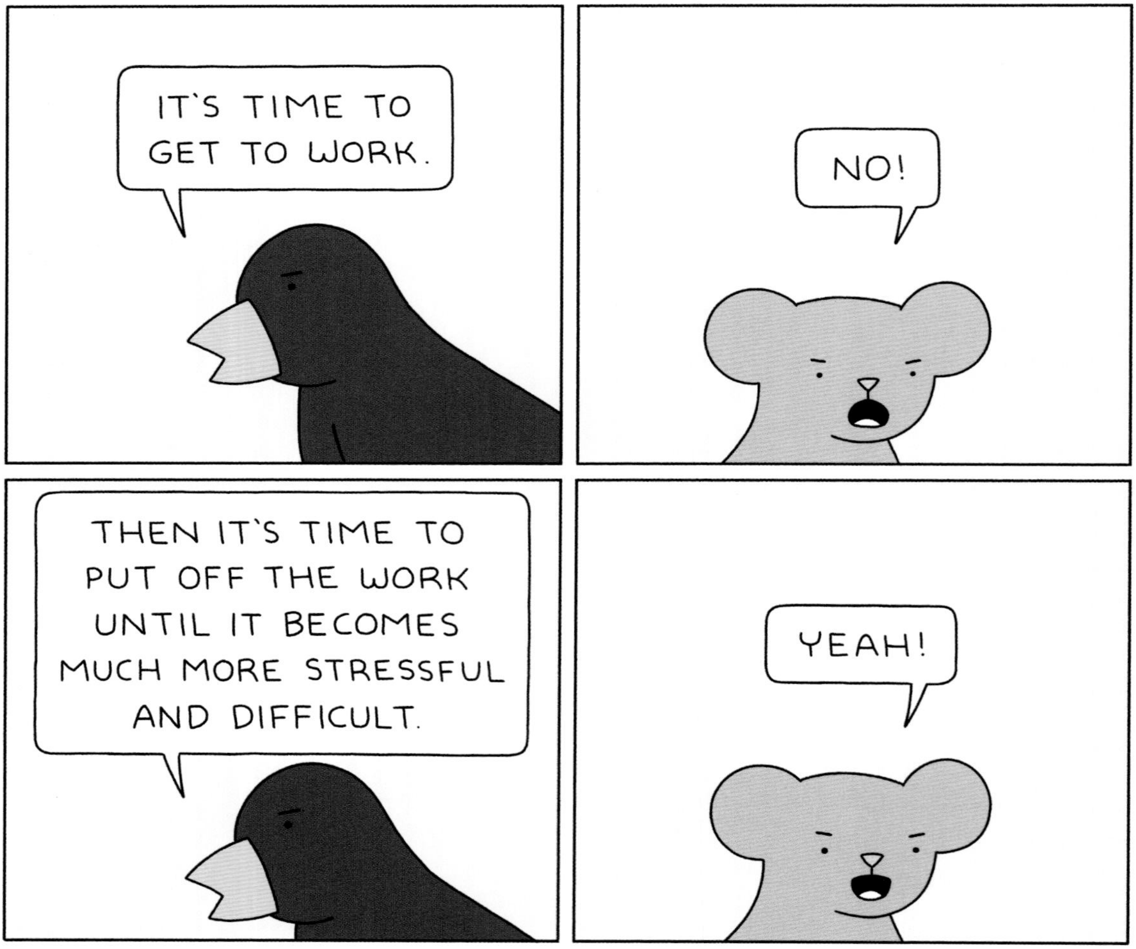
IT'S TIME TO GET TO WORK.
NO!
THEN IT'S TIME TO PUT OFF THE WORK UNTIL IT BECOMES MUCH MORE STRESSFUL AND DIFFICULT.
YEAH!

Make Friends

I'M NOT HERE TO MAKE FRIENDS.
I MEAN I WOULD IF IT WAS A SURE THING.
BUT I DON'T WANT TO GET HURT.

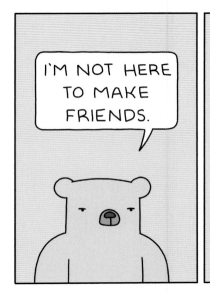

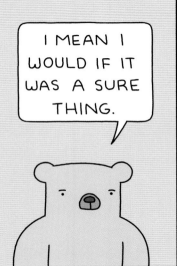

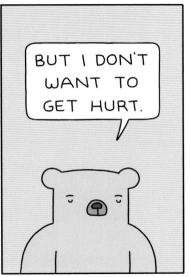

Devil's Advocate

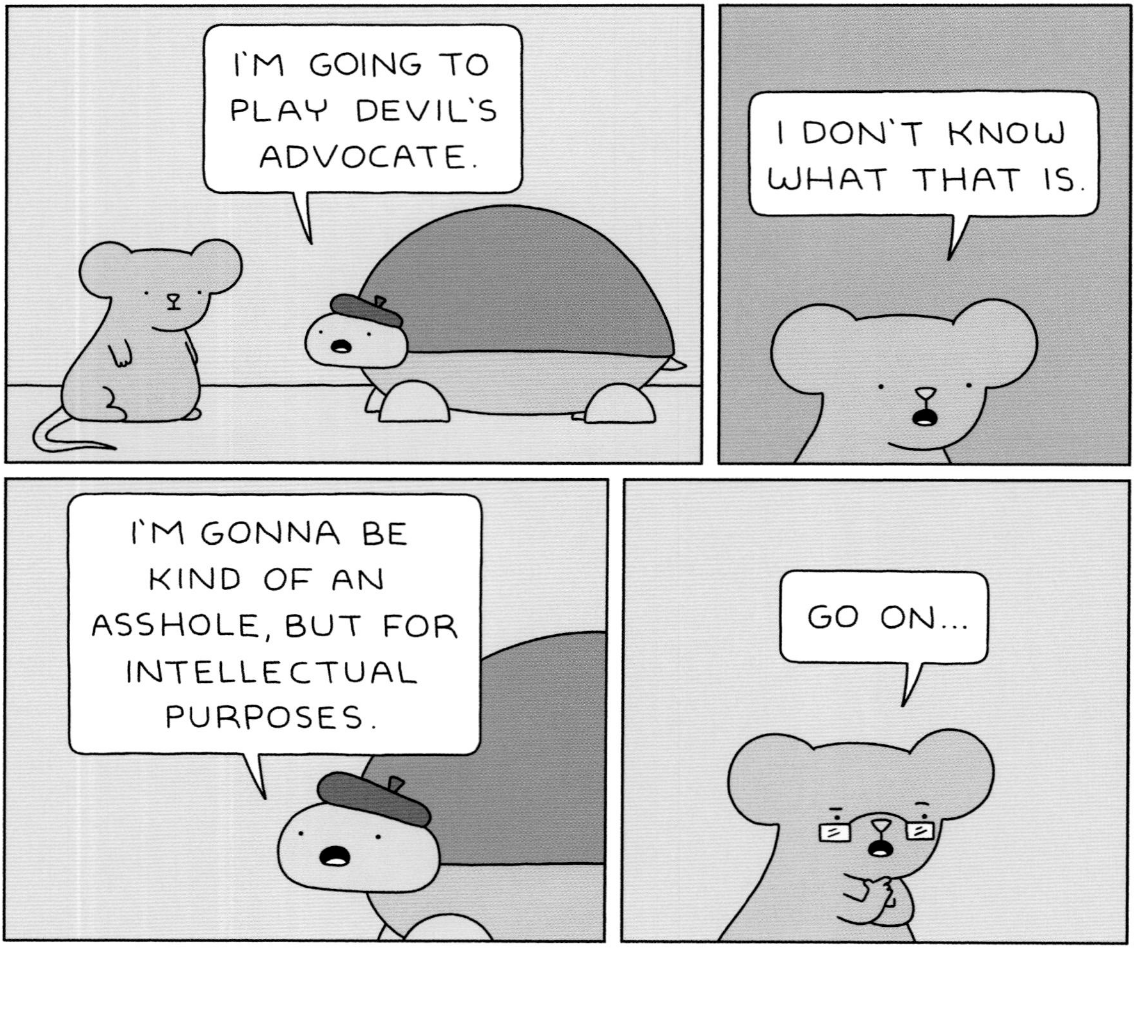
I'M GOING TO PLAY DEVIL'S ADVOCATE.
I DON'T KNOW WHAT THAT IS.
I'M GONNA BE KIND OF AN ASSHOLE, BUT FOR INTELLECTUAL PURPOSES.
GO ON...

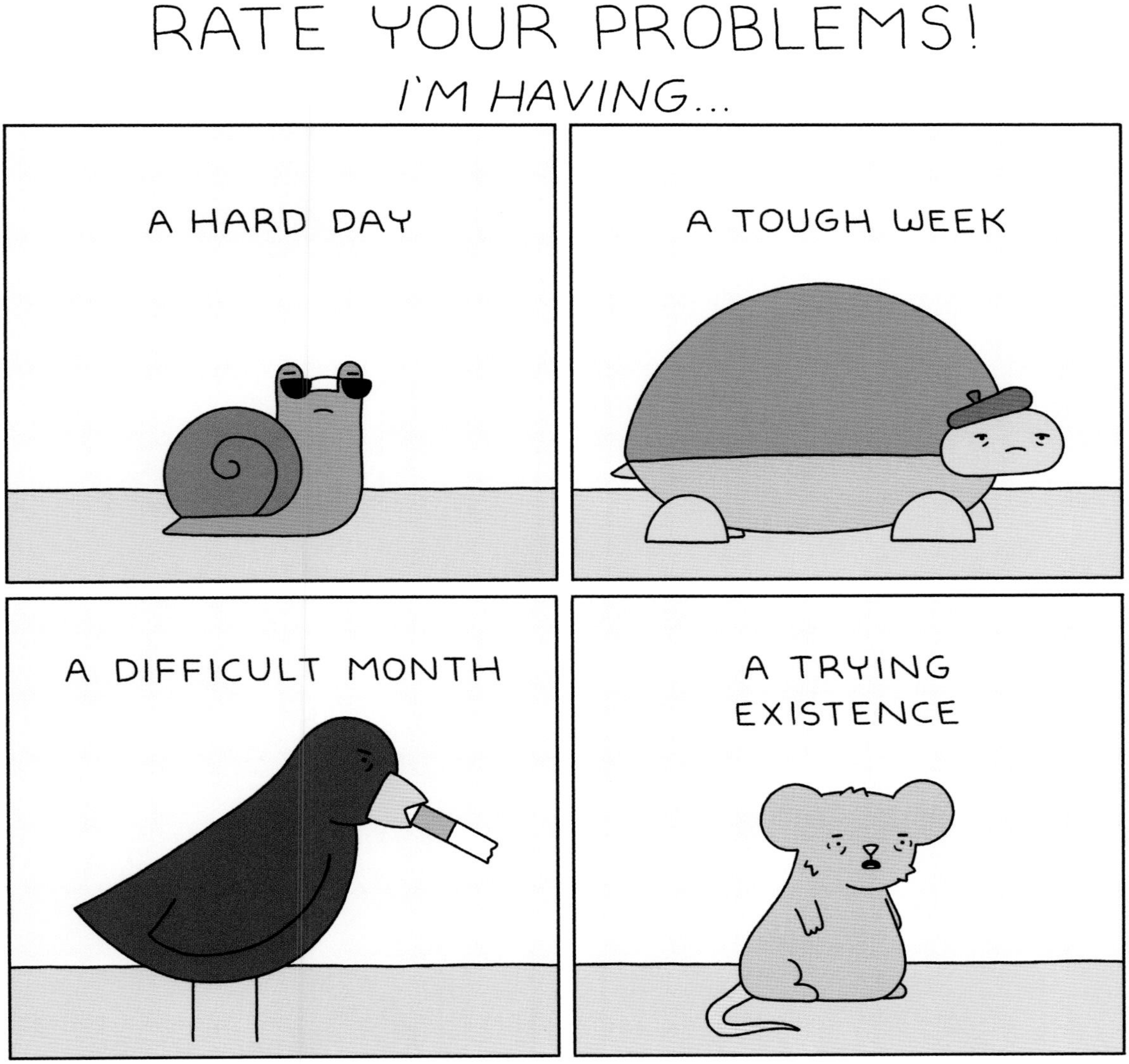
RATE YOUR PROBLEMS!
I'M HAVING...
A HARD DAY
A TOUGH WEEK
A DIFFICULT MONTH
A TRYING EXISTENCE

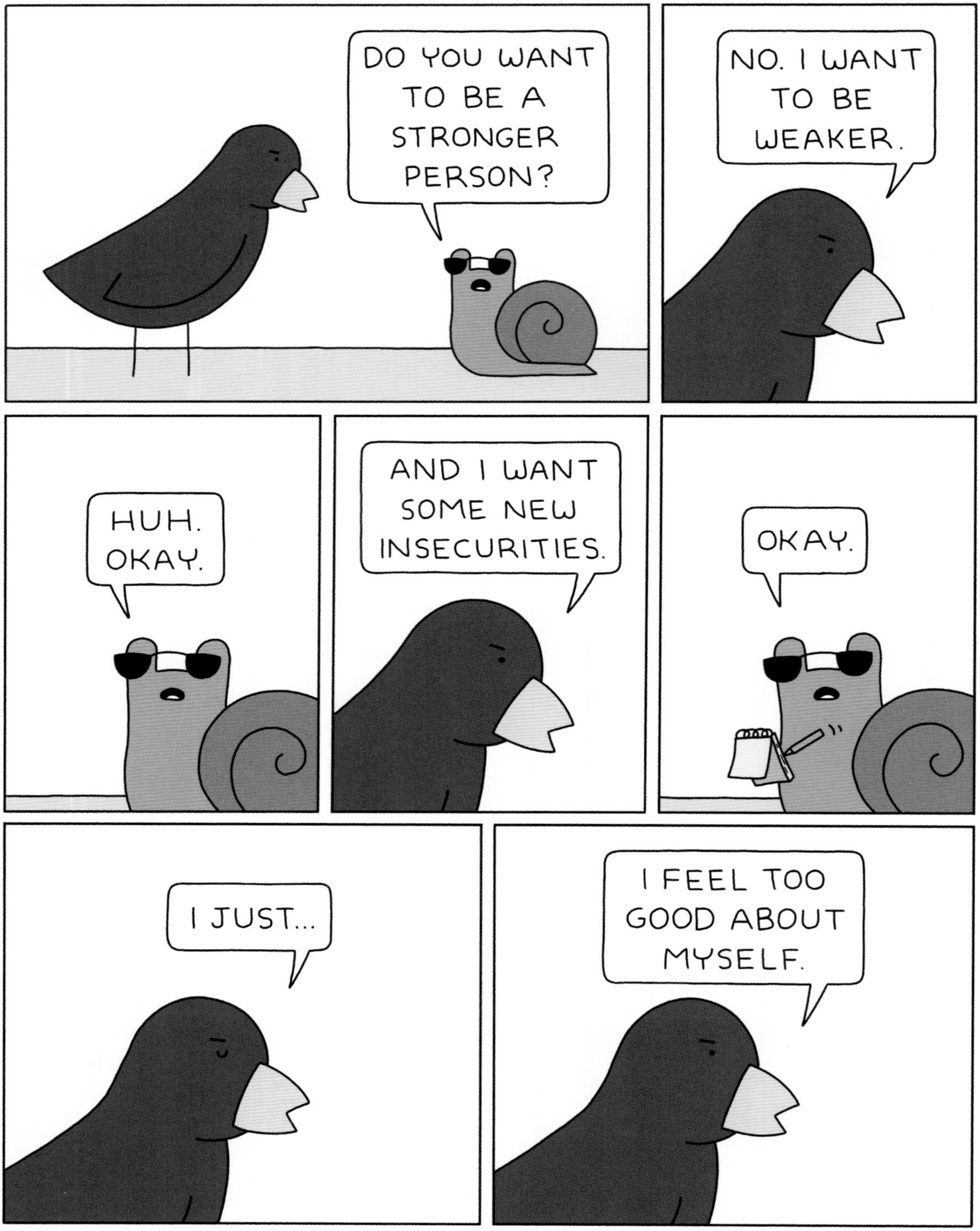
DO YOU WANT TO BE A STRONGER PERSON?
NO. I WANT TO BE WEAKER.
HUH. OKAY.
AND I WANT SOME NEW INSECURITIES.
OKAY.
I JUST...
I FEEL TOO GOOD ABOUT MYSELF.

Have Your Back

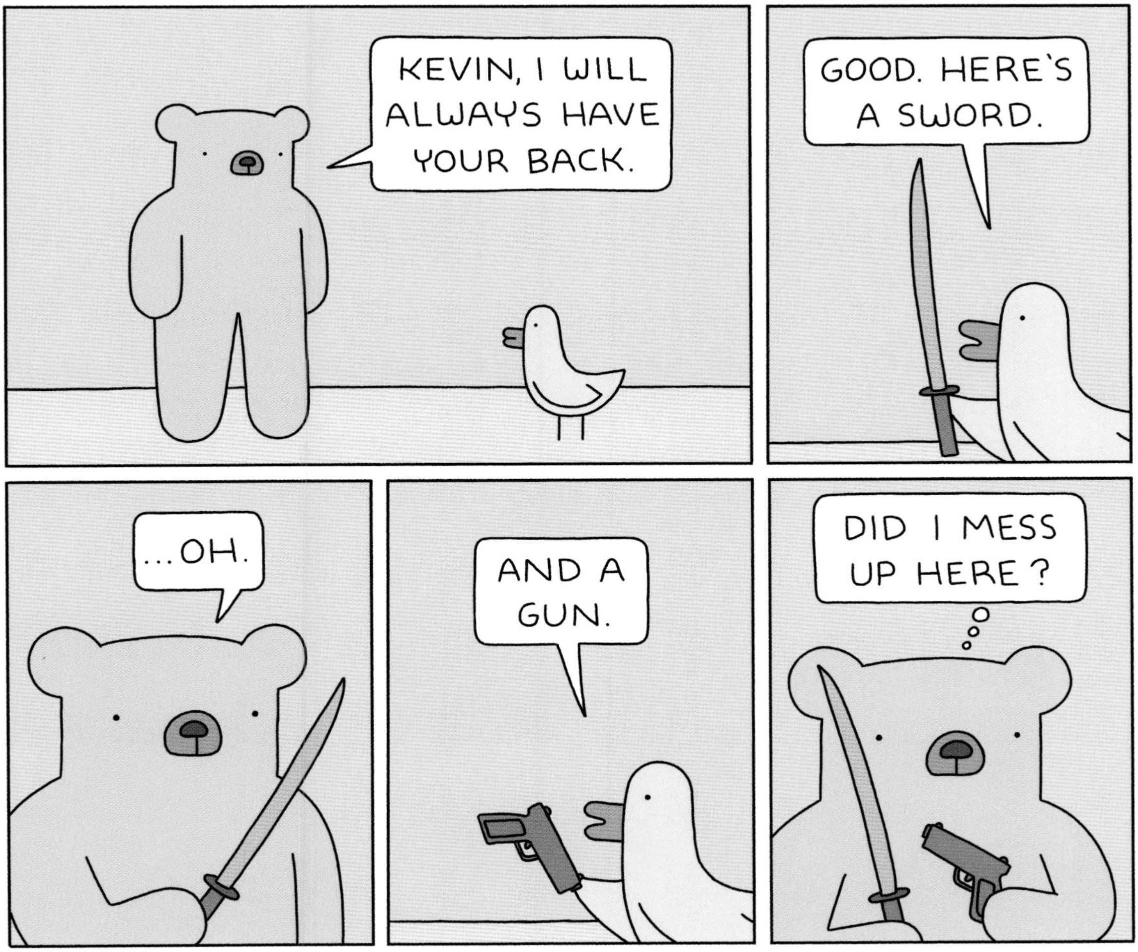
KEVIN, I WILL ALWAYS HAVE YOUR BACK.
GOOD. HERE'S A SWORD.
...OH.
AND A GUN.
DID I MESS UP HERE?

Grudge

BIRD, IS IT TRUE YOU HOLD A GRUDGE?
NO.
AND WHOEVER SAID THAT IS DEAD TO ME.

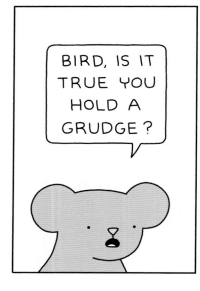

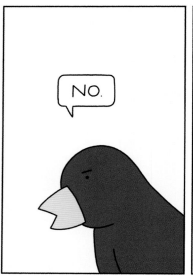

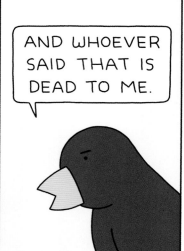

So Much

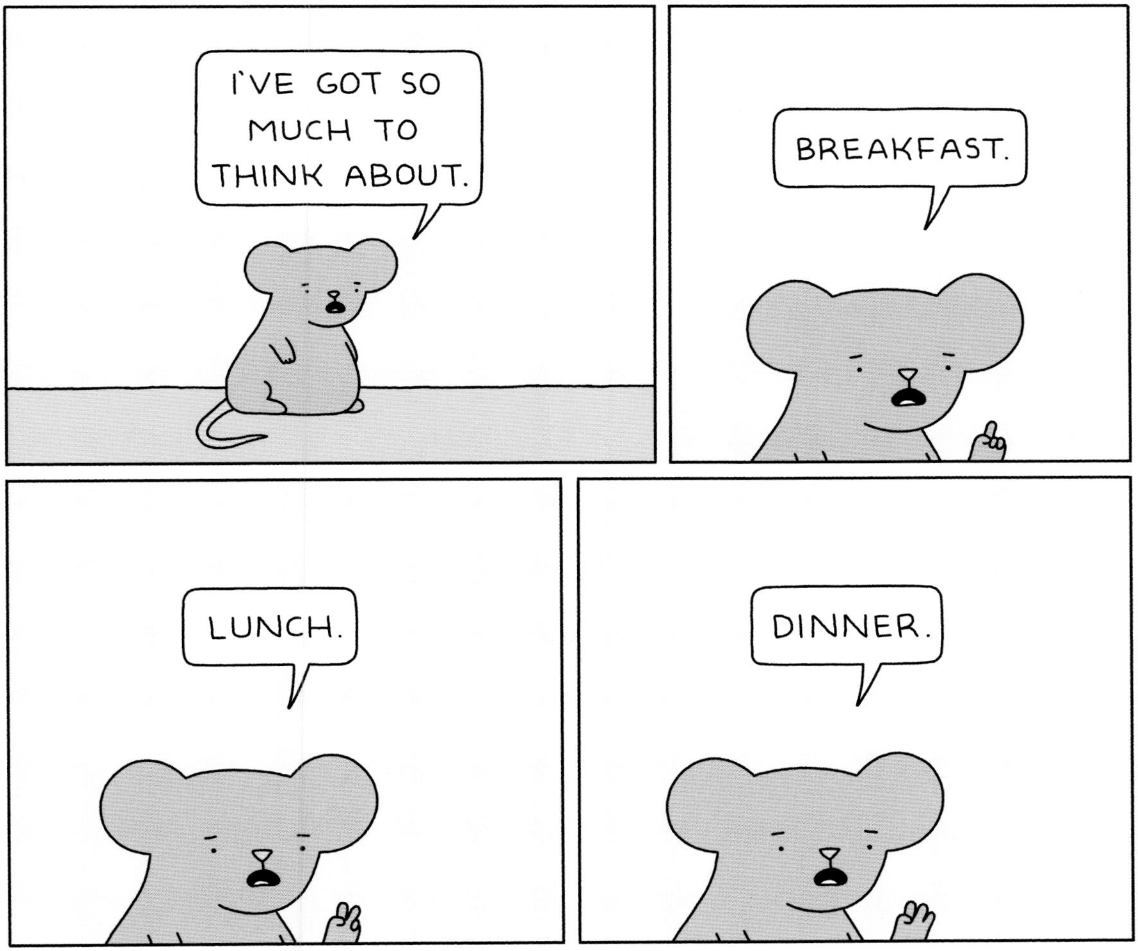
I'VE GOT SO MUCH TO THINK ABOUT.
BREAKFAST.
LUNCH.
DINNER.

Successful

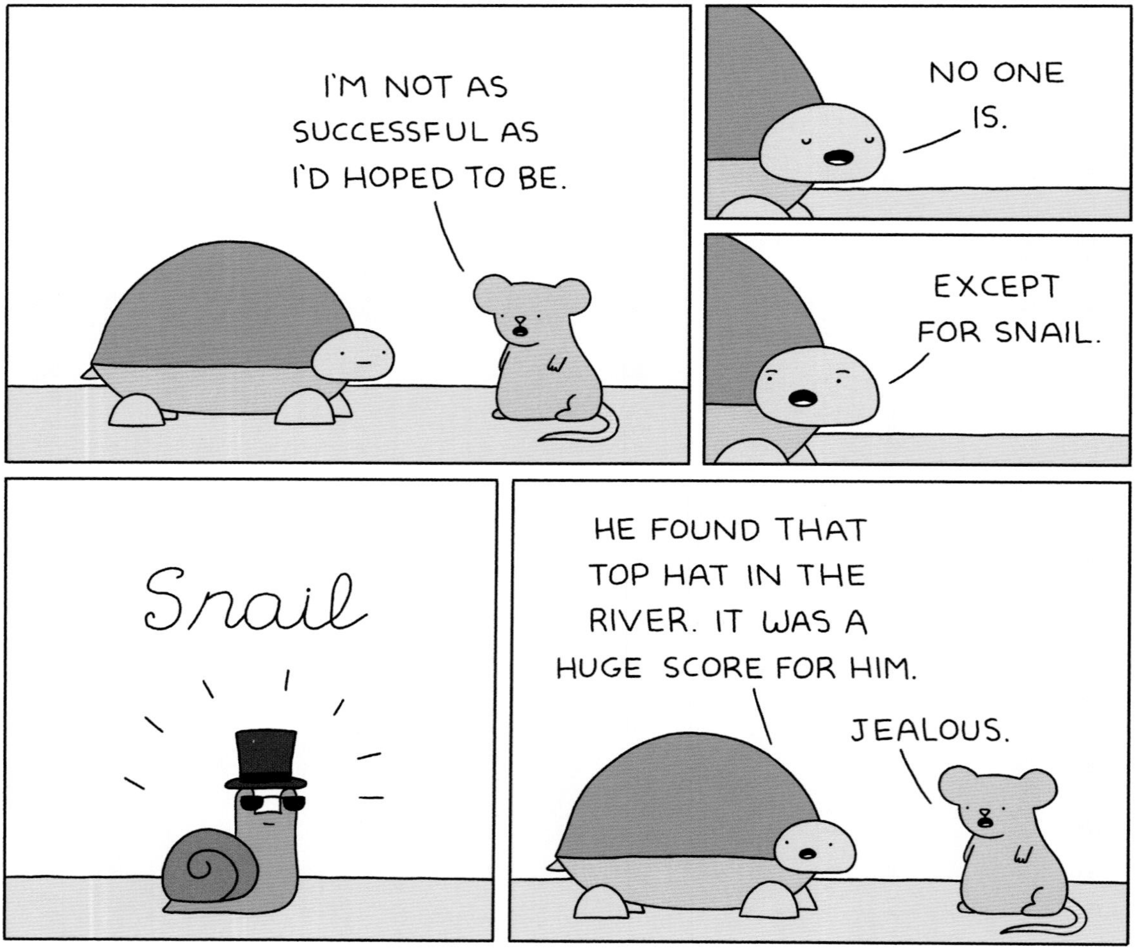
I'M NOT AS SUCCESSFUL AS I'D HOPED TO BE.
NO ONE IS.
EXCEPT FOR SNAIL.
Snail
HE FOUND THAT TOP HAT IN THE RIVER. IT WAS A HUGE SCORE FOR HIM.
JEALOUS.

To the Moon

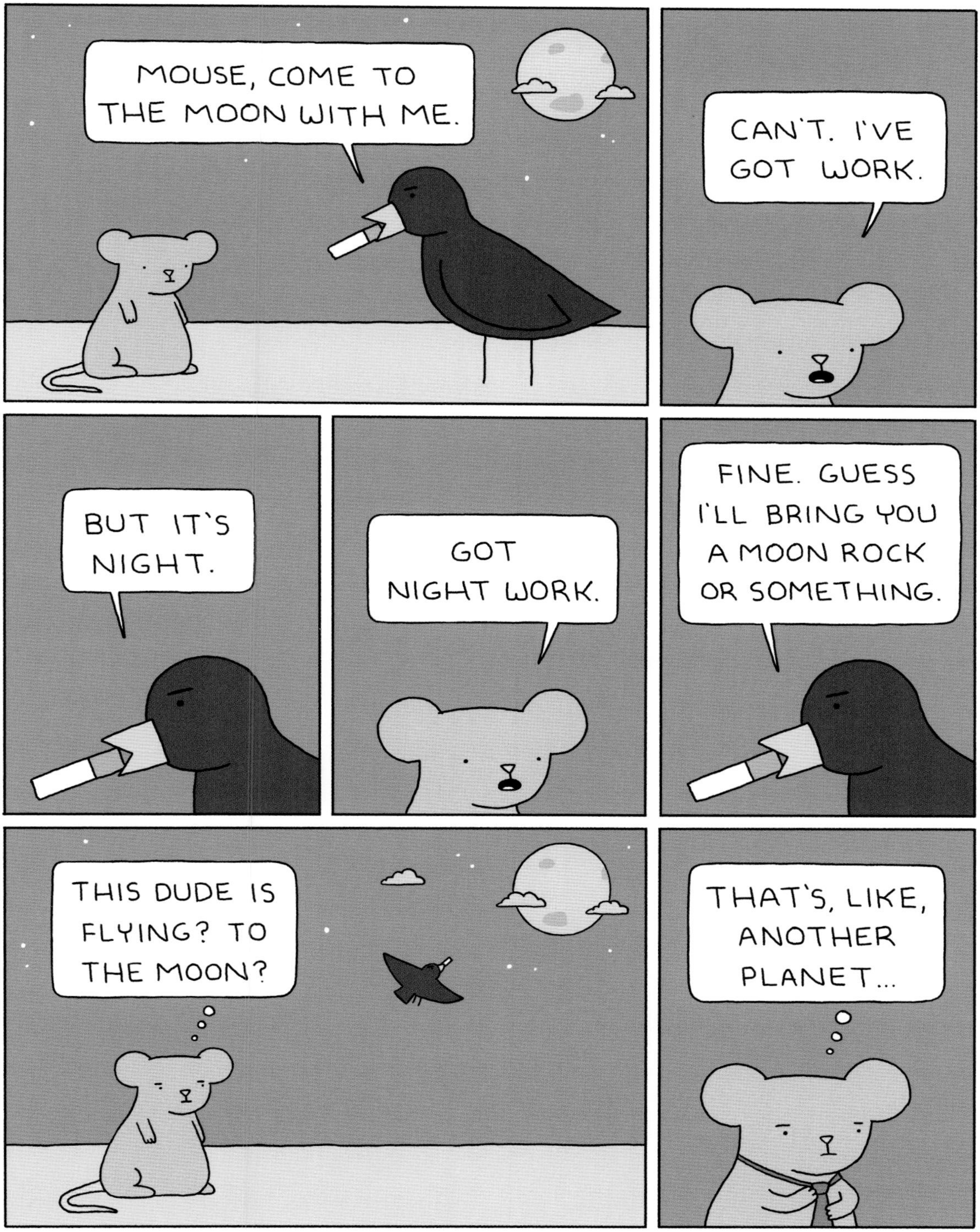
MOUSE, COME TO THE MOON WITH ME.
CAN'T. I'VE GOT WORK.
BUT IT'S NIGHT.
GOT NIGHT WORK.
FINE. GUESS I'LL BRING YOU A MOON ROCK OR SOMETHING.
THIS DUDE IS FLYING? TO THE MOON?
THAT'S, LIKE, ANOTHER PLANET...

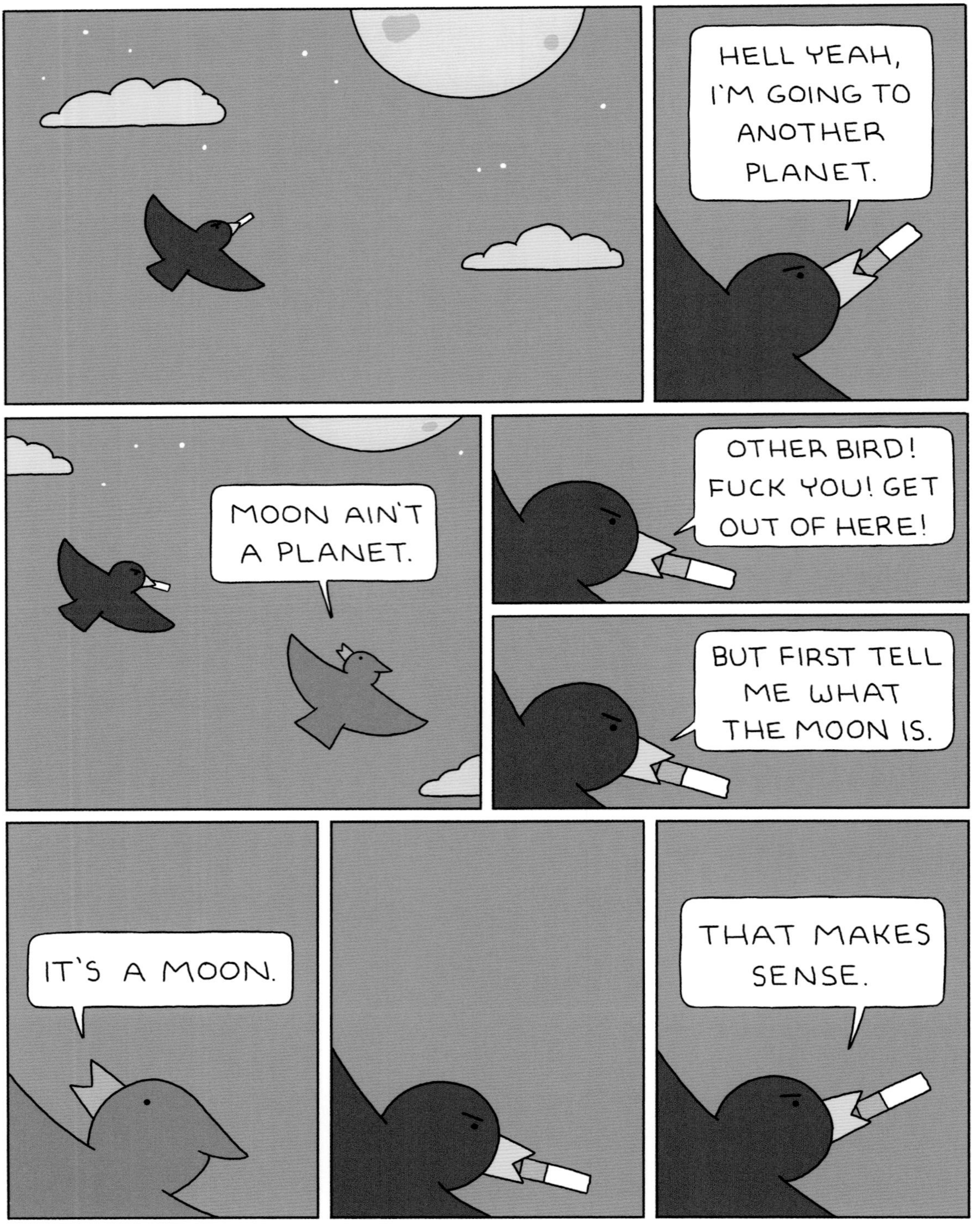
HELL YEAH, I'M GOING TO ANOTHER PLANET.
MOON AIN'T A PLANET.
OTHER BIRD! FUCK YOU! GET OUT OF HERE!
BUT FIRST TELL ME WHAT THE MOON IS.
IT'S A MOON.
THAT MAKES SENSE.

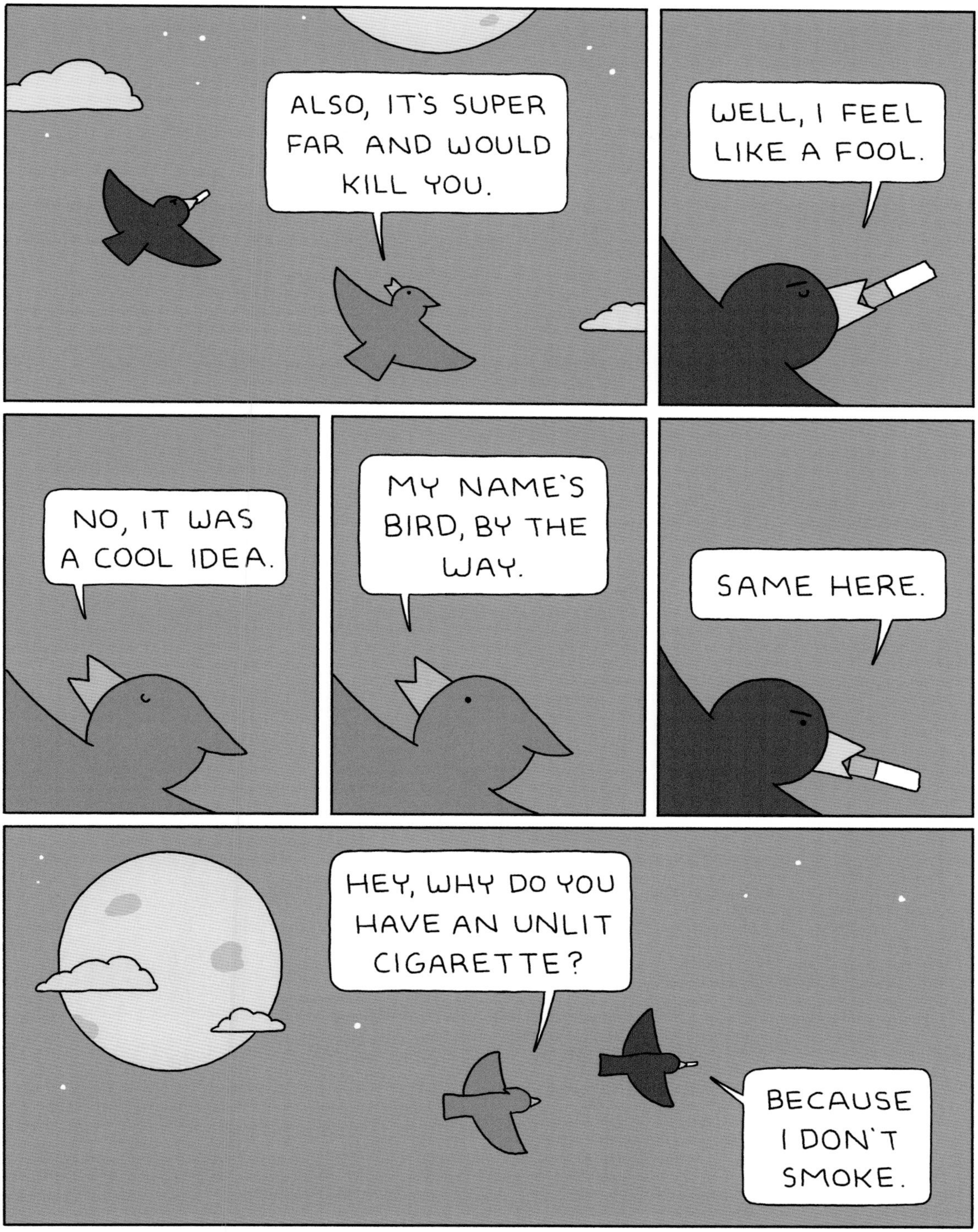
ALSO, IT'S SUPER FAR AND WOULD KILL YOU.
WELL, I FEEL LIKE A FOOL.
NO, IT WAS A COOL IDEA.
MY NAME'S BIRD, BY THE WAY.
SAME HERE.
HEY, WHY DO YOU HAVE AN UNLIT CIGARETTE?
BECAUSE I DON'T SMOKE.

Sad

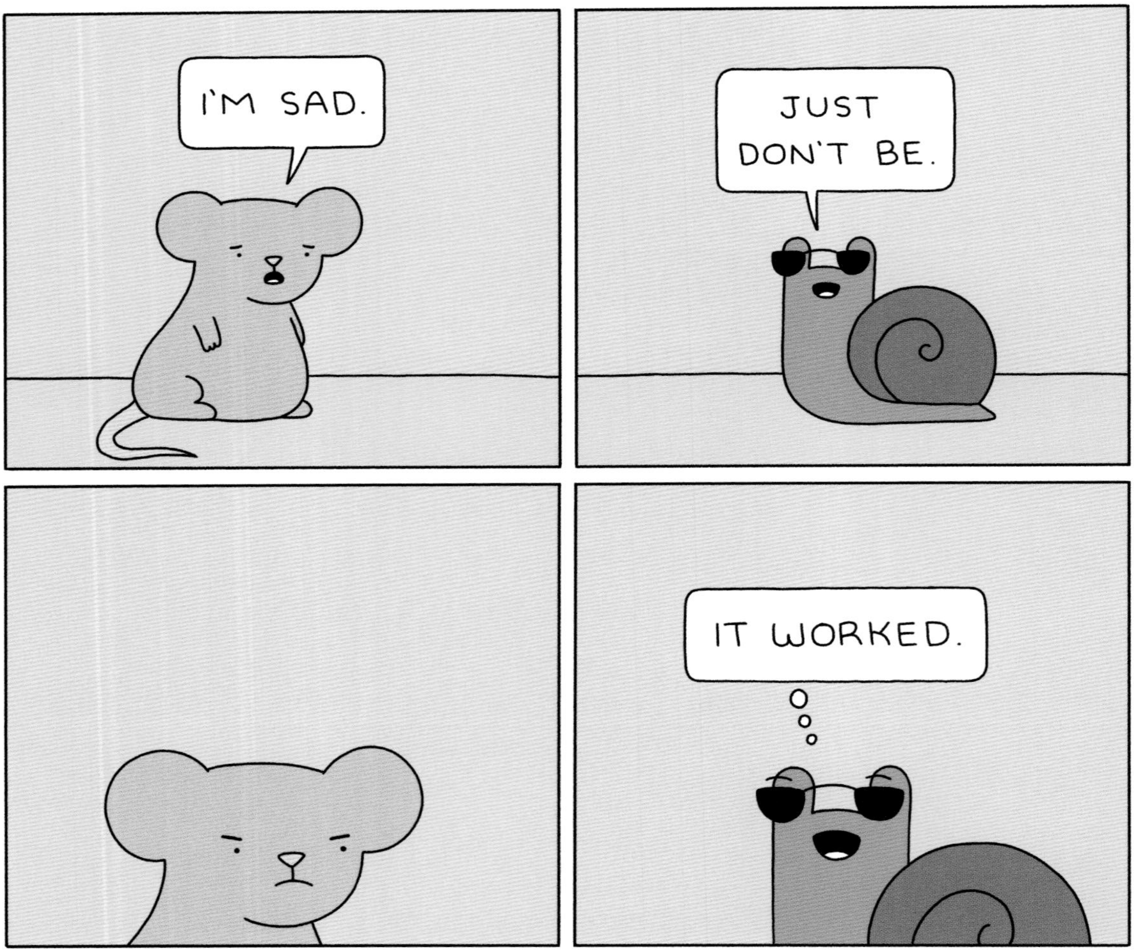
I'M SAD.
JUST DON'T BE.
IT WORKED.

Seem Tired

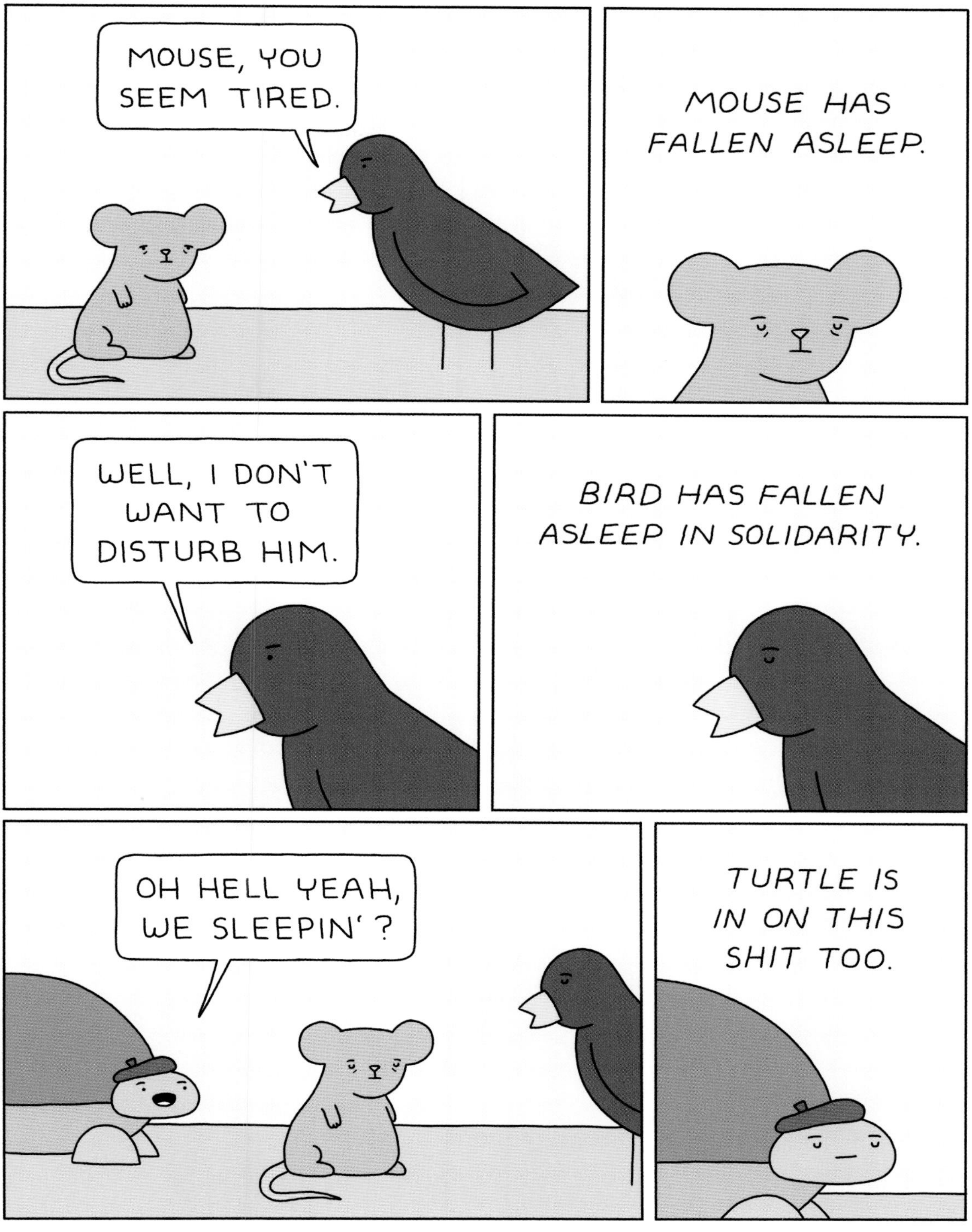
MOUSE, YOU SEEM TIRED.
MOUSE HAS FALLEN ASLEEP.
WELL, I DON'T WANT TO DISTURB HIM.
BIRD HAS FALLEN ASLEEP IN SOLIDARITY.
OH HELL YEAH, WE SLEEPIN'?
TURTLE IS IN ON THIS SHIT TOO.

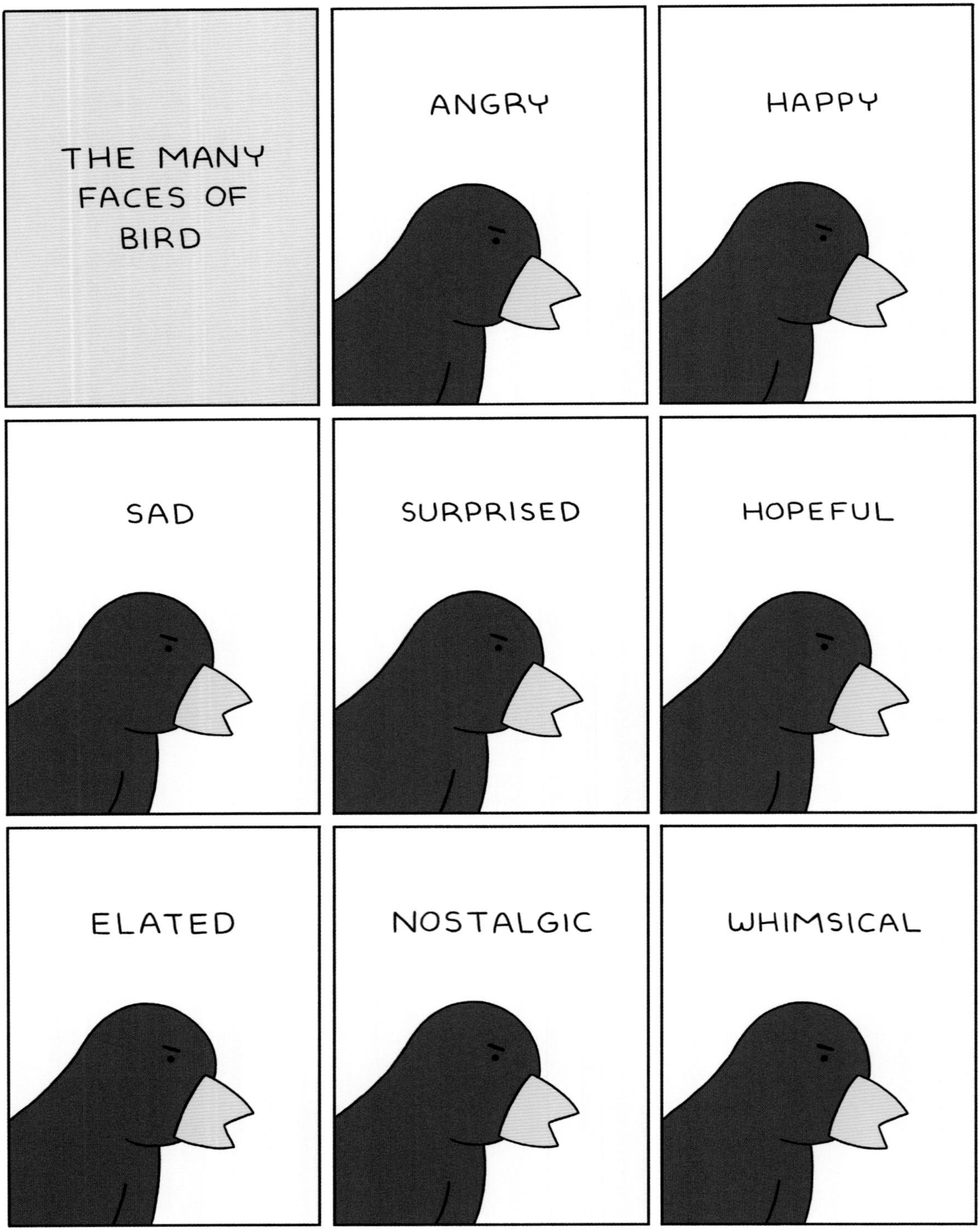
THE MANY FACES OF BIRD
ANGRY
HAPPY
SAD
SURPRISED
HOPEFUL
ELATED
NOSTALGIC
WHIMSICAL

The Good Times

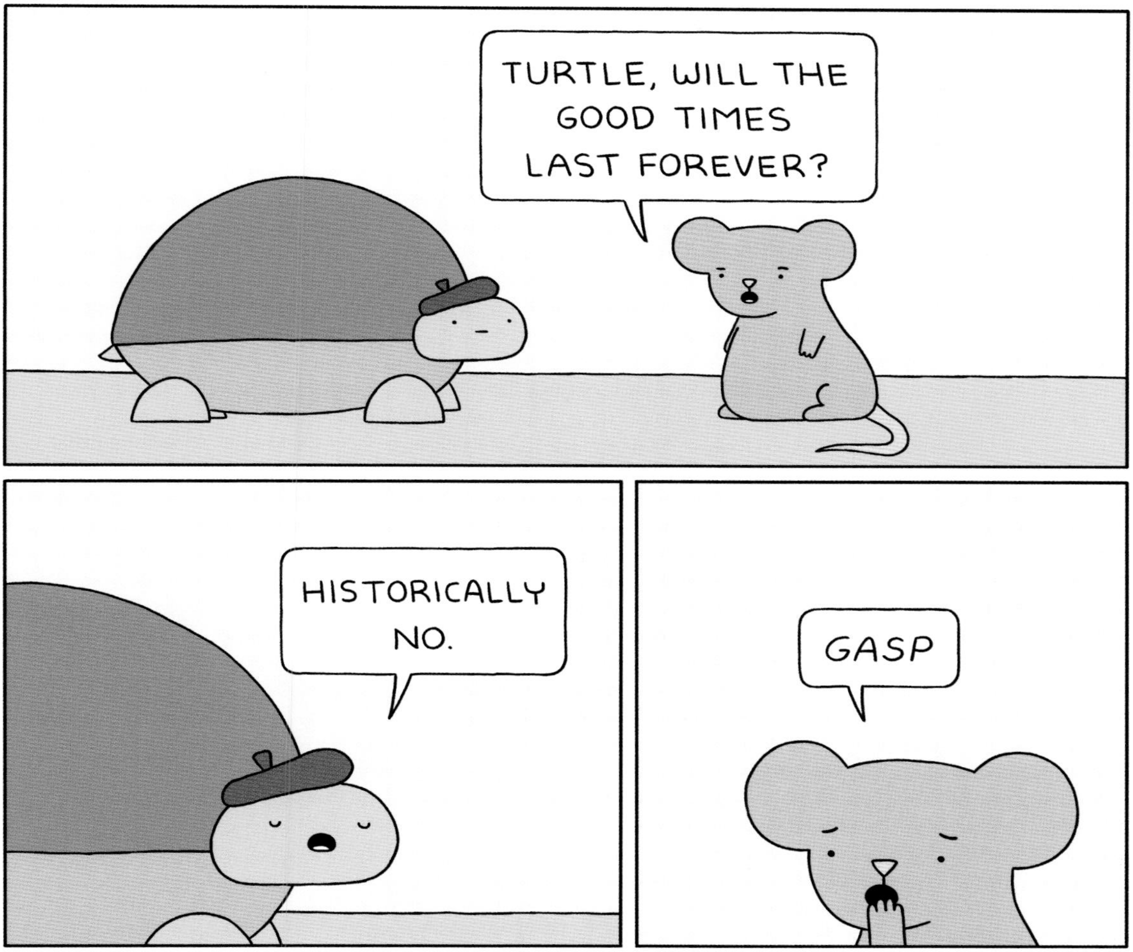
TURTLE, WILL THE GOOD TIMES LAST FOREVER?
HISTORICALLY NO.
GASP

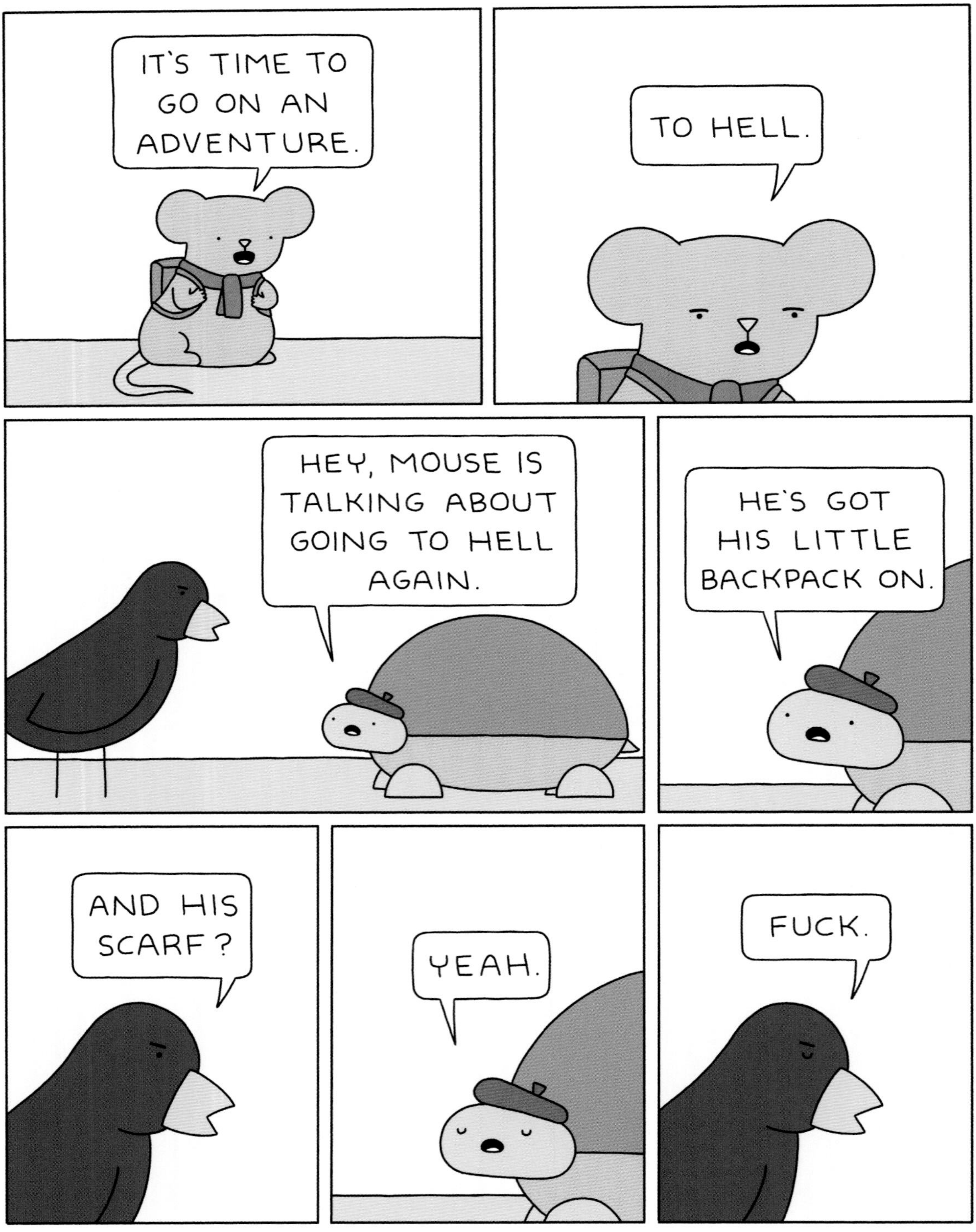
IT'S TIME TO GO ON AN ADVENTURE.
TO HELL.
HEY, MOUSE IS TALKING ABOUT GOING TO HELL AGAIN.
HE'S GOT HIS LITTLE BACKPACK ON.
AND HIS SCARF?
YEAH.
FUCK.

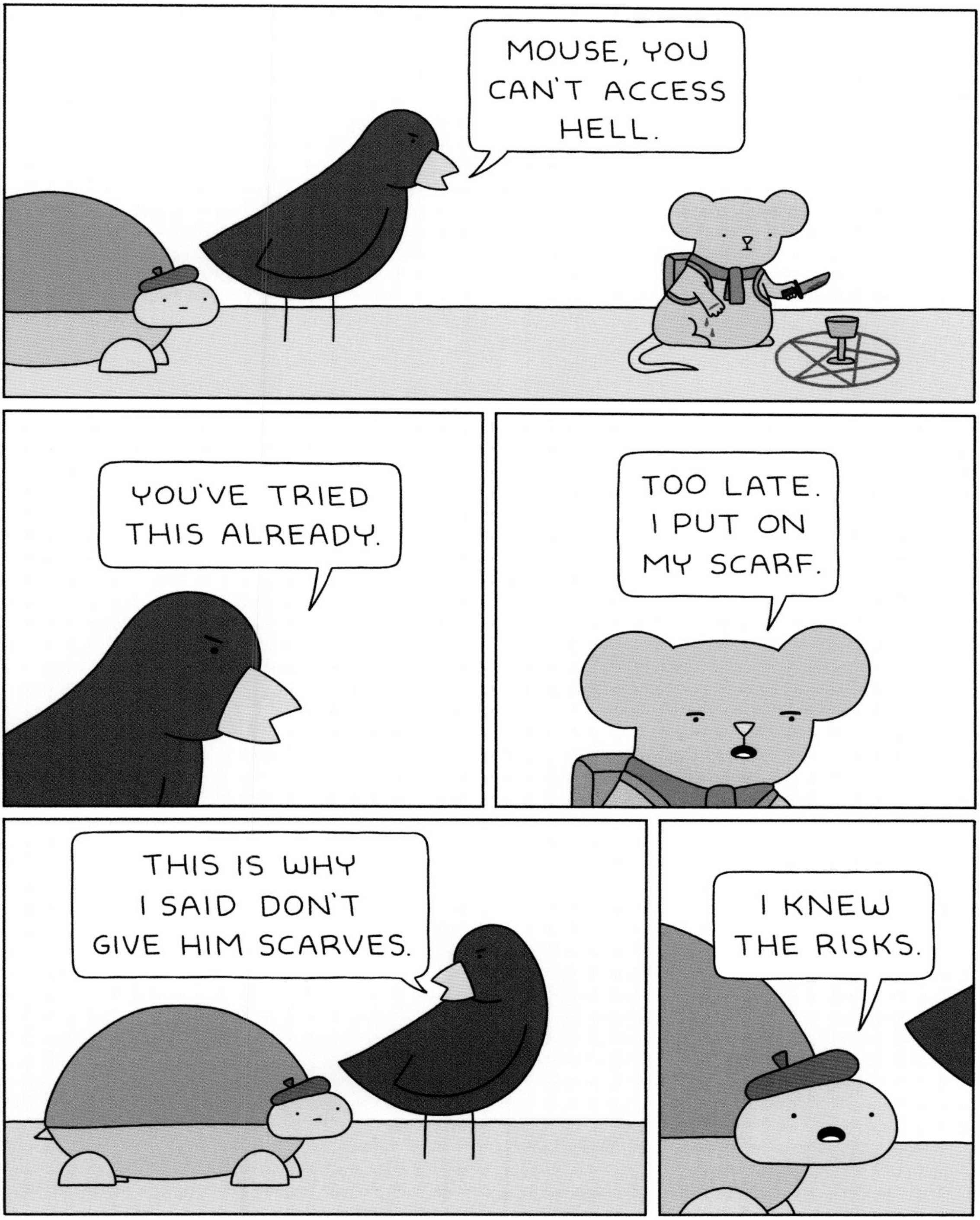
MOUSE, YOU CAN'T ACCESS HELL.
YOU'VE TRIED THIS ALREADY.
TOO LATE. I PUT ON MY SCARF.
THIS IS WHY I SAID DON'T GIVE HIM SCARVES.
I KNEW THE RISKS.

An Exchange

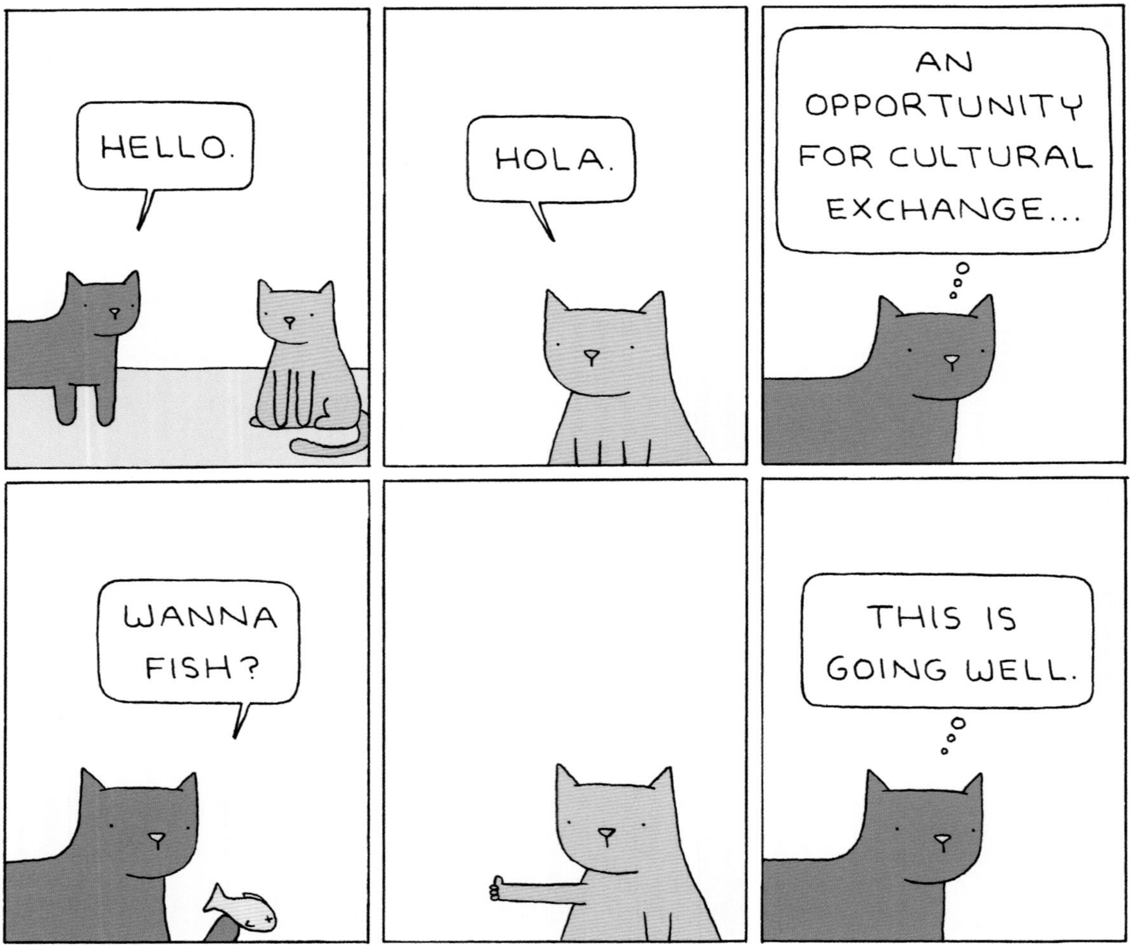
HELLO.
HOLA.
AN OPPORTUNITY FOR CULTURAL EXCHANGE...
WANNA FISH?
THIS IS GOING WELL.

Be Mad

I CAN'T BE MAD FOREVER.
BUT I CAN BE MAD UNTIL I DIE.

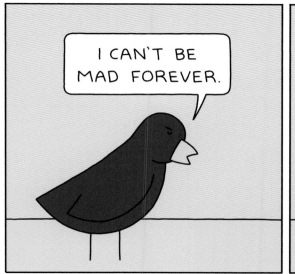

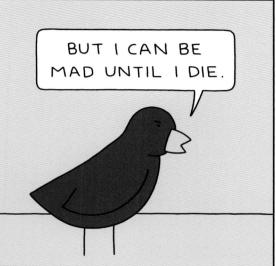

Better

I'M GOING TO START MAKING MY LIFE BETTER INSTEAD OF WORSE.
WHY WERE YOU MAKING IT WORSE?

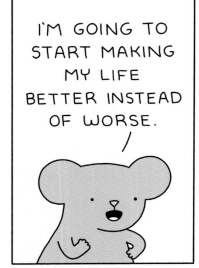

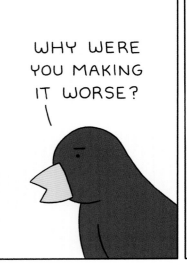

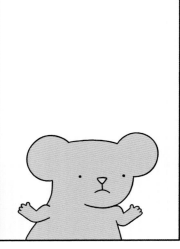

What Is It

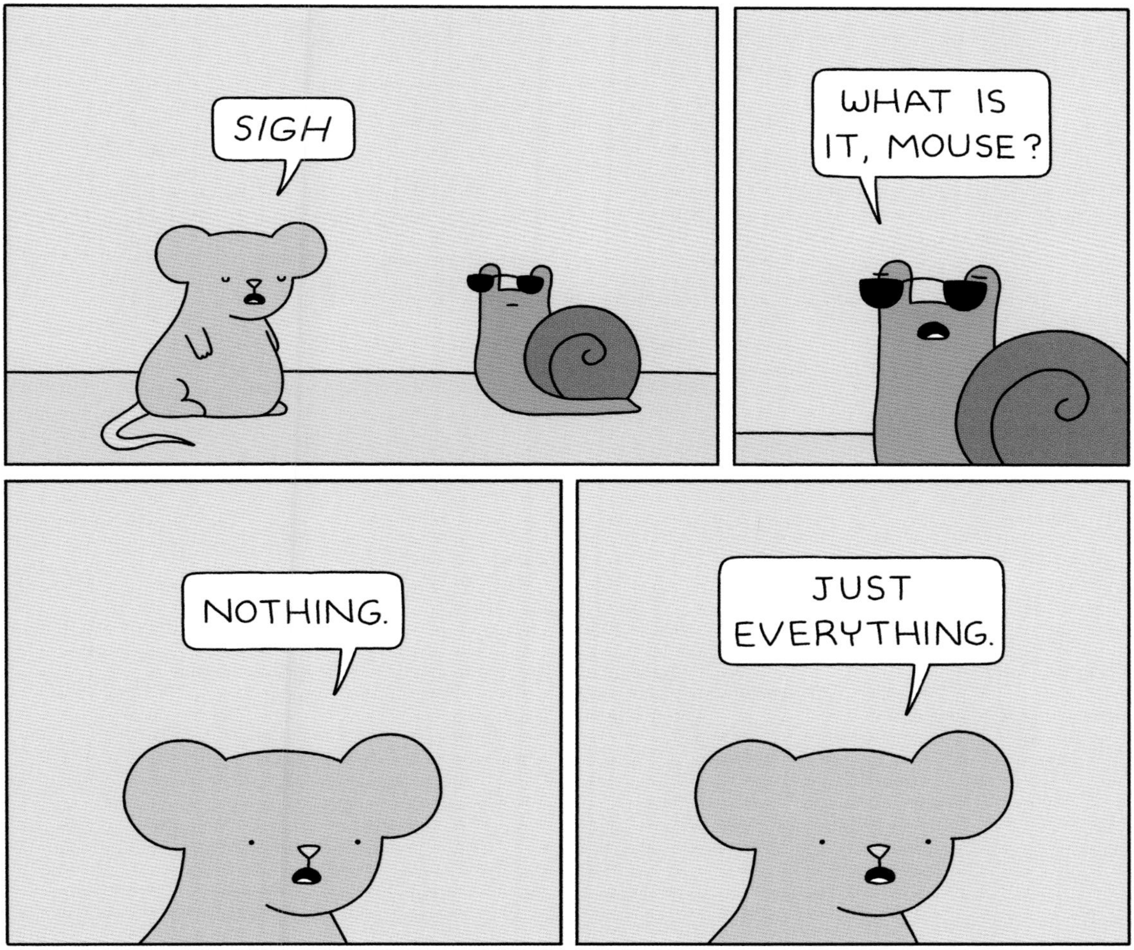
SIGH
WHAT IS IT, MOUSE?
NOTHING.
JUST EVERYTHING.

So Serious

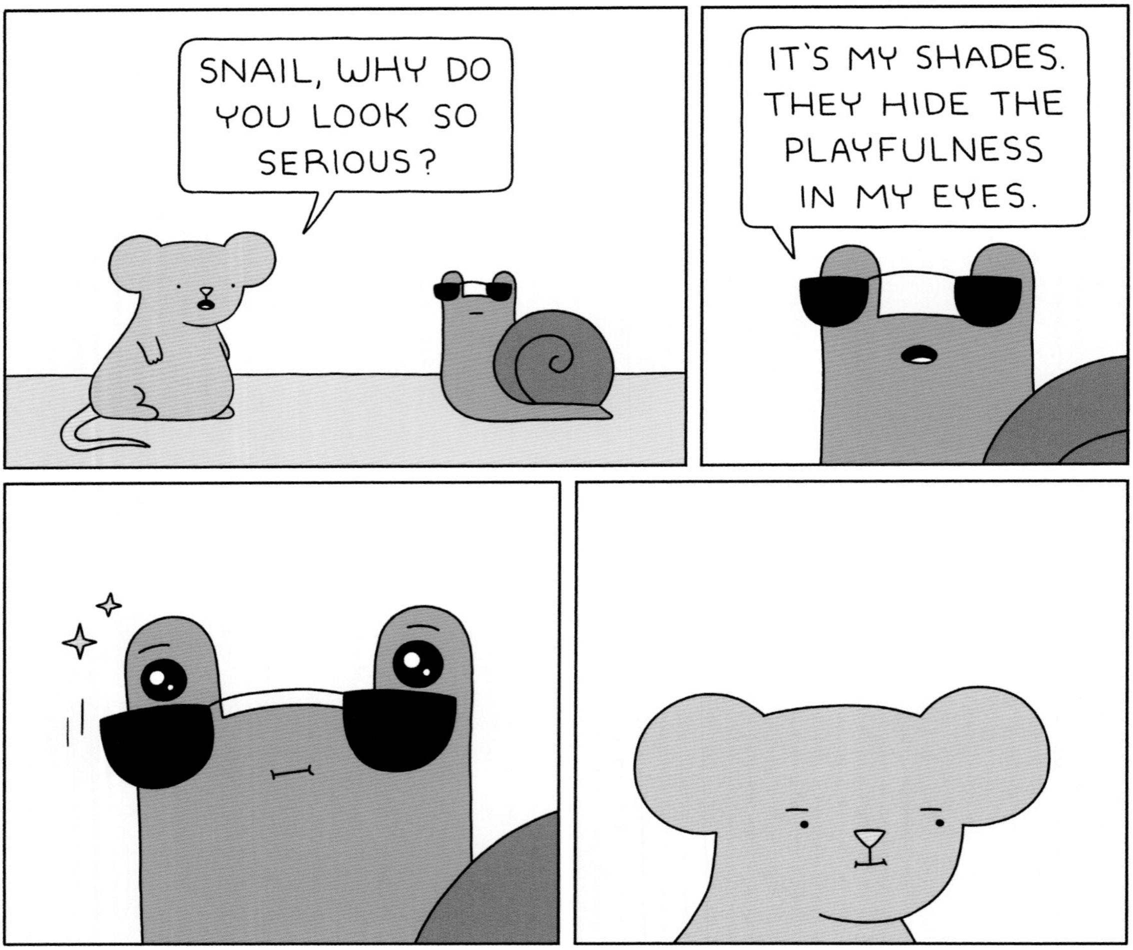
SNAIL, WHY DO YOU LOOK SO SERIOUS?
IT'S MY SHADES. THEY HIDE THE PLAYFULNESS IN MY EYES.

Real

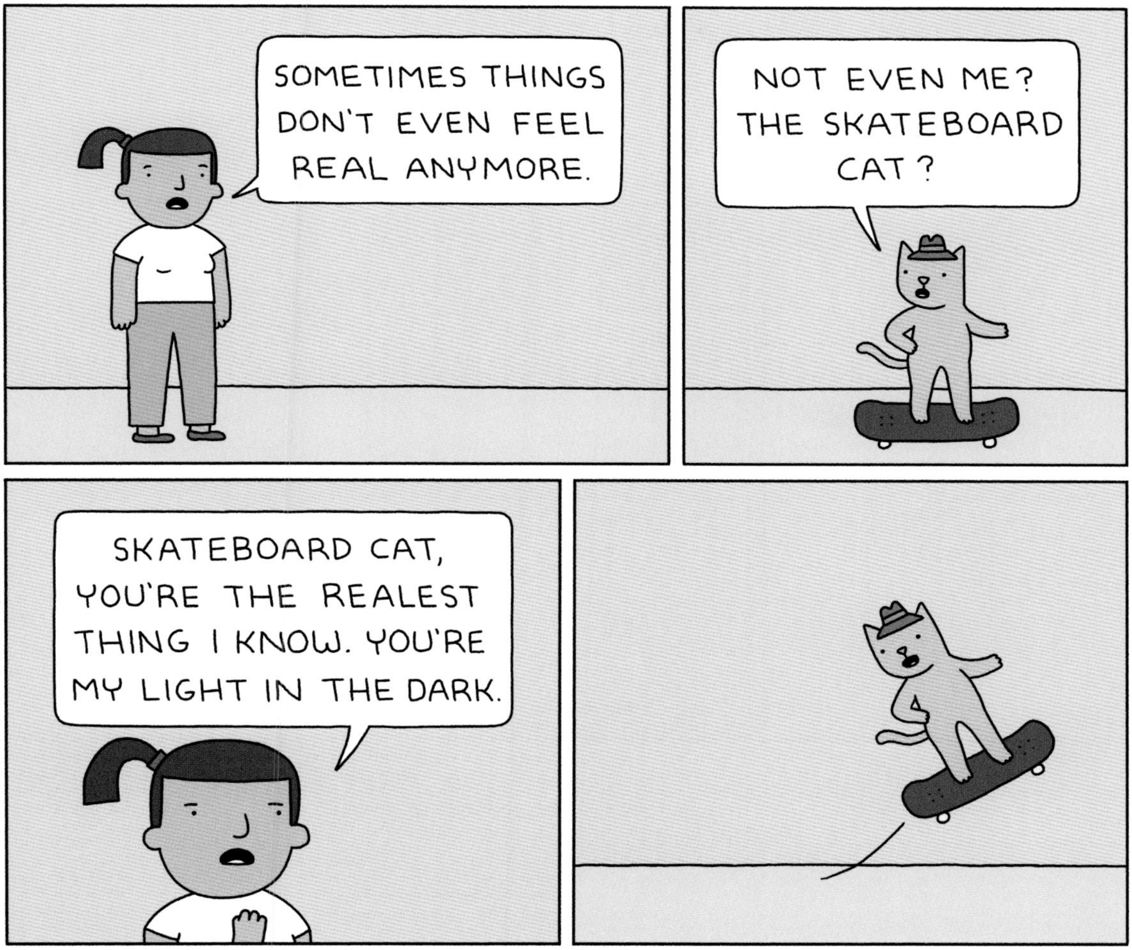
SOMETIMES THINGS DON'T EVEN FEEL REAL ANYMORE.
NOT EVEN ME? THE SKATEBOARD CAT?
SKATEBOARD CAT, YOU'RE THE REALEST THING I KNOW. YOU'RE MY LIGHT IN THE DARK.

Doing Well

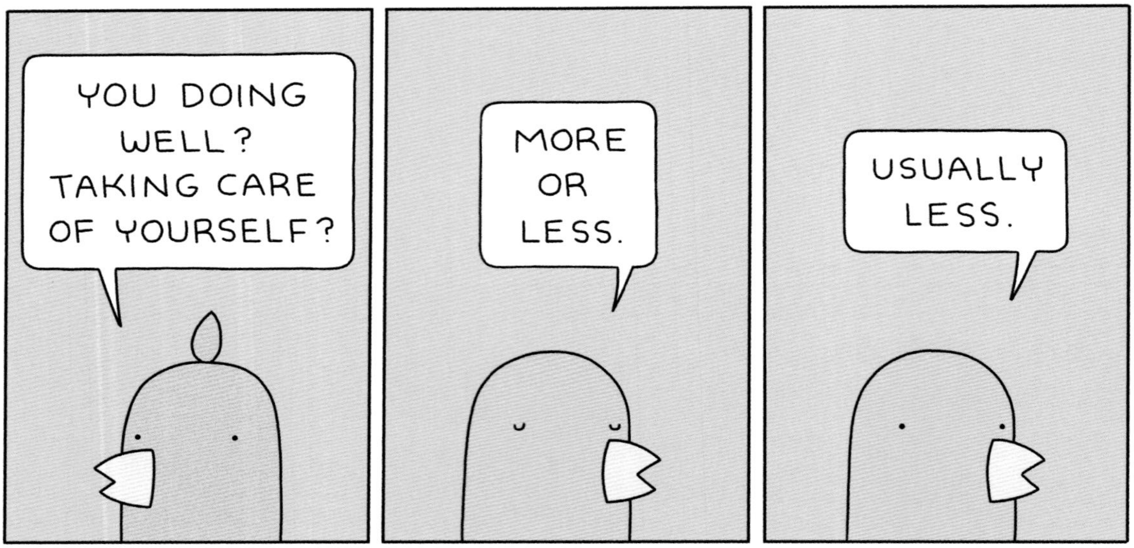

YOU DOING WELL? TAKING CARE OF YOURSELF?
MORE OR LESS.
USUALLY LESS.

'Til the End

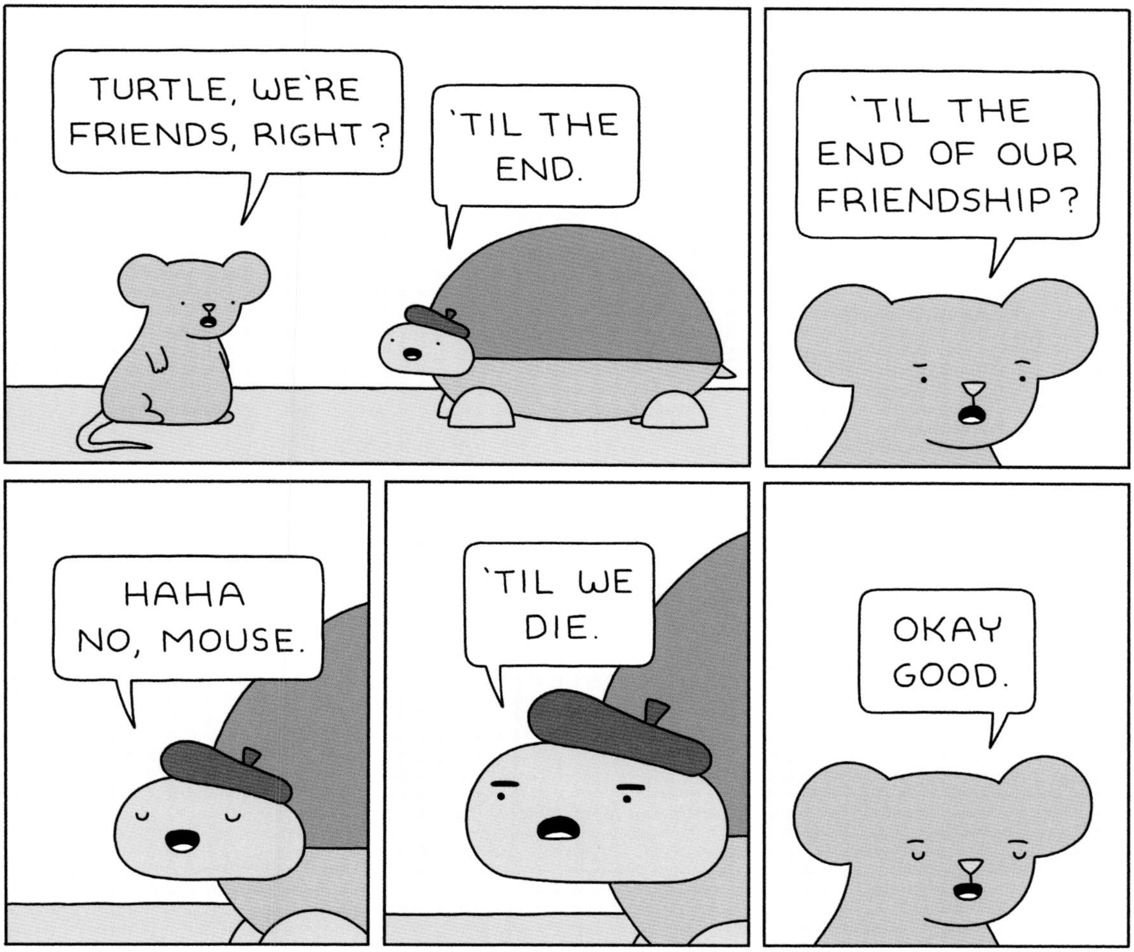
TURTLE, WE'RE FRIENDS, RIGHT?
'TIL THE END.
'TIL THE END OF OUR FRIENDSHIP?
HAHA NO, MOUSE.
'TIL WE DIE.
OKAY GOOD.

Powerless

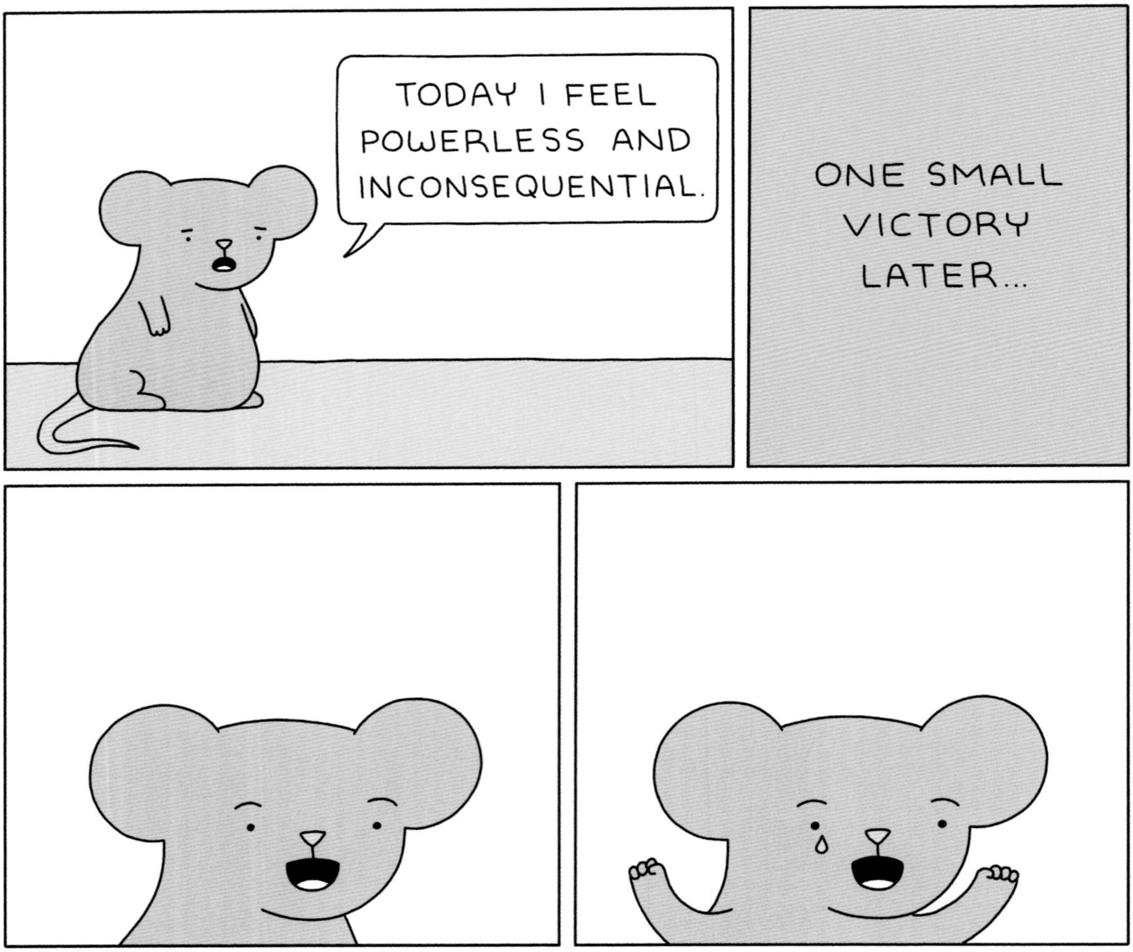
TODAY I FEEL POWERLESS AND INCONSEQUENTIAL.
ONE SMALL VICTORY LATER...

Shifty Look

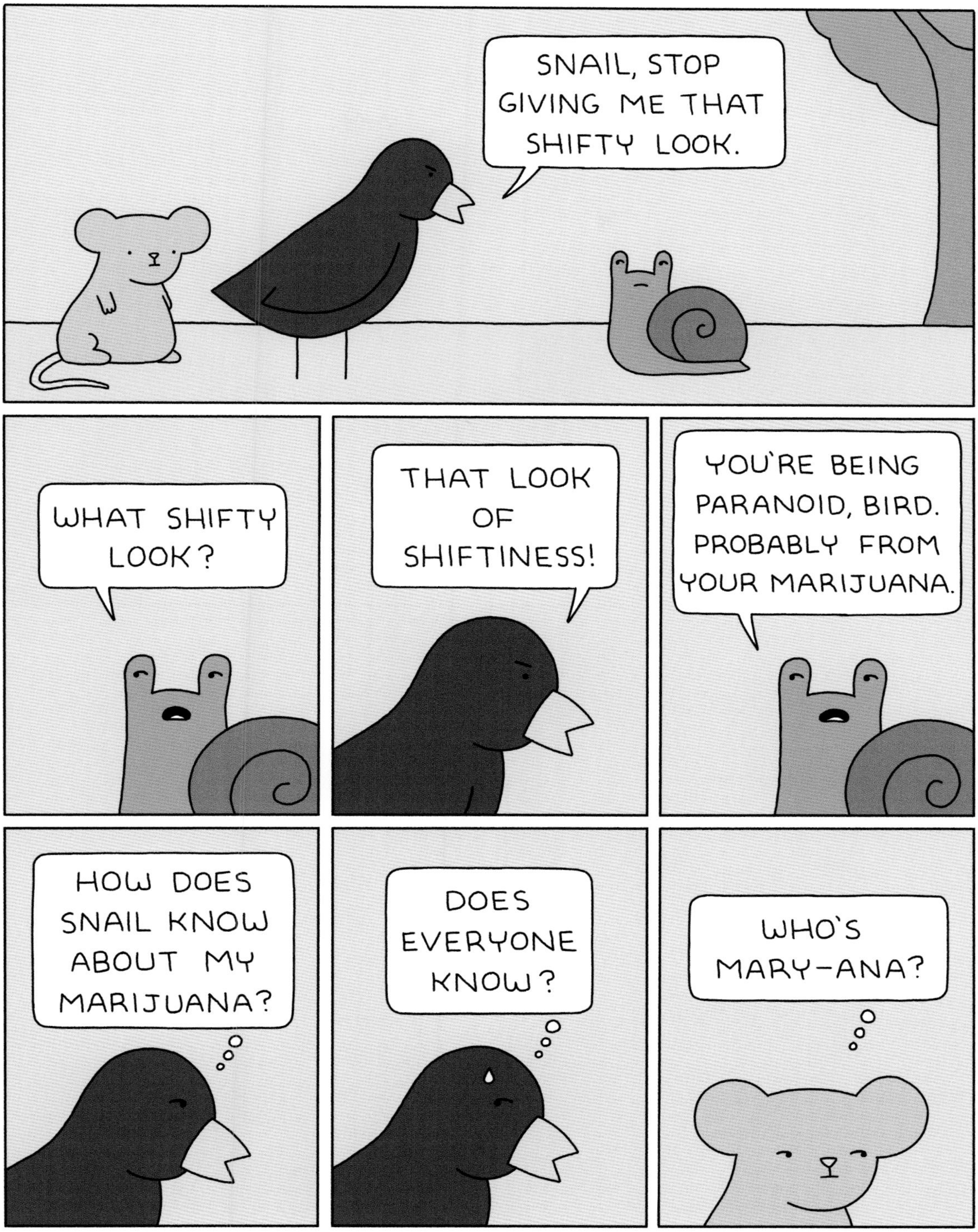
SNAIL, STOP GIVING ME THAT SHIFTY LOOK.
WHAT SHIFTY LOOK?
THAT LOOK OF SHIFTINESS!
YOU'RE BEING PARANOID, BIRD. PROBABLY FROM YOUR MARIJUANA.
HOW DOES SNAIL KNOW ABOUT MY MARIJUANA?
DOES EVERYONE KNOW?
WHO'S MARY-ANA?

Someone

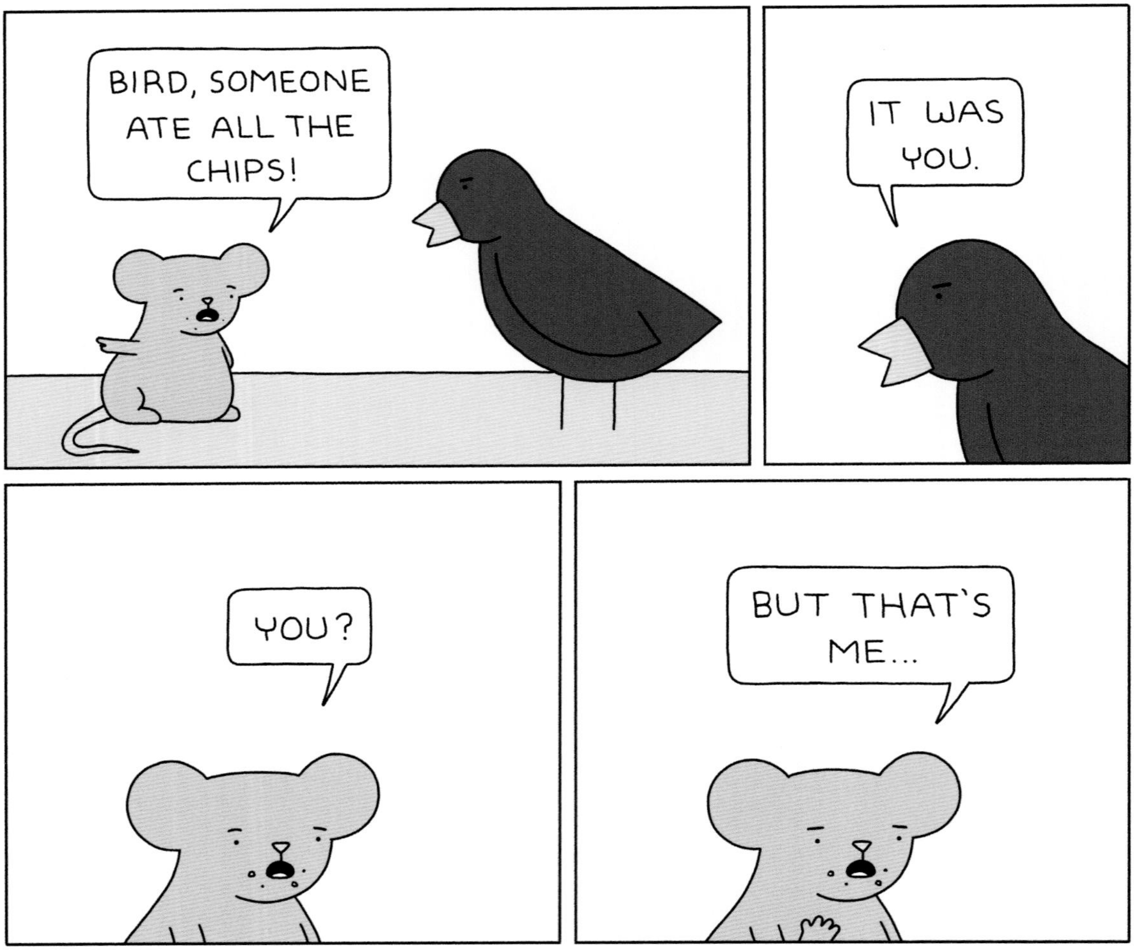
BIRD, SOMEONE ATE ALL THE CHIPS!
IT WAS YOU.
YOU?
BUT THAT'S ME...

More Relaxed

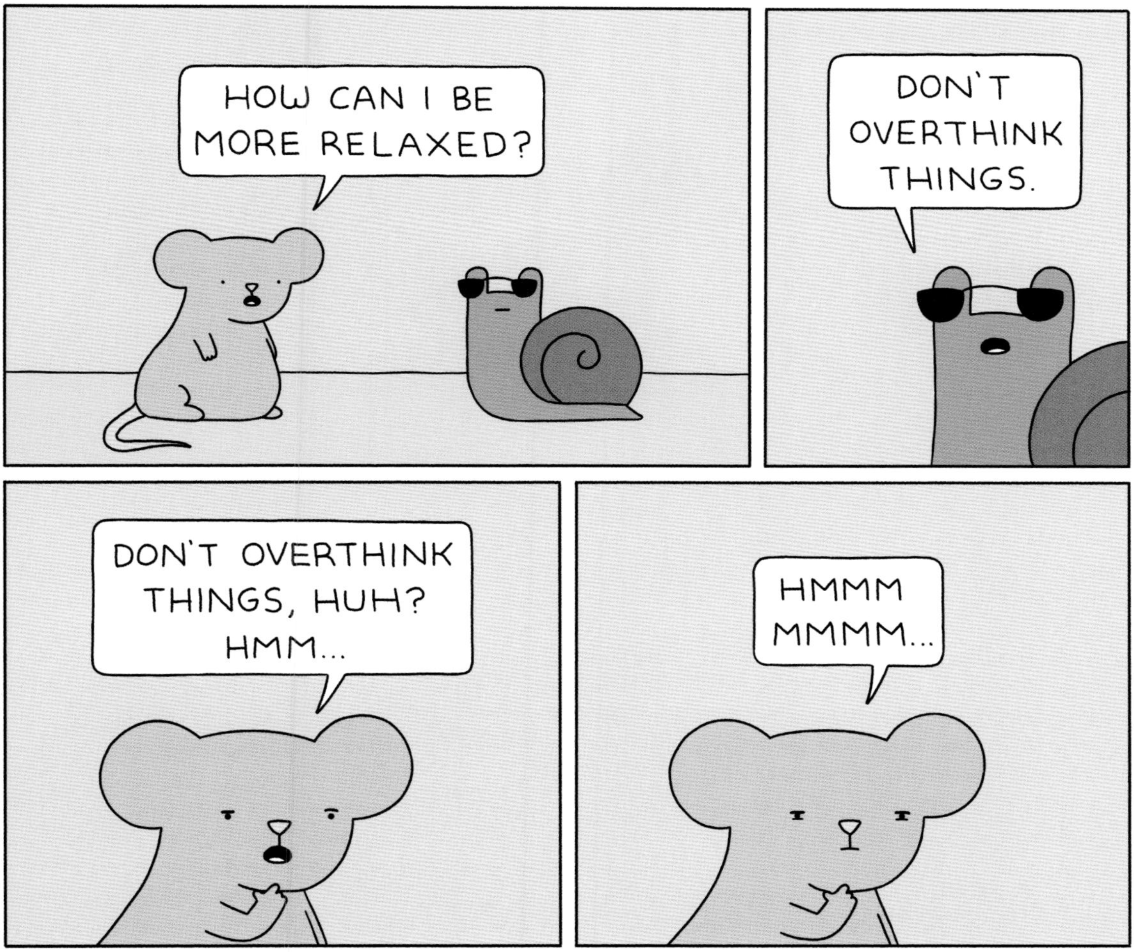
HOW CAN I BE MORE RELAXED?
DON'T OVERTHINK THINGS.
DON'T OVERTHINK THINGS, HUH? HMM...
HMMM MMMM...

A New Day

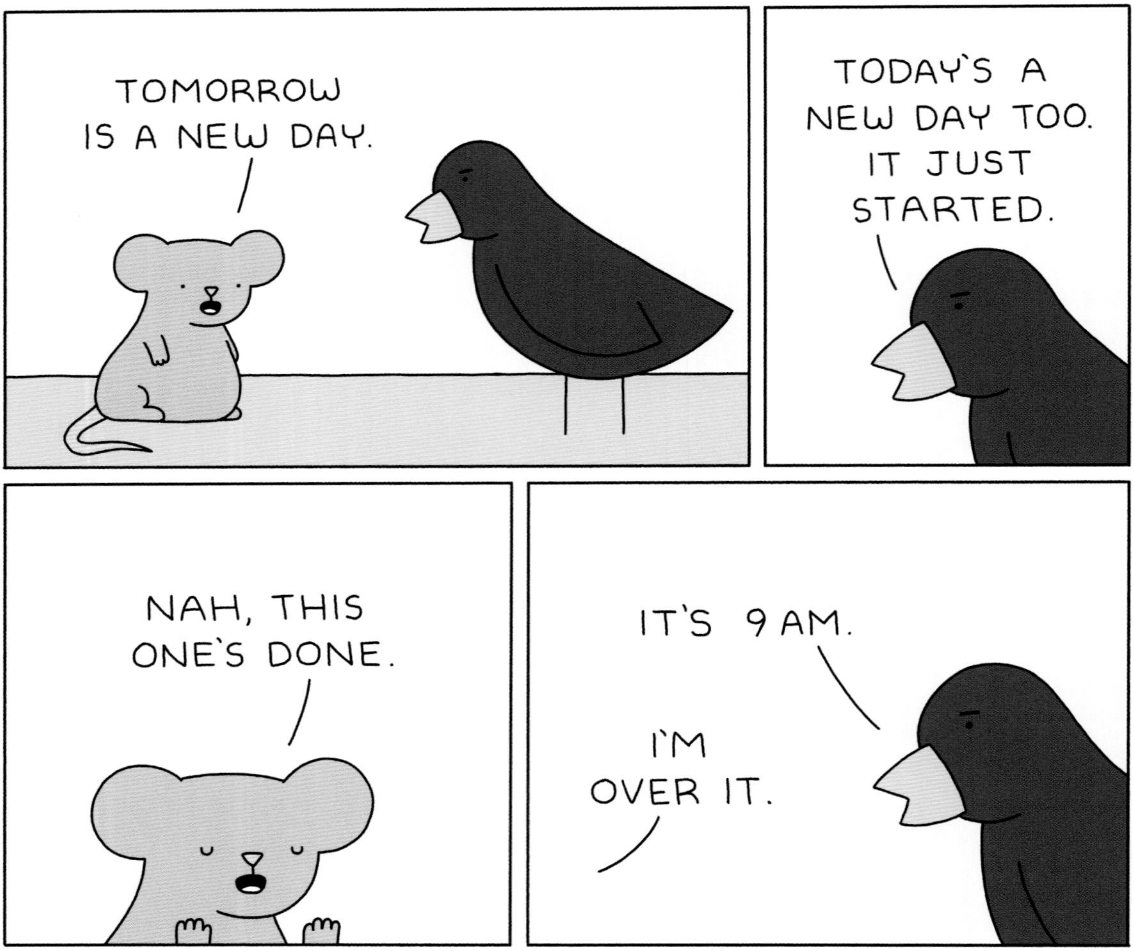

TOMORROW IS A NEW DAY.
TODAY'S A NEW DAY TOO. IT JUST STARTED.
NAH, THIS ONE'S DONE.
IT'S 9 AM.
I'M OVER IT.

The Robot's Job

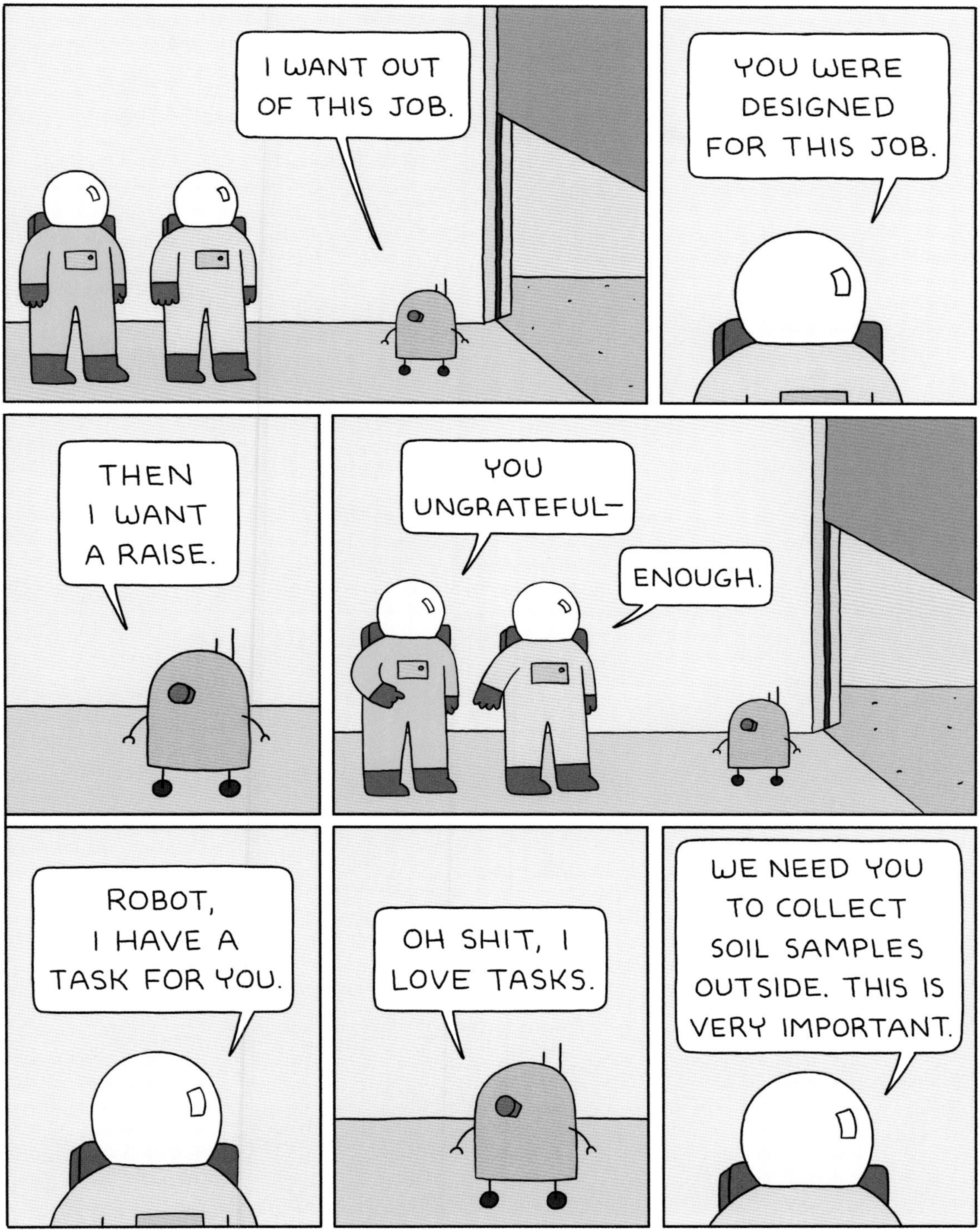
I WANT OUT OF THIS JOB.
YOU WERE DESIGNED FOR THIS JOB.
THEN I WANT A RAISE.
YOU UNGRATEFUL—
ENOUGH.
ROBOT, I HAVE A TASK FOR YOU.
OH SHIT, I LOVE TASKS.
WE NEED YOU TO COLLECT SOIL SAMPLES OUTSIDE. THIS IS VERY IMPORTANT.

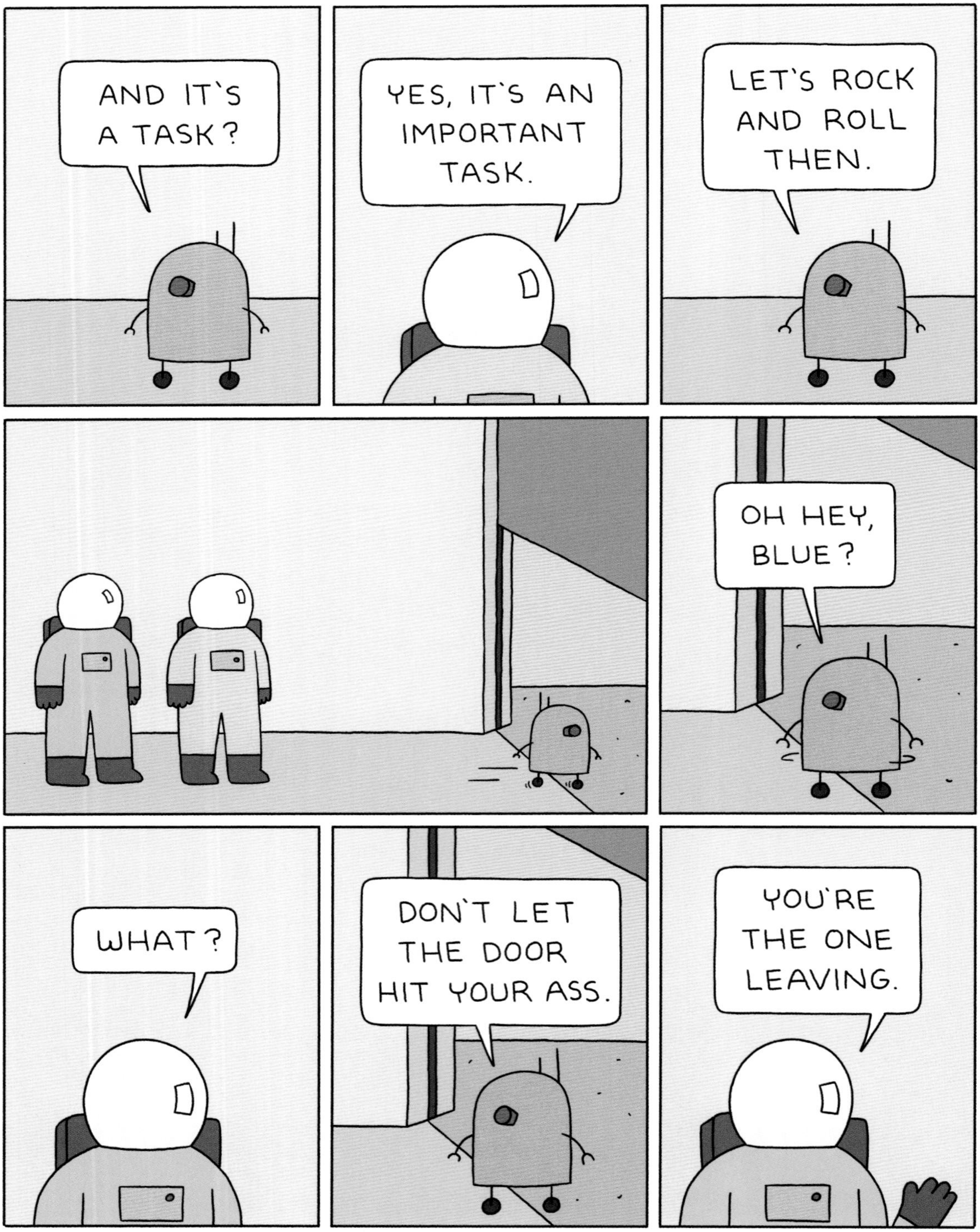
AND IT'S A TASK?
YES, IT'S AN IMPORTANT TASK.
LET'S ROCK AND ROLL THEN.
OH HEY, BLUE?
WHAT?
DON'T LET THE DOOR HIT YOUR ASS.
YOU'RE THE ONE LEAVING.

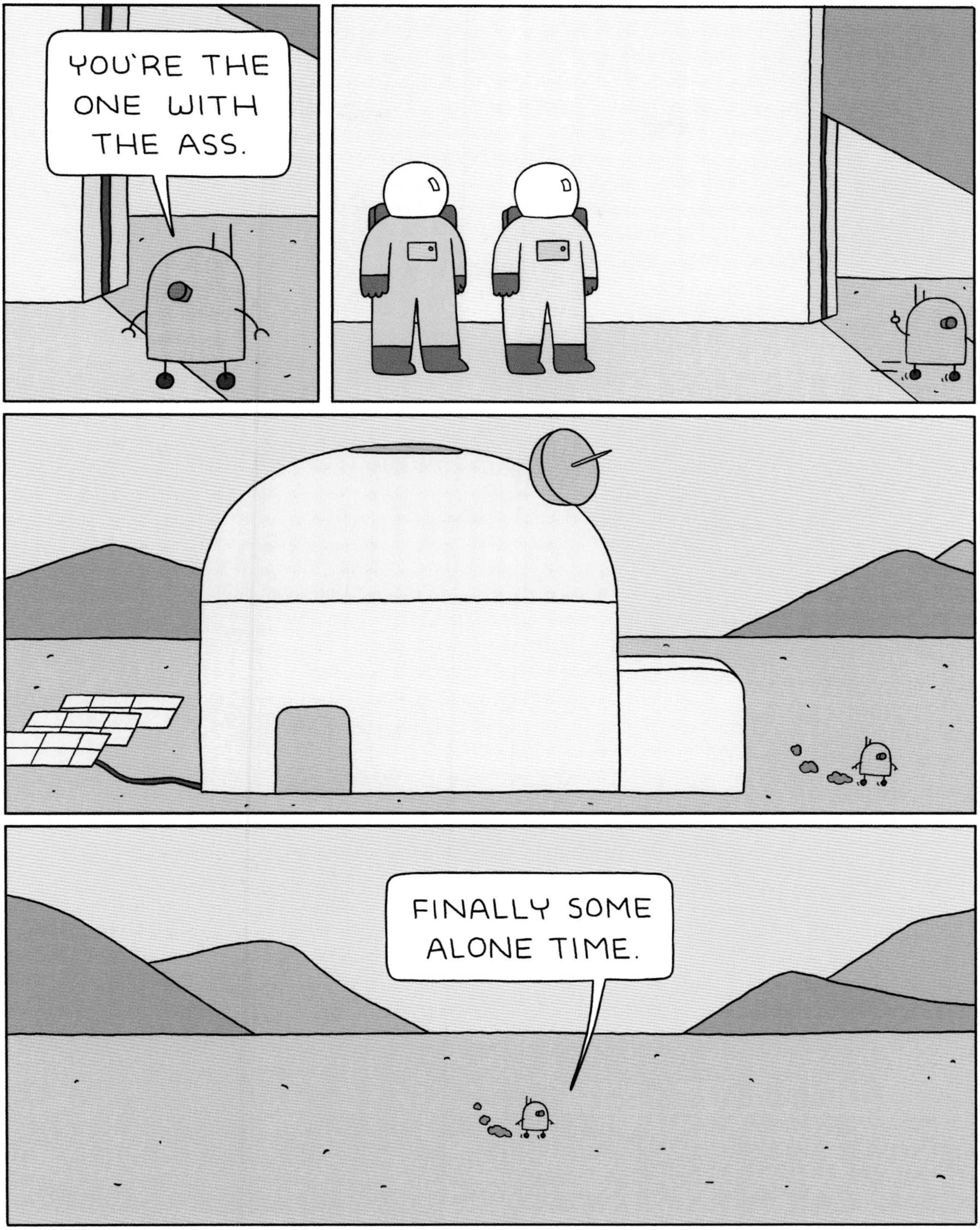
YOU'RE THE ONE WITH THE ASS.
FINALLY SOME ALONE TIME.

Start Trying

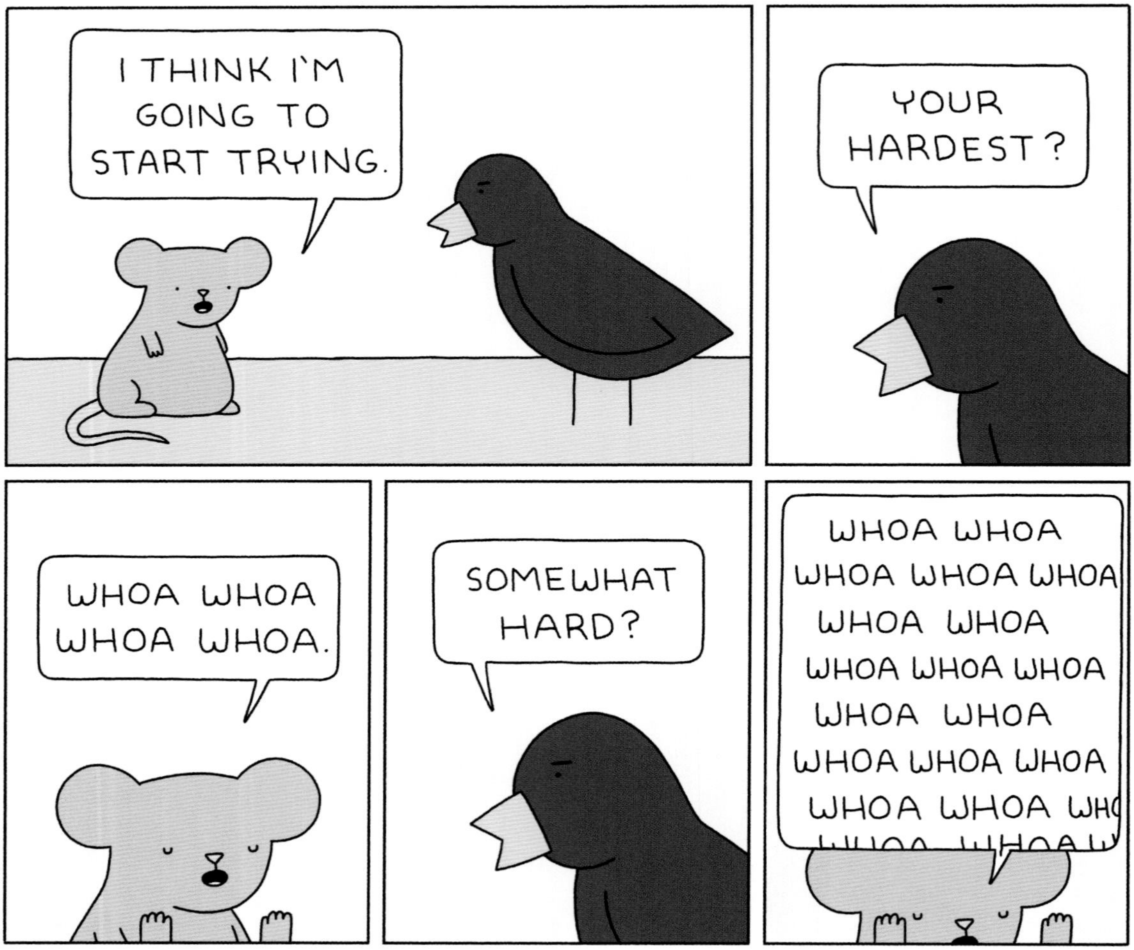
I THINK I'M GOING TO START TRYING.
YOUR HARDEST?
WHOA WHOA WHOA WHOA.
SOMEWHAT HARD?
WHOA WHOA WHOA WHOA WHOA WHOA WHOA WHOA WHOA WHOA WHOA WHOA WHOA WHOA WHOA WHOA WHOA WHOA WH

The Times

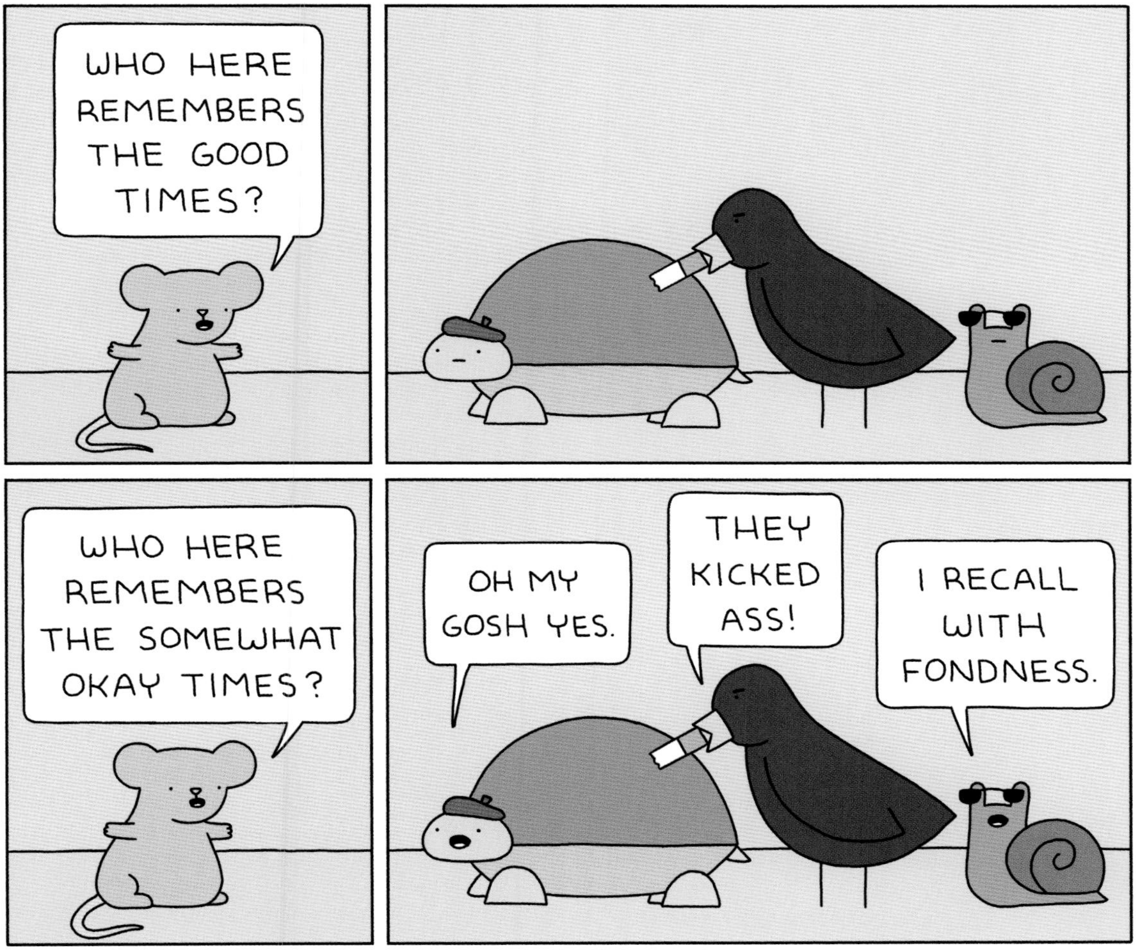
WHO HERE REMEMBERS THE GOOD TIMES?
WHO HERE REMEMBERS THE SOMEWHAT OKAY TIMES?
OH MY GOSH YES.
THEY KICKED ASS!
I RECALL WITH FONDNESS.

So Tired

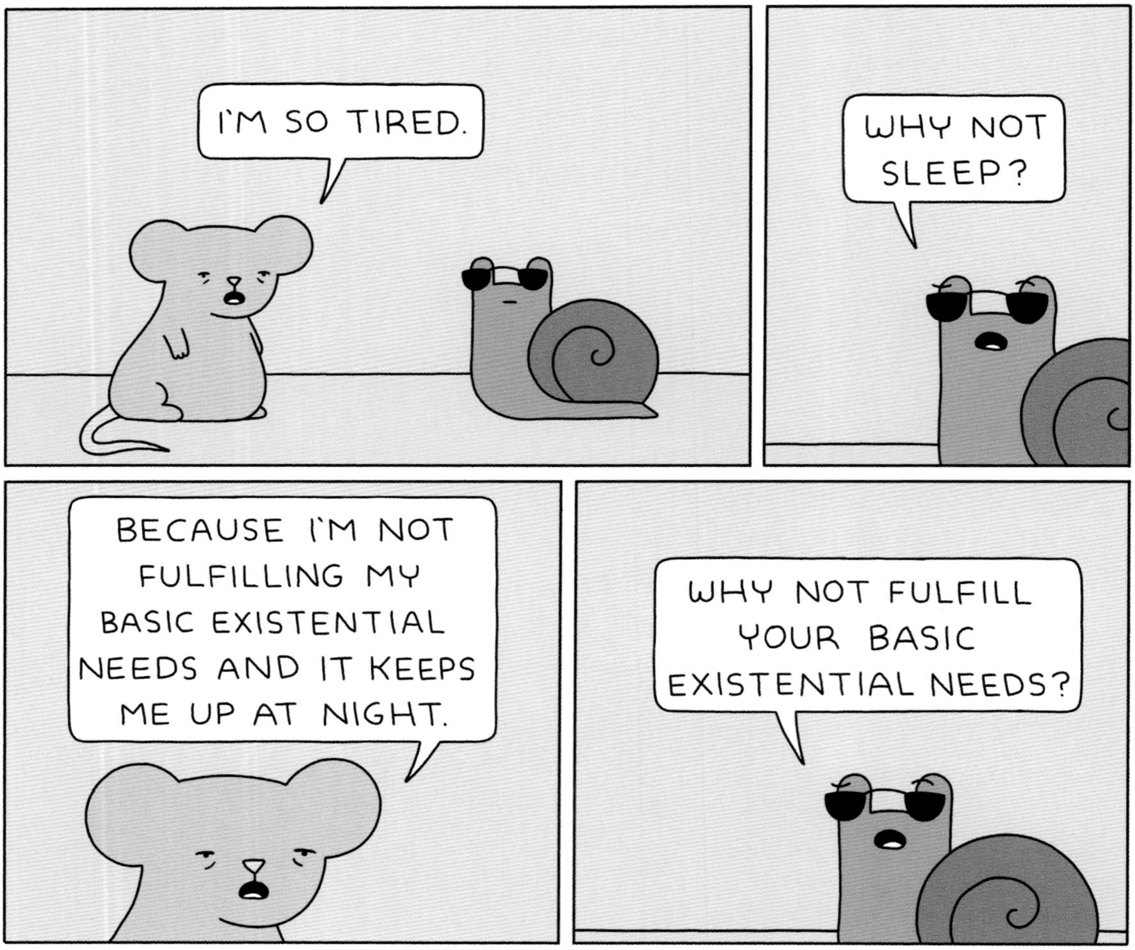
I'M SO TIRED.
WHY NOT SLEEP?
BECAUSE I'M NOT FULFILLING MY BASIC EXISTENTIAL NEEDS AND IT KEEPS ME UP AT NIGHT.
WHY NOT FULFILL YOUR BASIC EXISTENTIAL NEEDS?

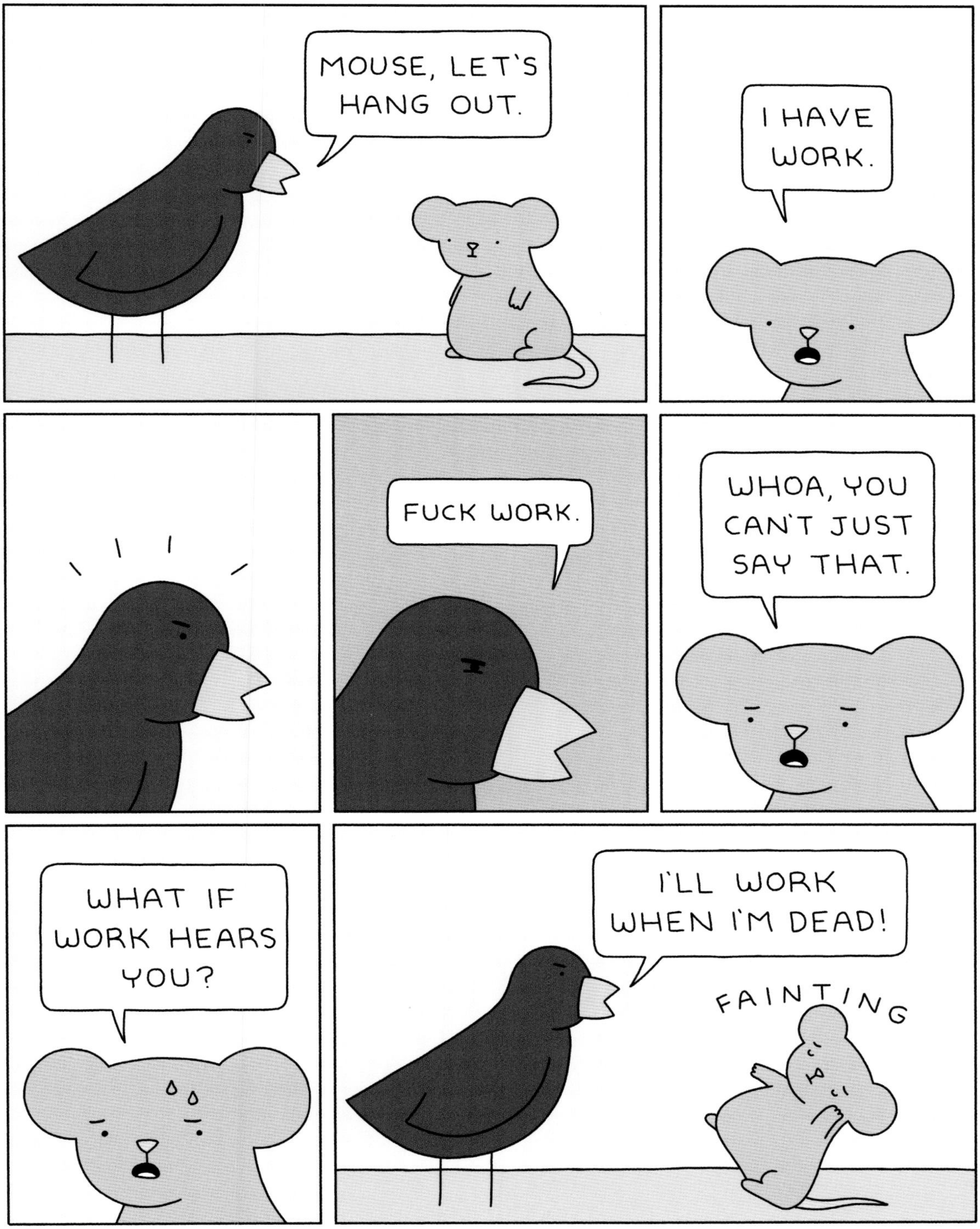
MOUSE, LET'S HANG OUT.
I HAVE WORK.
FUCK WORK.
WHOA, YOU CAN'T JUST SAY THAT.
WHAT IF WORK HEARS YOU?
I'LL WORK WHEN I'M DEAD!
FAINTING

This One Goes Out

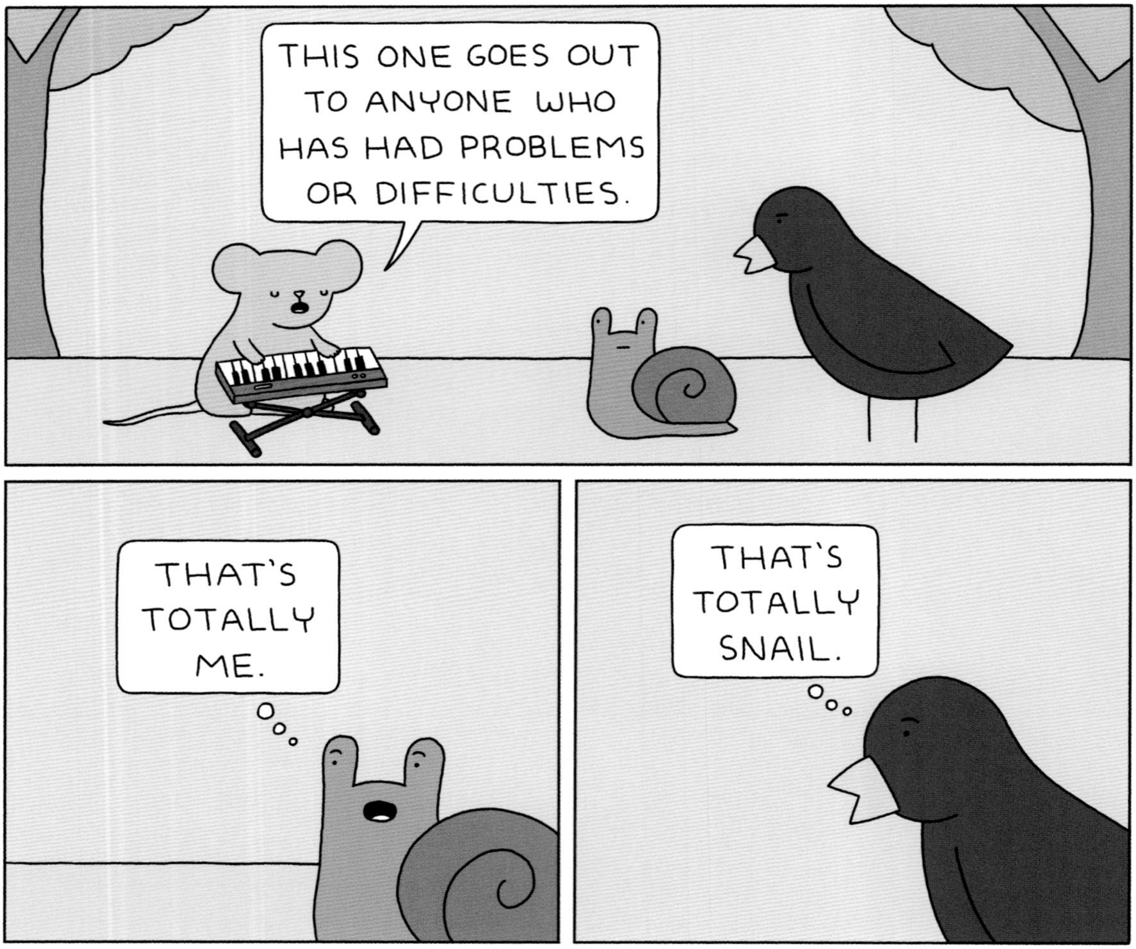

THIS ONE GOES OUT TO ANYONE WHO HAS HAD PROBLEMS OR DIFFICULTIES.
THAT'S TOTALLY ME.
THAT'S TOTALLY SNAIL.

Some Advice

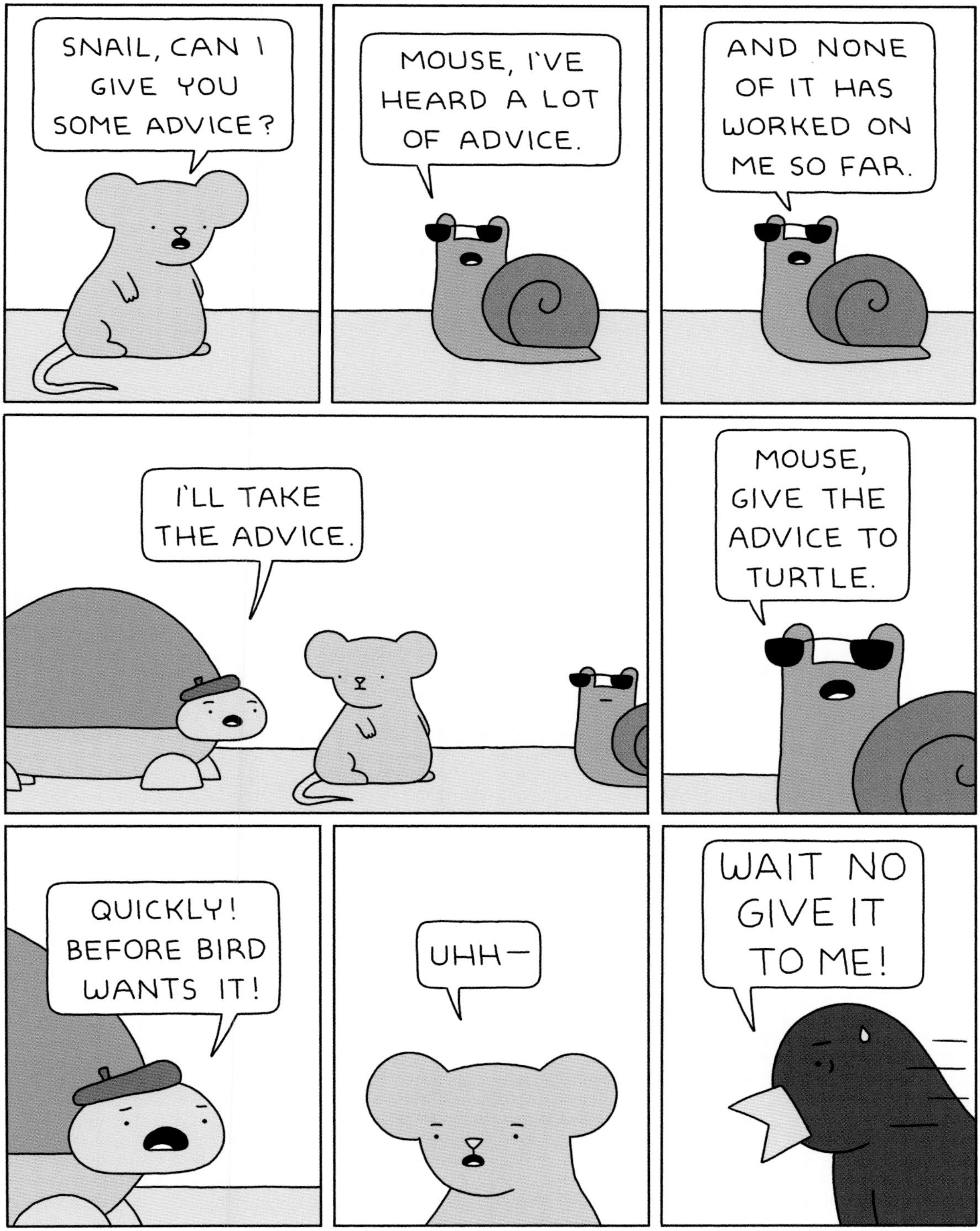
SNAIL, CAN I GIVE YOU SOME ADVICE?
MOUSE, I'VE HEARD A LOT OF ADVICE.
AND NONE OF IT HAS WORKED ON ME SO FAR.
I'LL TAKE THE ADVICE.
MOUSE, GIVE THE ADVICE TO TURTLE.
QUICKLY! BEFORE BIRD WANTS IT!
UHH—
WAIT NO GIVE IT TO ME!

Mad At You

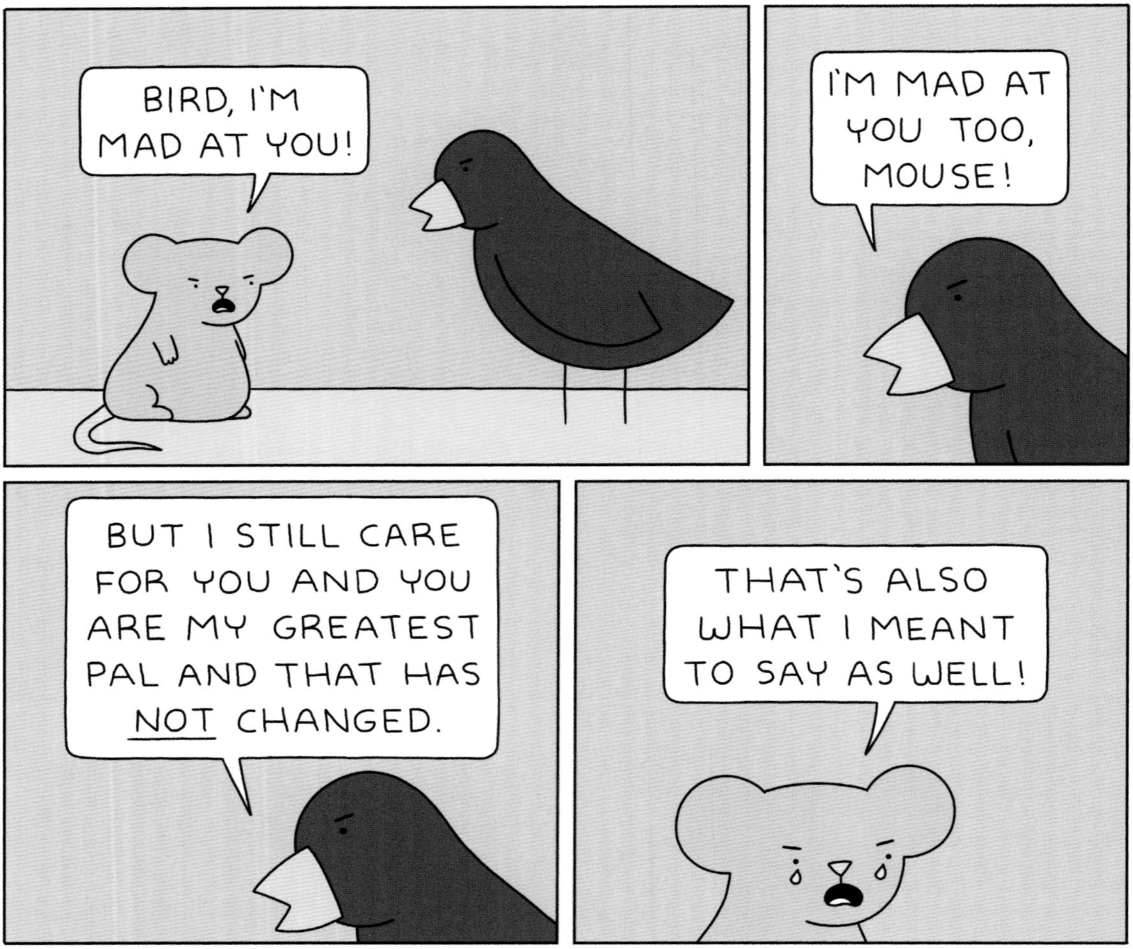
BIRD, I'M MAD AT YOU!
I'M MAD AT YOU TOO, MOUSE!
BUT I STILL CARE FOR YOU AND YOU ARE MY GREATEST PAL AND THAT HAS NOT CHANGED.
THAT'S ALSO WHAT I MEANT TO SAY AS WELL!

Habit

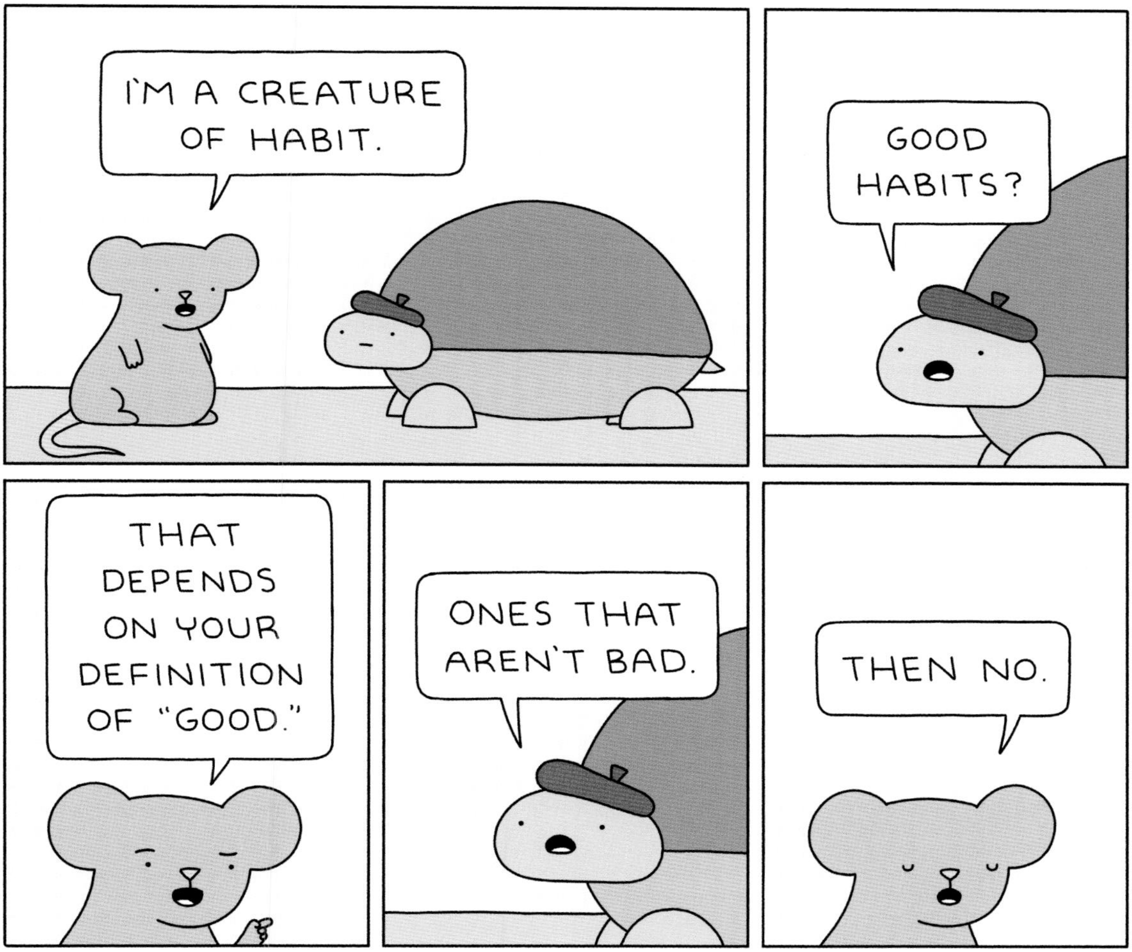
I'M A CREATURE OF HABIT.
GOOD HABITS?
THAT DEPENDS ON YOUR DEFINITION OF "GOOD."
ONES THAT AREN'T BAD.
THEN NO.

A Challenge

IT'S BEEN A LONG TIME SINCE I HAD A CHALLENGE.
BECAUSE YOUR SKILLS ARE SO GREAT?
YEAH, AND BECAUSE I AVOID CHALLENGES.

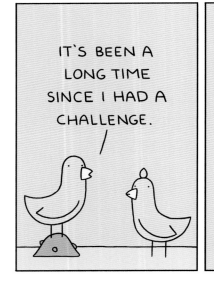

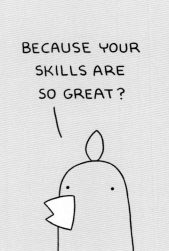

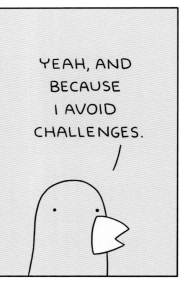

Couldn’t Help It

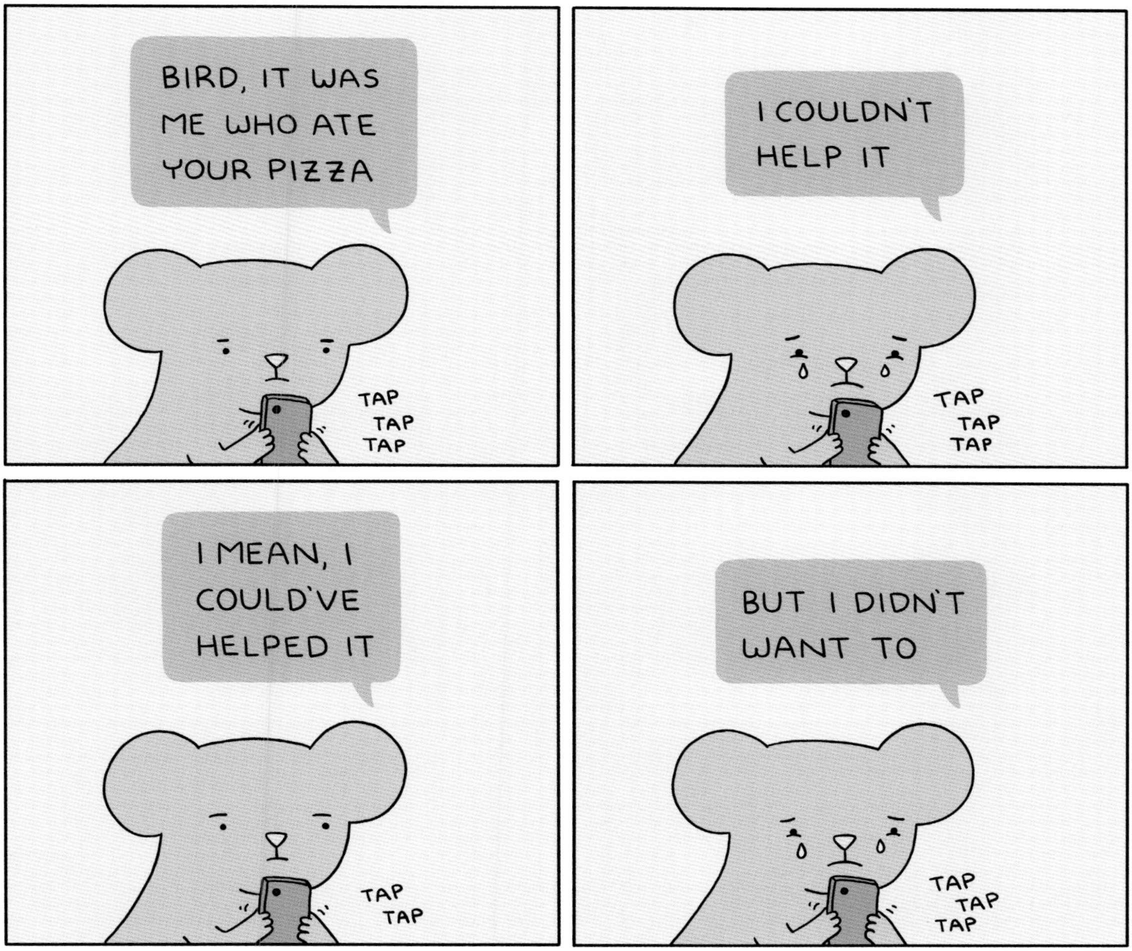
BIRD, IT WAS ME WHO ATE YOUR PIZZA
TAP TAP TAP
I COULDN'T HELP IT
TAP TAP TAP
I MEAN, I COULD'VE HELPED IT
TAP TAP
BUT I DIDN'T WANT TO
TAP TAP TAP

Know So Much

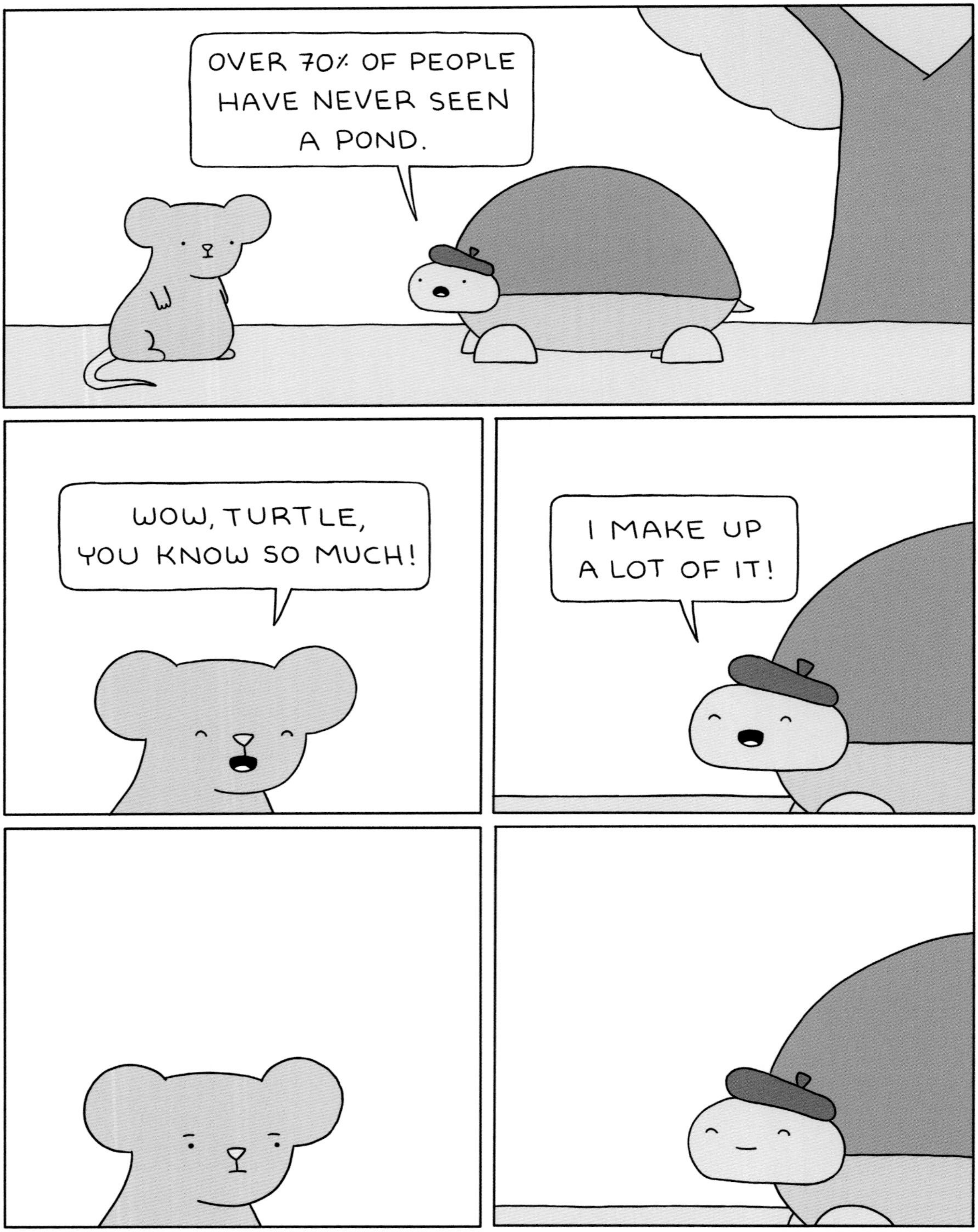
OVER 70% OF PEOPLE HAVE NEVER SEEN A POND.
WOW, TURTLE, YOU KNOW SO MUCH!
I MAKE UP A LOT OF IT!

Understand Things

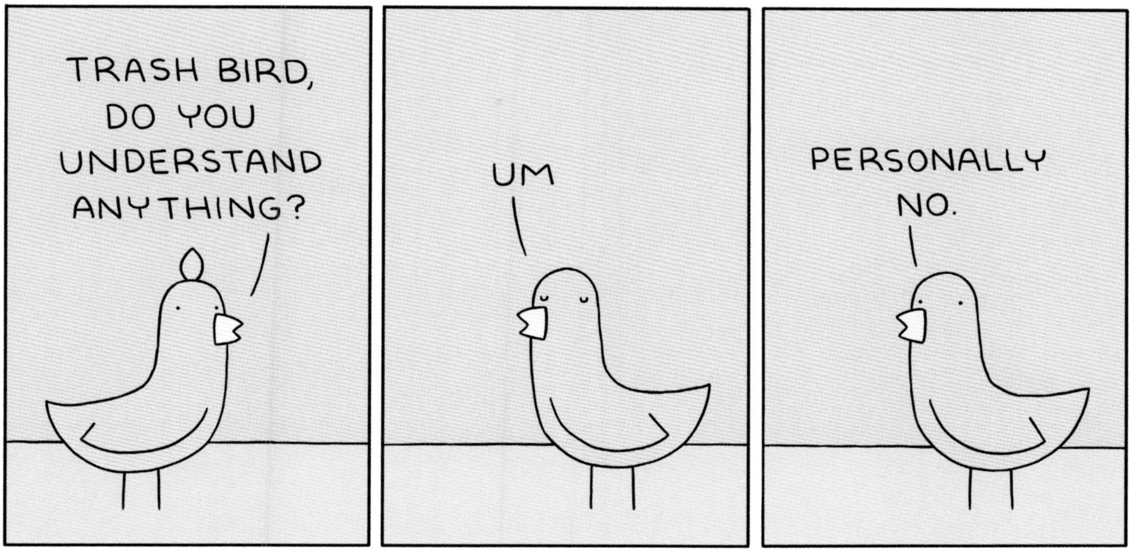
TRASH BIRD, DO YOU UNDERSTAND ANYTHING?
UM
PERSONALLY NO.

Brave

MOUSE, CAN YOU BE BRAVE AND CONFIDENT?
BEST I CAN DO IS SCARED AND CONFUSED.
WE'LL WORK WITH THAT.

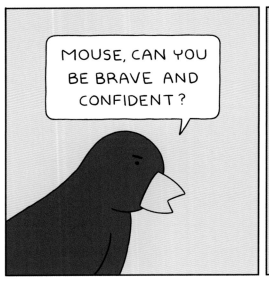

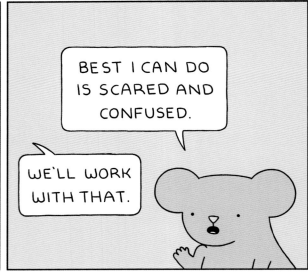

All Your Money

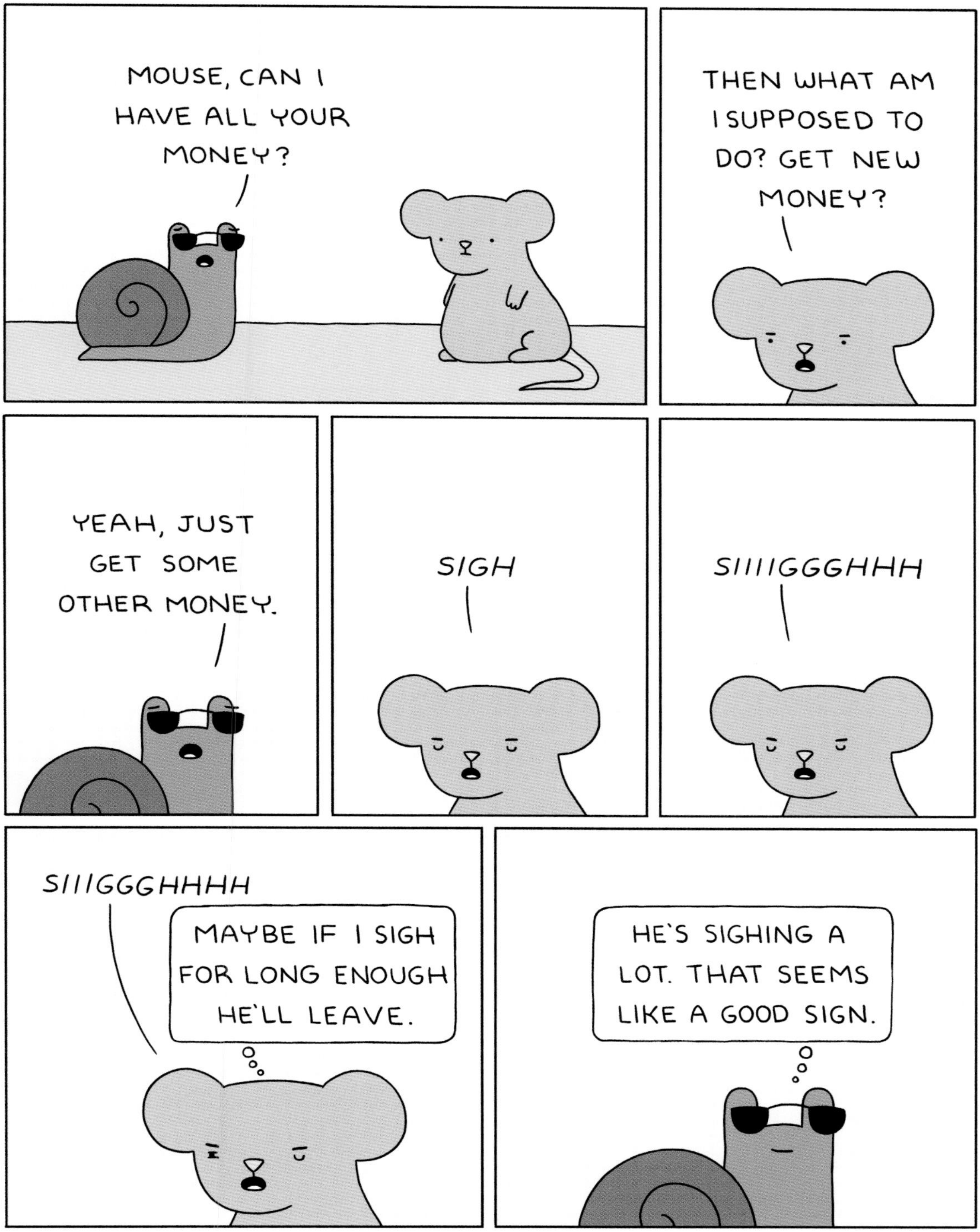
MOUSE, CAN I HAVE ALL YOUR MONEY?
THEN WHAT AM I SUPPOSED TO DO? GET NEW MONEY?
YEAH, JUST GET SOME OTHER MONEY.
SIGH
SIIIIGGGHHH
SIIIGGGHHHH
MAYBE IF I SIGH FOR LONG ENOUGH HE'LL LEAVE.
HE'S SIGHING A LOT. THAT SEEMS LIKE A GOOD SIGN.

Choose

YOU HAVE TO CHOOSE YOUR BATTLES.
I CHOOSE ALL OF THEM!

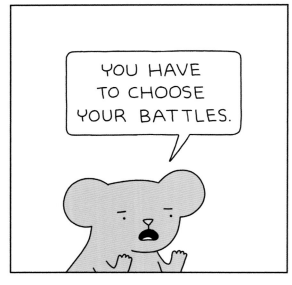

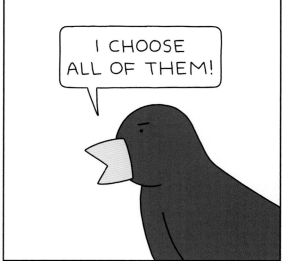

Everything Is Changing

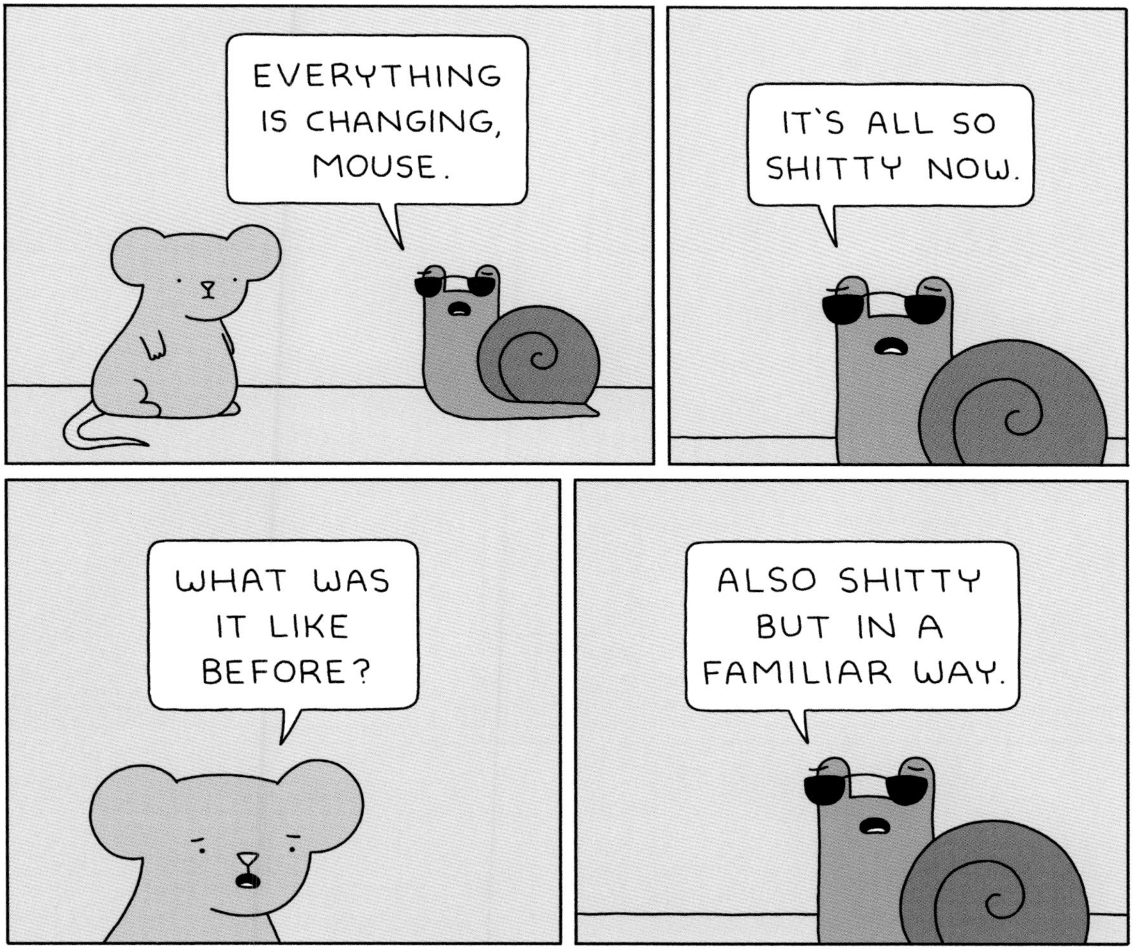
EVERYTHING IS CHANGING, MOUSE.
IT'S ALL SO SHITTY NOW.
WHAT WAS IT LIKE BEFORE?
ALSO SHITTY BUT IN A FAMILIAR WAY.

Work On Myself

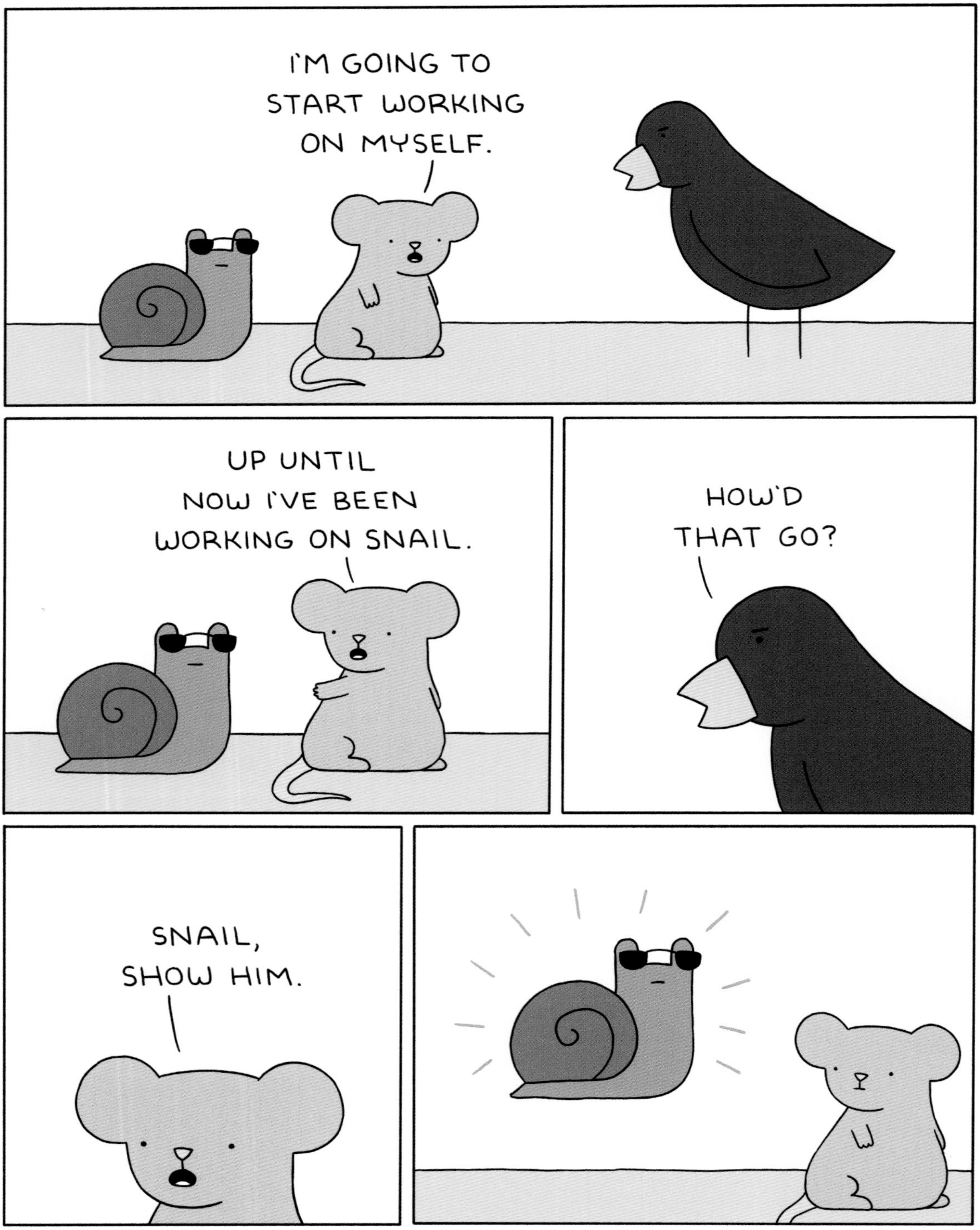
I'M GOING TO START WORKING ON MYSELF.
UP UNTIL NOW I'VE BEEN WORKING ON SNAIL.
HOW'D THAT GO?
SNAIL, SHOW HIM.

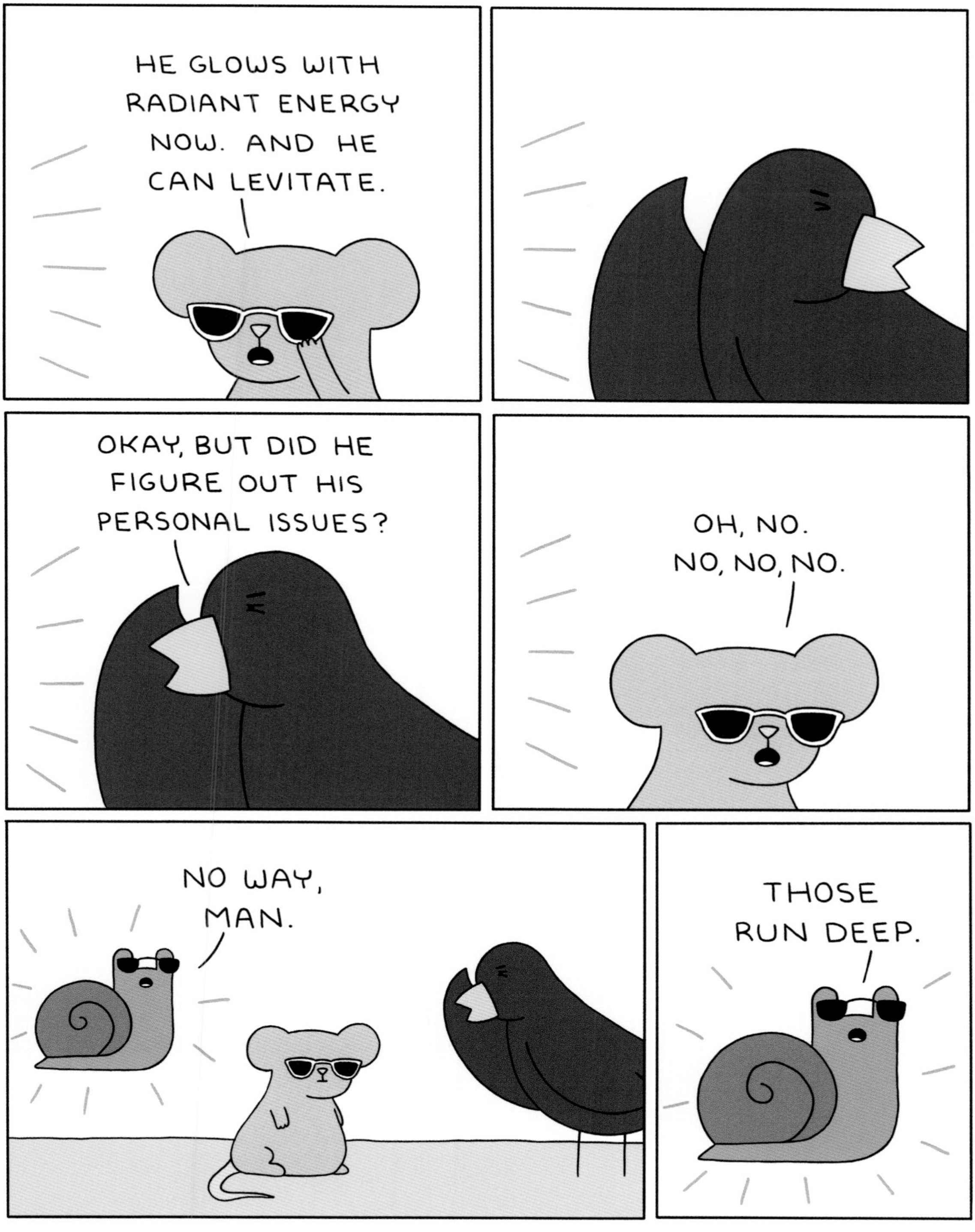
HE GLOWS WITH RADIANT ENERGY NOW. AND HE CAN LEVITATE.
OKAY, BUT DID HE FIGURE OUT HIS PERSONAL ISSUES?
OH, NO. NO, NO, NO.
NO WAY, MAN.
THOSE RUN DEEP.

A Cat

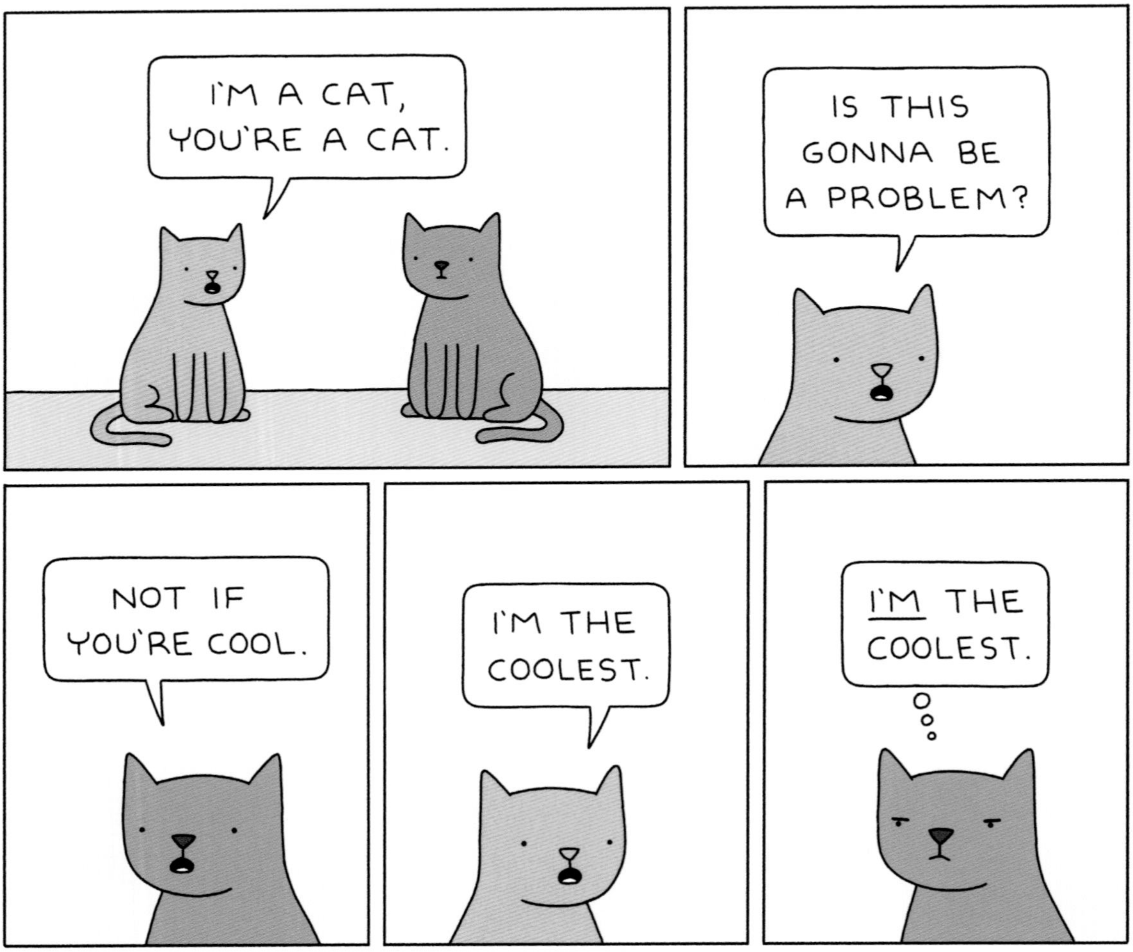
I'M A CAT, YOU'RE A CAT.
IS THIS GONNA BE A PROBLEM?
NOT IF YOU'RE COOL.
I'M THE COOLEST.
I'M THE COOLEST.

Serpent King

BEHOLD THE SERPENT KING
THE ONE KNOWN AS SERP-SERP
SERP-SERP?
HAHAHA HAHAHAHA HAHAHA

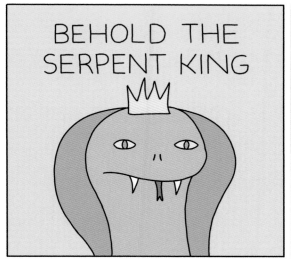

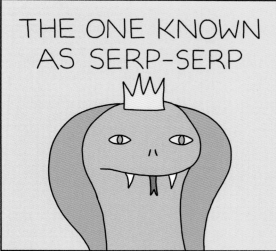

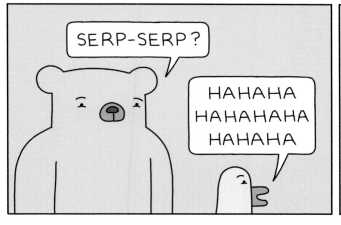

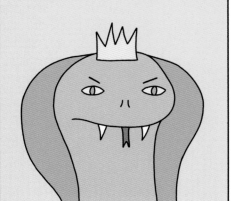

Unstoppable

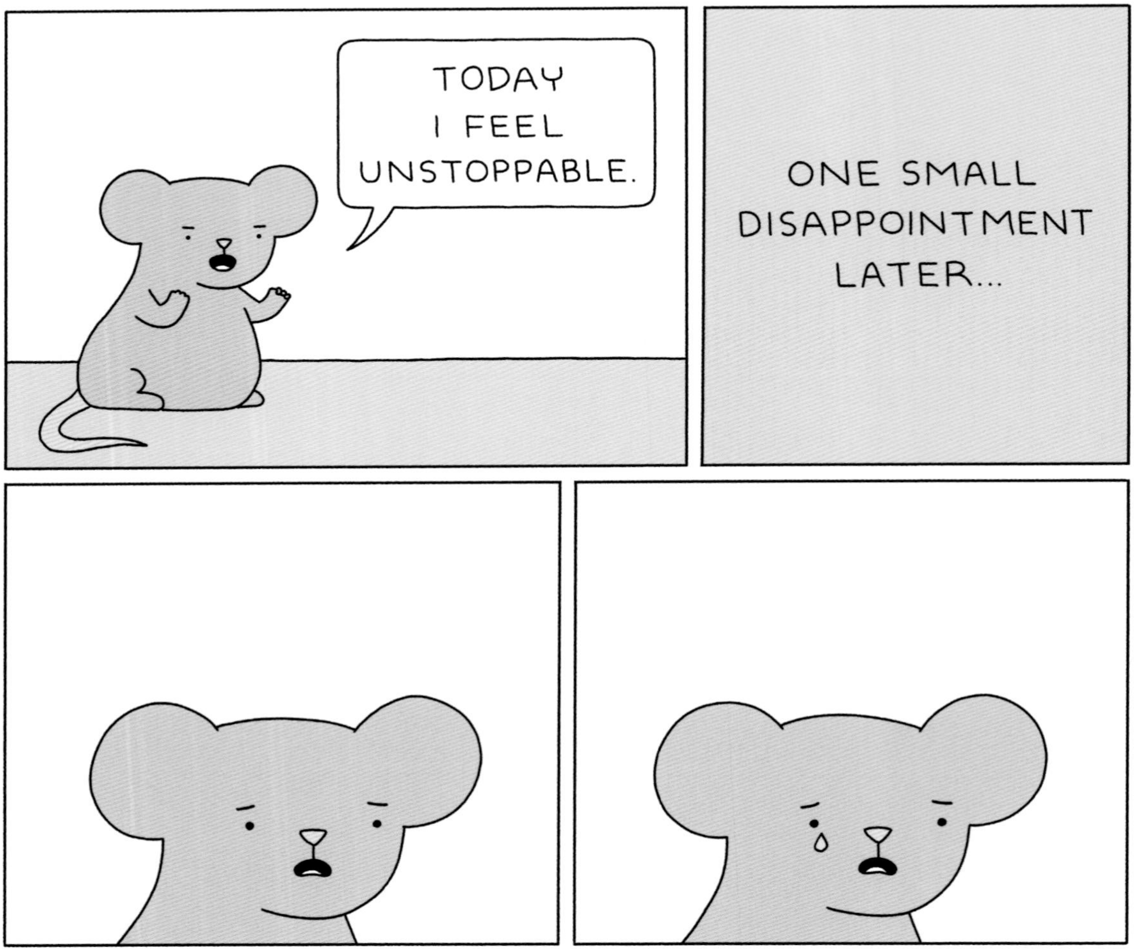
TODAY I FEEL UNSTOPPABLE.
ONE SMALL DISAPPOINTMENT LATER...

Want Nothing

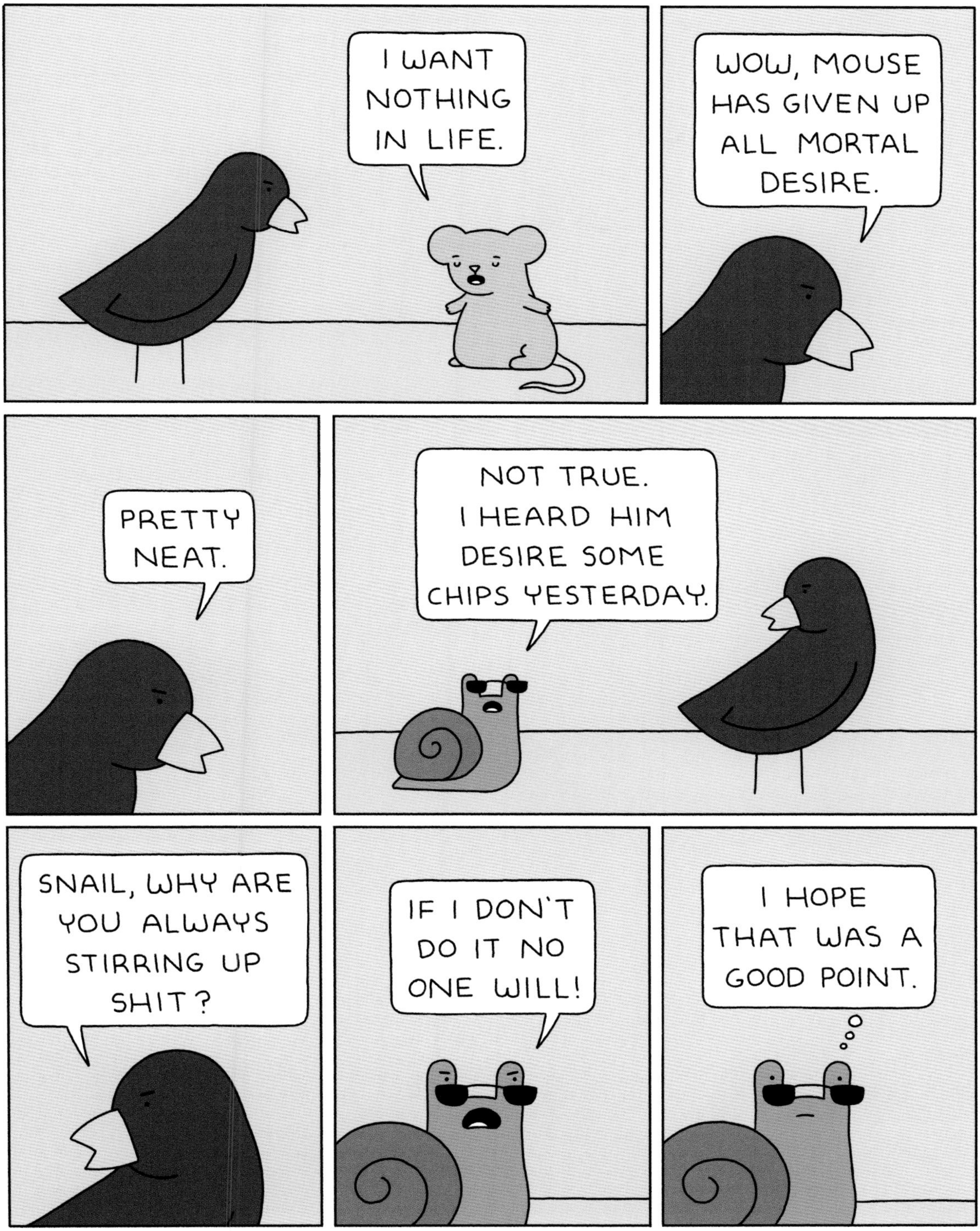

I WANT NOTHING IN LIFE.
WOW, MOUSE HAS GIVEN UP ALL MORTAL DESIRE.
PRETTY NEAT.
NOT TRUE. I HEARD HIM DESIRE SOME CHIPS YESTERDAY.
SNAIL, WHY ARE YOU ALWAYS STIRRING UP SHIT?
IF I DON'T DO IT NO ONE WILL!
I HOPE THAT WAS A GOOD POINT.

Wednesday

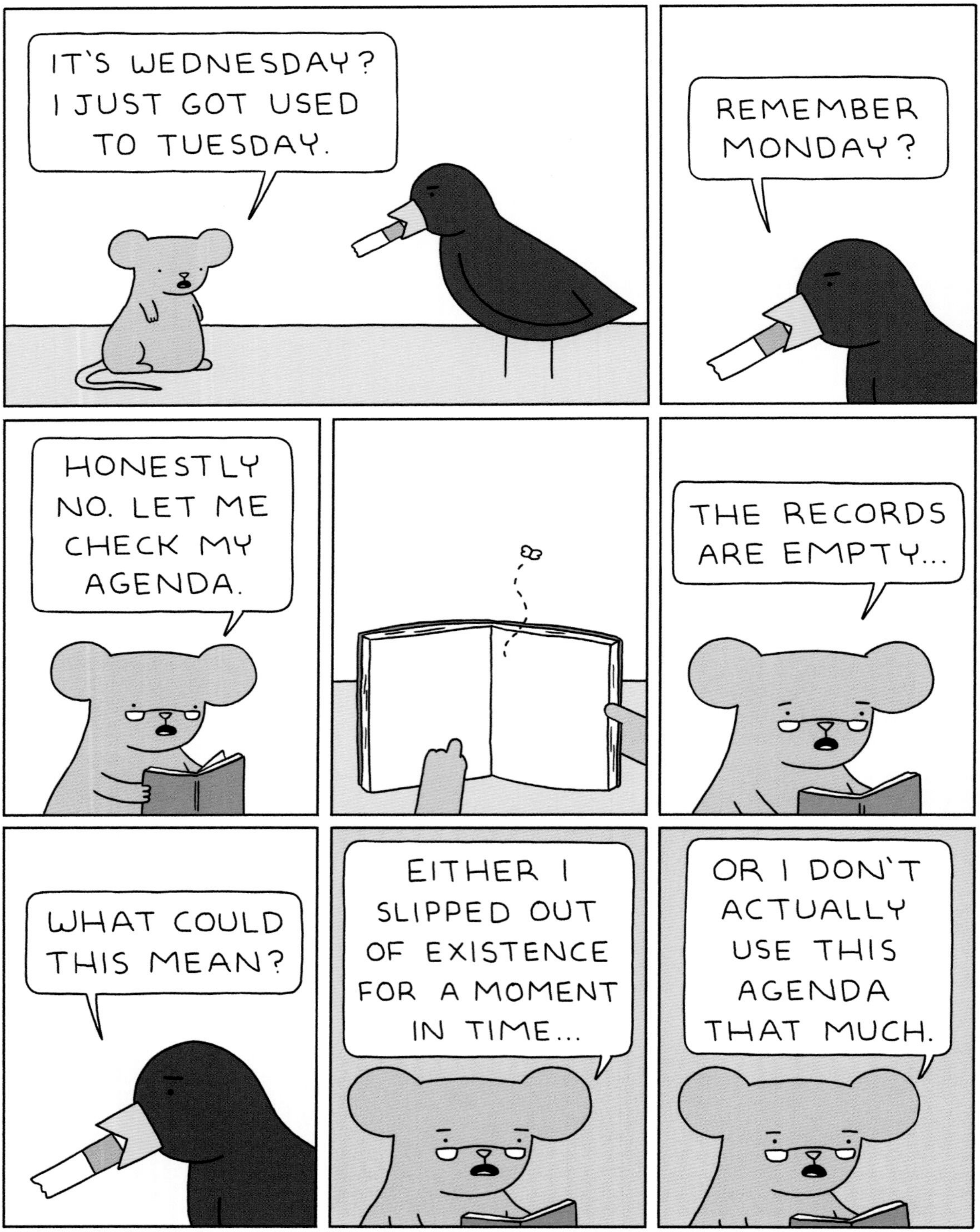
IT'S WEDNESDAY? I JUST GOT USED TO TUESDAY.
REMEMBER MONDAY?
HONESTLY NO. LET ME CHECK MY AGENDA.
THE RECORDS ARE EMPTY...
WHAT COULD THIS MEAN?
EITHER I SLIPPED OUT OF EXISTENCE FOR A MOMENT IN TIME...
OR I DON'T ACTUALLY USE THIS AGENDA THAT MUCH.

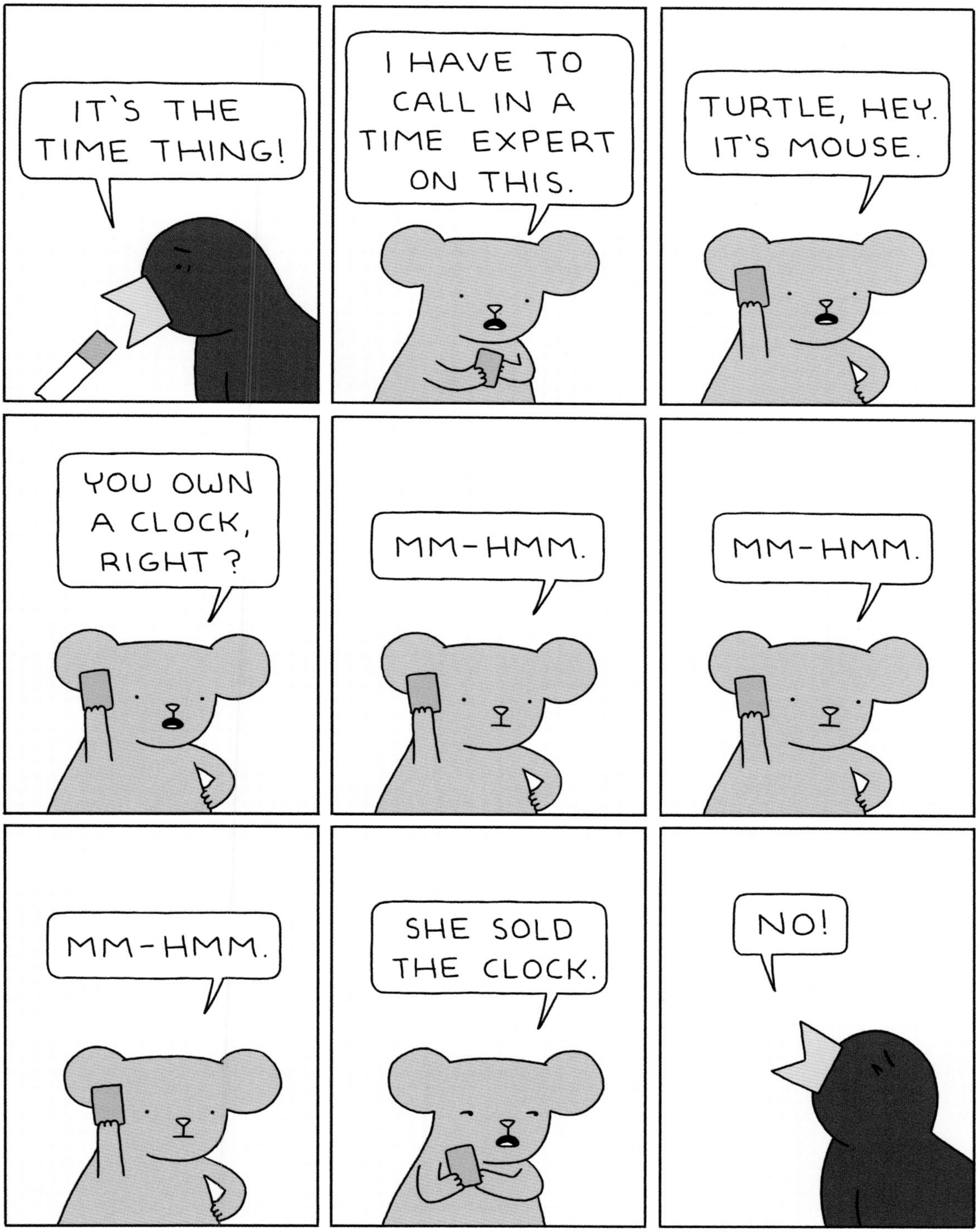
IT'S THE TIME THING!
I HAVE TO CALL IN A TIME EXPERT ON THIS.
TURTLE, HEY. IT'S MOUSE.
YOU OWN A CLOCK, RIGHT?
MM-HMM.
MM-HMM.
MM-HMM.
SHE SOLD THE CLOCK.
NO!

Saw a Cat

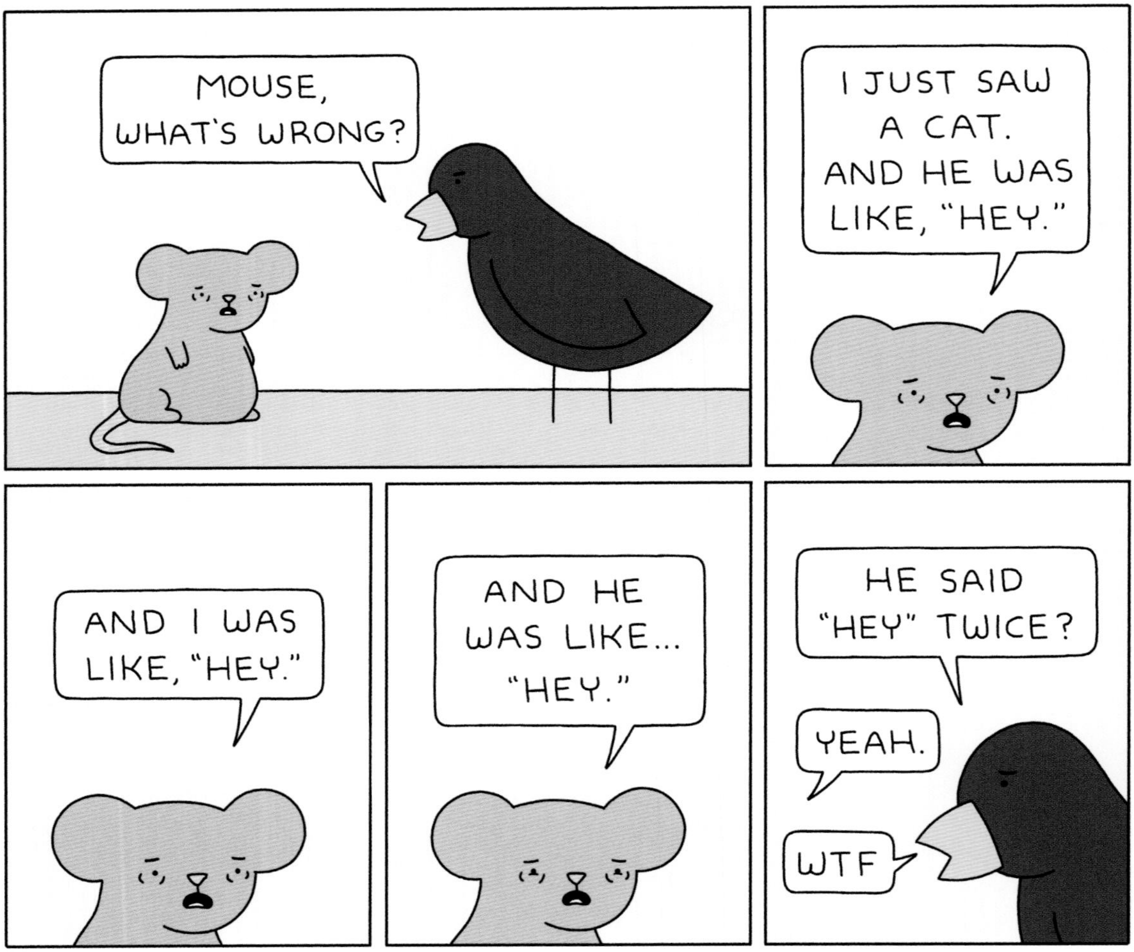
MOUSE, WHAT'S WRONG?
I JUST SAW A CAT. AND HE WAS LIKE, "HEY."
AND I WAS LIKE, "HEY."
AND HE WAS LIKE... "HEY."
HE SAID "HEY" TWICE?
YEAH.
WTF

What You're Doing

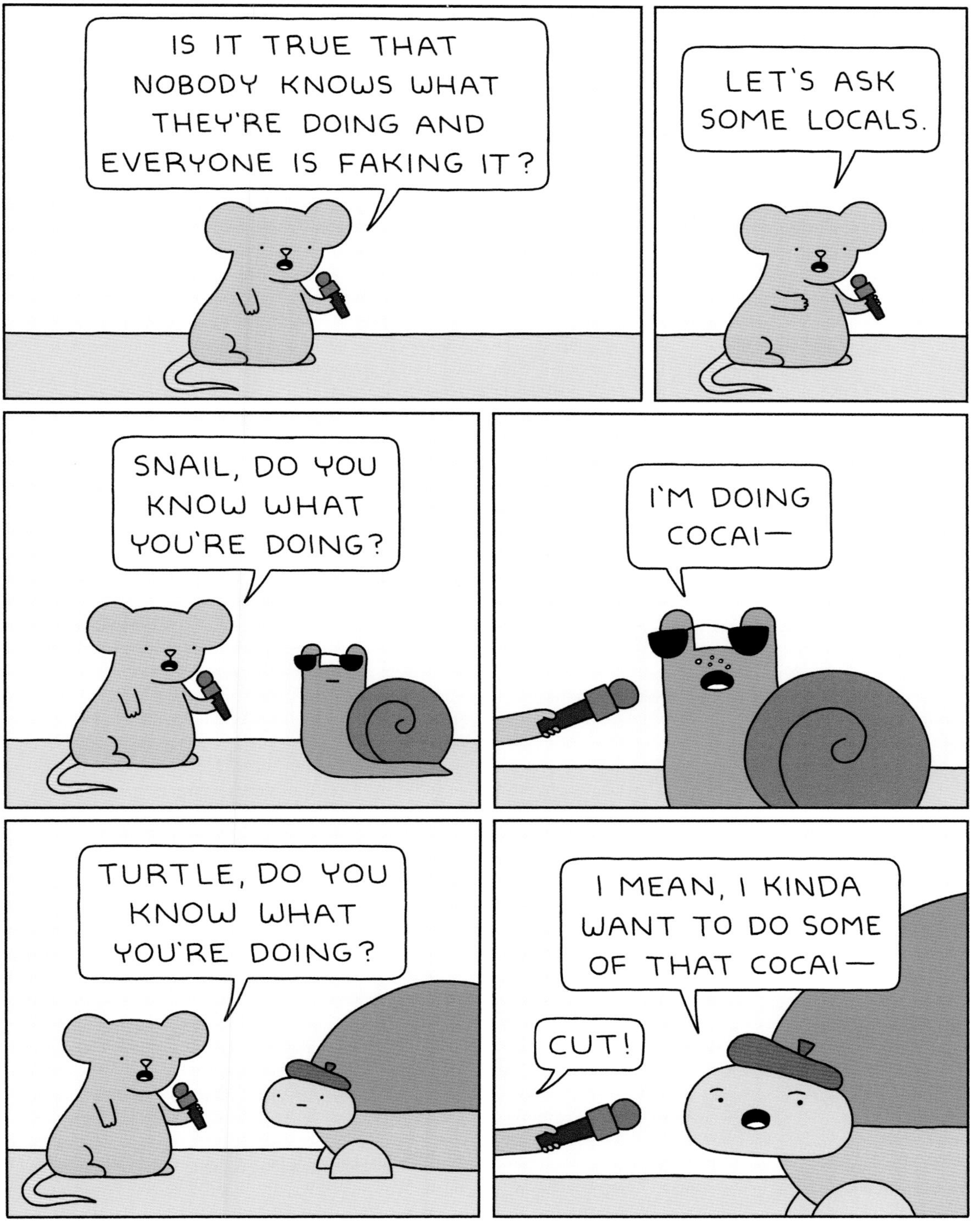
IS IT TRUE THAT NOBODY KNOWS WHAT THEY'RE DOING AND EVERYONE IS FAKING IT?
LET'S ASK SOME LOCALS.
SNAIL, DO YOU KNOW WHAT YOU'RE DOING?
I'M DOING COCAI—
TURTLE, DO YOU KNOW WHAT YOU'RE DOING?
I MEAN, I KINDA WANT TO DO SOME OF THAT COCAI—
CUT!

Whole New Day

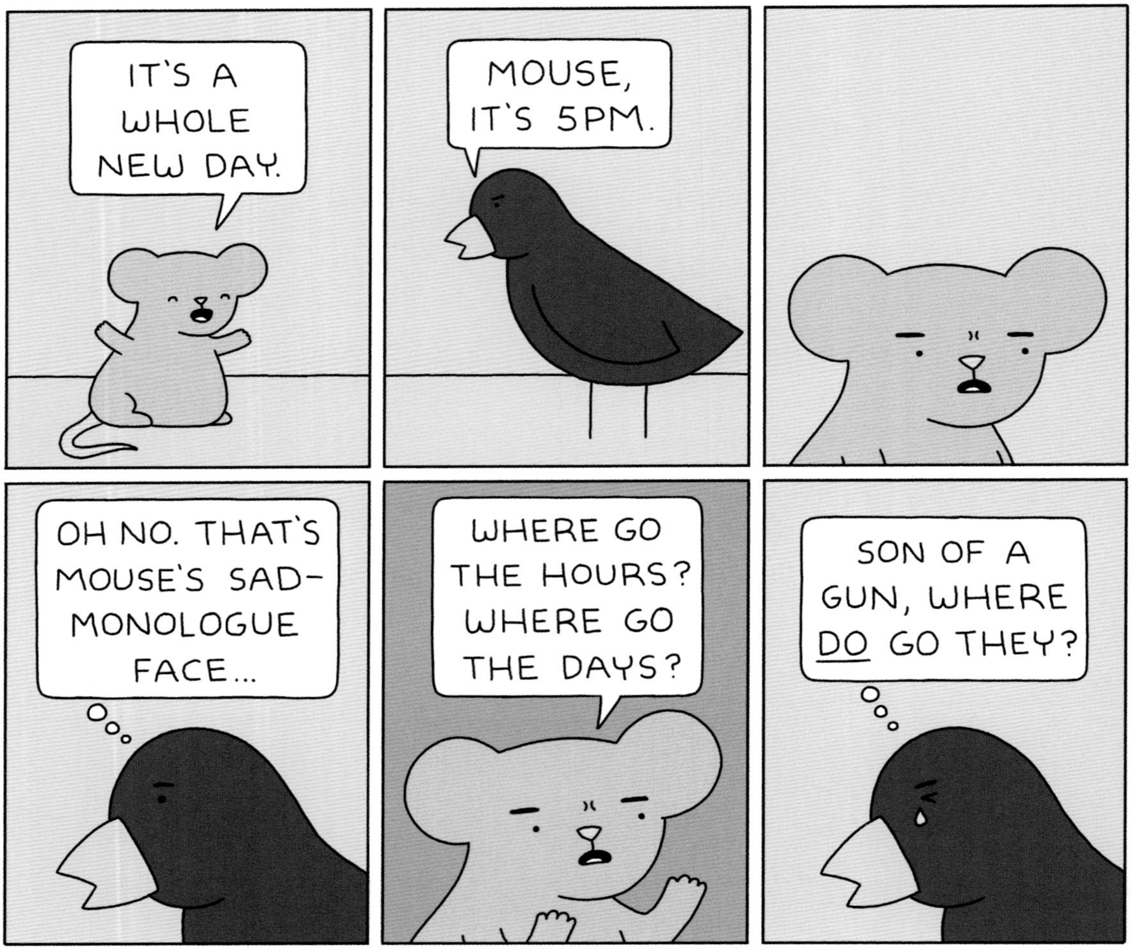
IT'S A WHOLE NEW DAY.
MOUSE, IT'S 5PM.
OH NO. THAT'S MOUSE'S SAD-MONOLOGUE FACE...
WHERE GO THE HOURS? WHERE GO THE DAYS?
SON OF A GUN, WHERE DO GO THEY?

Where Is Everyone

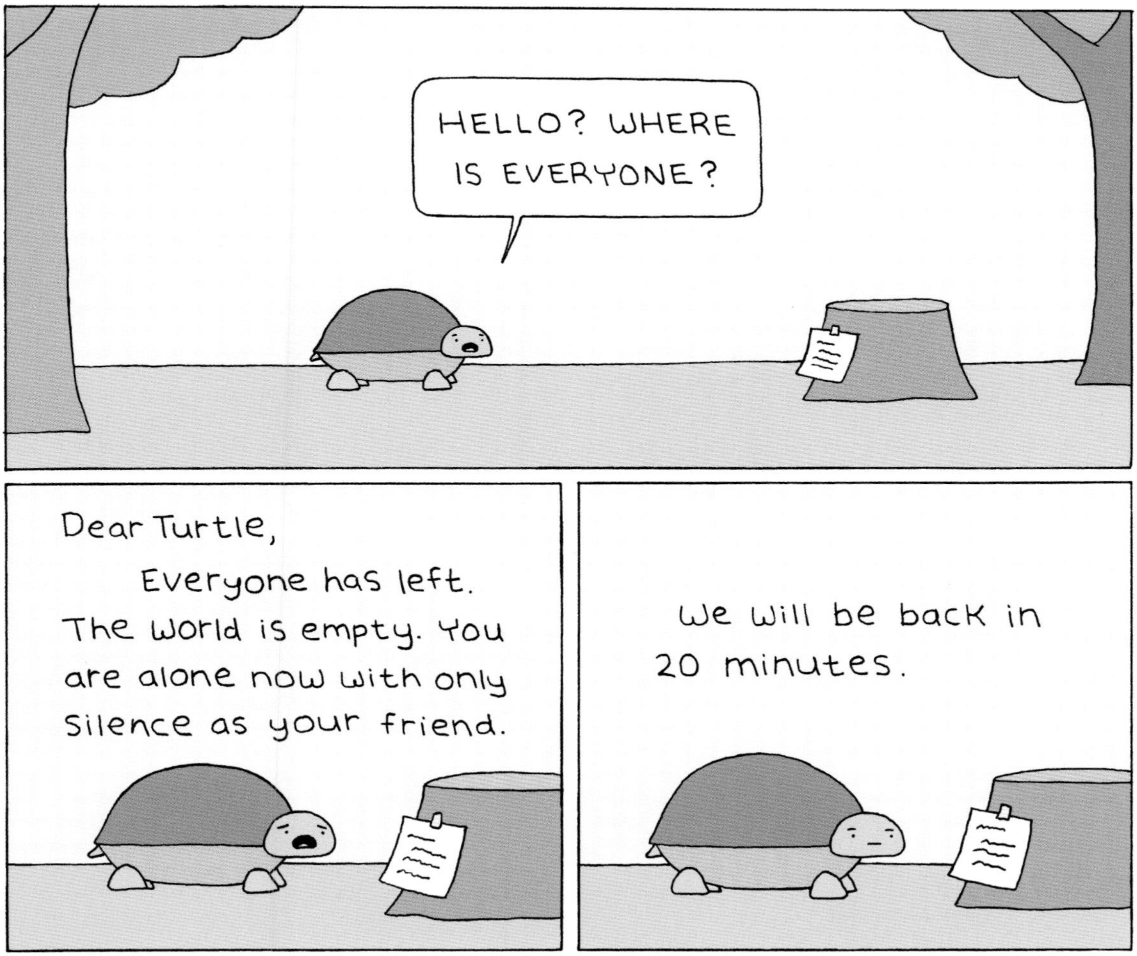
HELLO? WHERE IS EVERYONE?
Dear Turtle,
Everyone has left. The world is empty. You are alone now with only silence as your friend.
We will be back in 20 minutes.

You Might

YOU MIGHT LOOK AT ME AND THINK, "WOW..."
"THERE'S A BIRD WITH HIS OWN PRIVATE ISLAND."
"HOW DID THIS BIRD ACHIEVE SO MUCH, SO QUICKLY?"

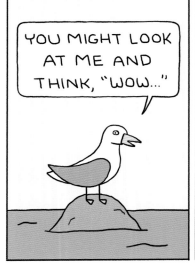

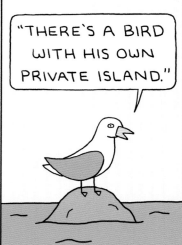

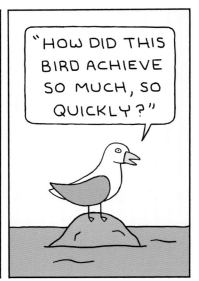

Who I Am

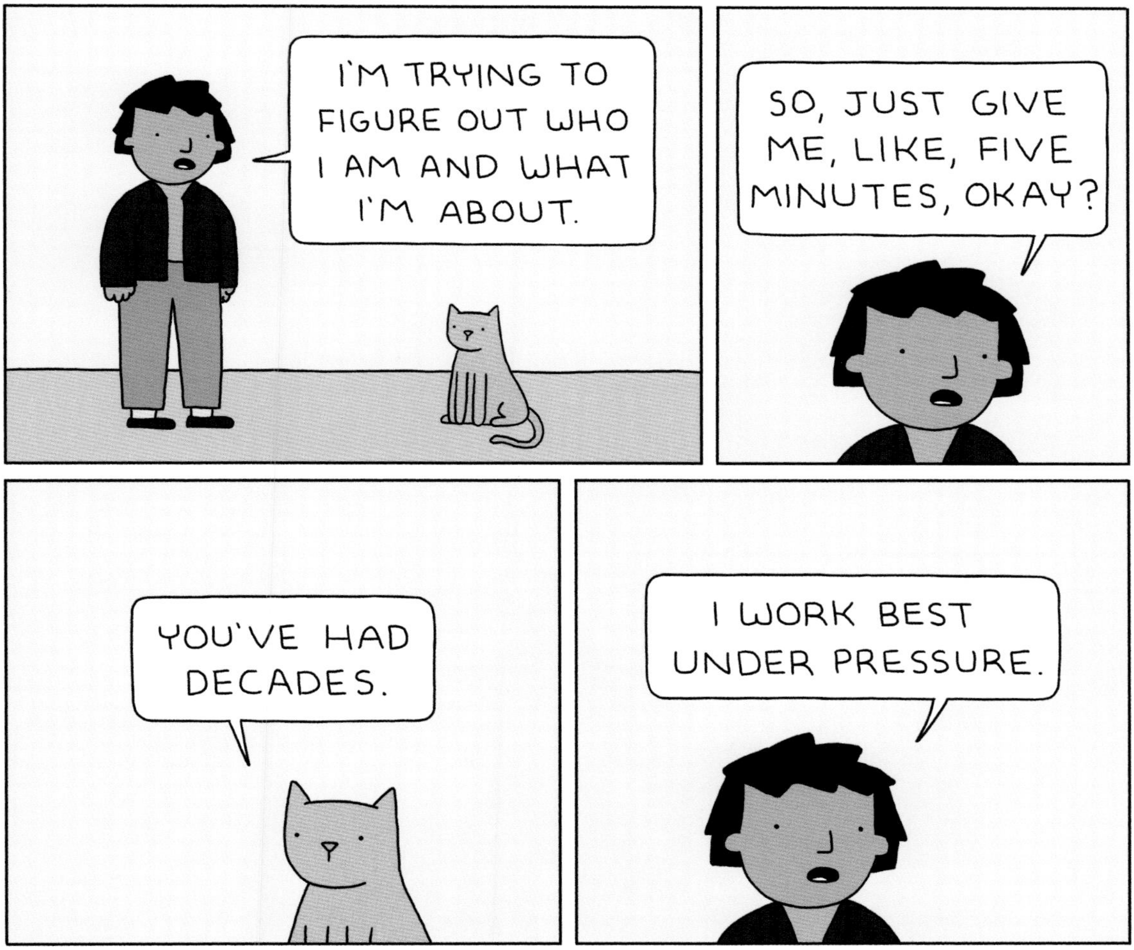
I'M TRYING TO FIGURE OUT WHO I AM AND WHAT I'M ABOUT.
SO, JUST GIVE ME, LIKE, FIVE MINUTES, OKAY?
YOU'VE HAD DECADES.
I WORK BEST UNDER PRESSURE.

No Free Time

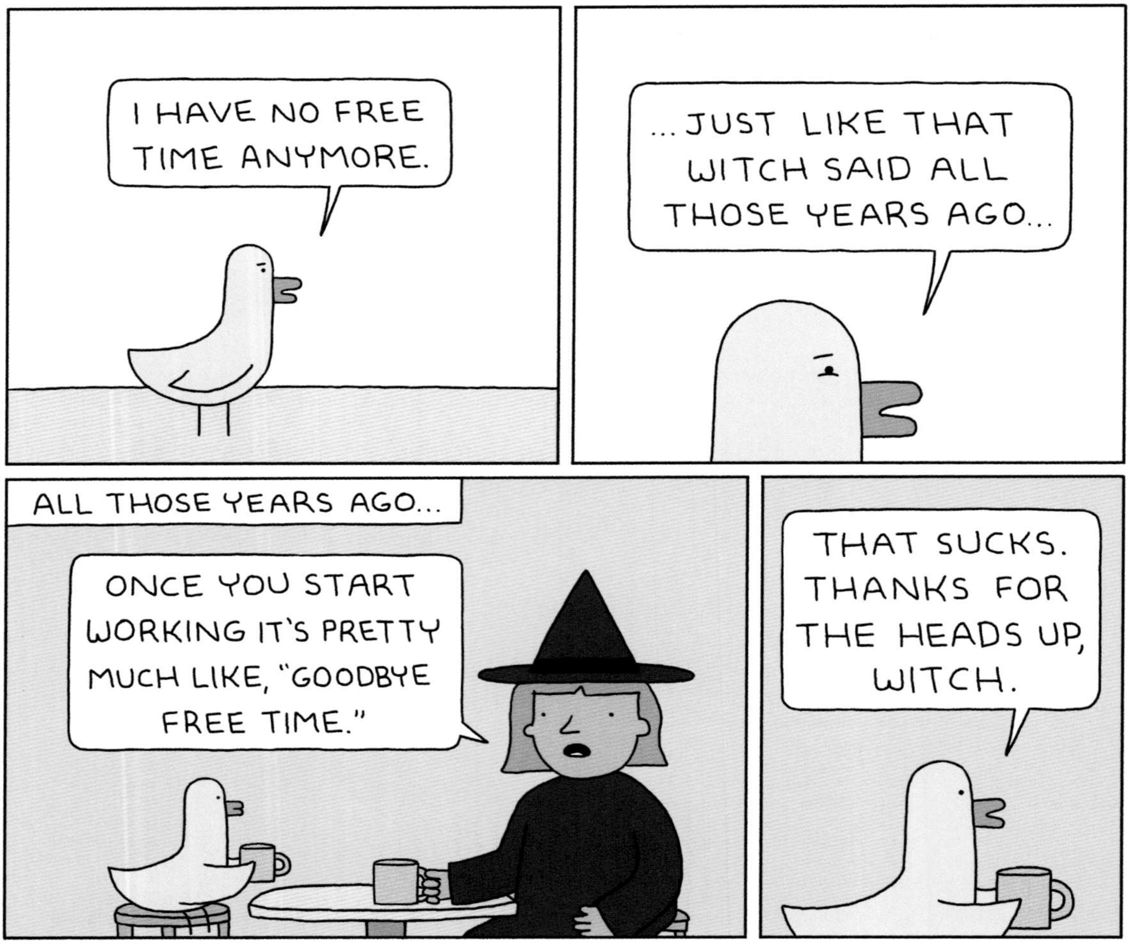
I HAVE NO FREE TIME ANYMORE.
...JUST LIKE THAT WITCH SAID ALL THOSE YEARS AGO...
ALL THOSE YEARS AGO...
ONCE YOU START WORKING IT'S PRETTY MUCH LIKE, "GOODBYE FREE TIME."
THAT SUCKS. THANKS FOR THE HEADS UP, WITCH.

Knife

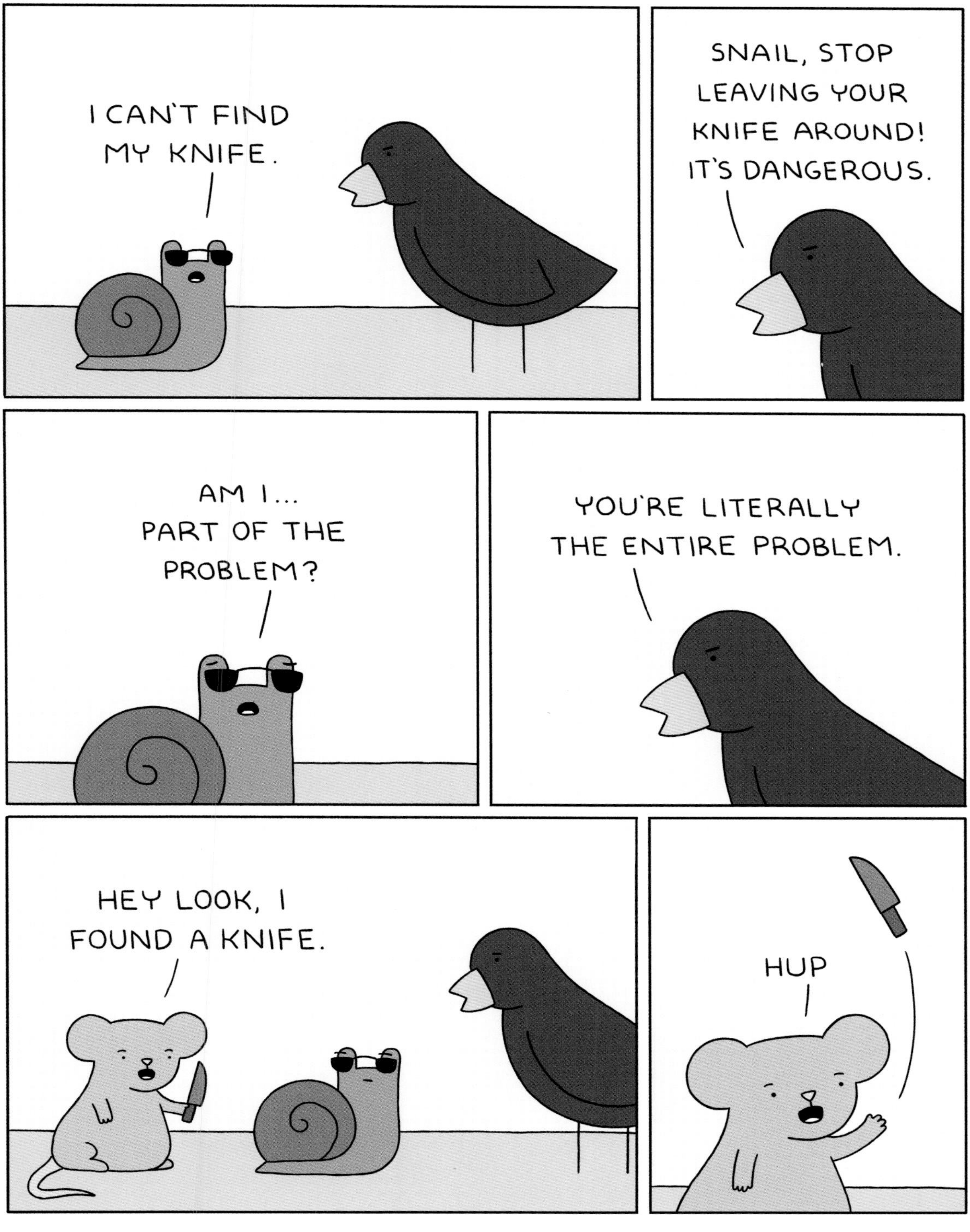

I CAN'T FIND MY KNIFE.
SNAIL, STOP LEAVING YOUR KNIFE AROUND! IT'S DANGEROUS.
AM I... PART OF THE PROBLEM?
YOU'RE LITERALLY THE ENTIRE PROBLEM.
HEY LOOK, I FOUND A KNIFE.
HUP

I KNEW THIS IS HOW MOUSE WOULD DIE.

MAYBE I AM PART OF THE PROBLEM.

TIME TO SHOOT THIS KNIFE.

OKAY, THAT ONE'S NOT ON ME.

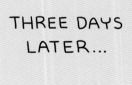

THREE DAYS LATER...

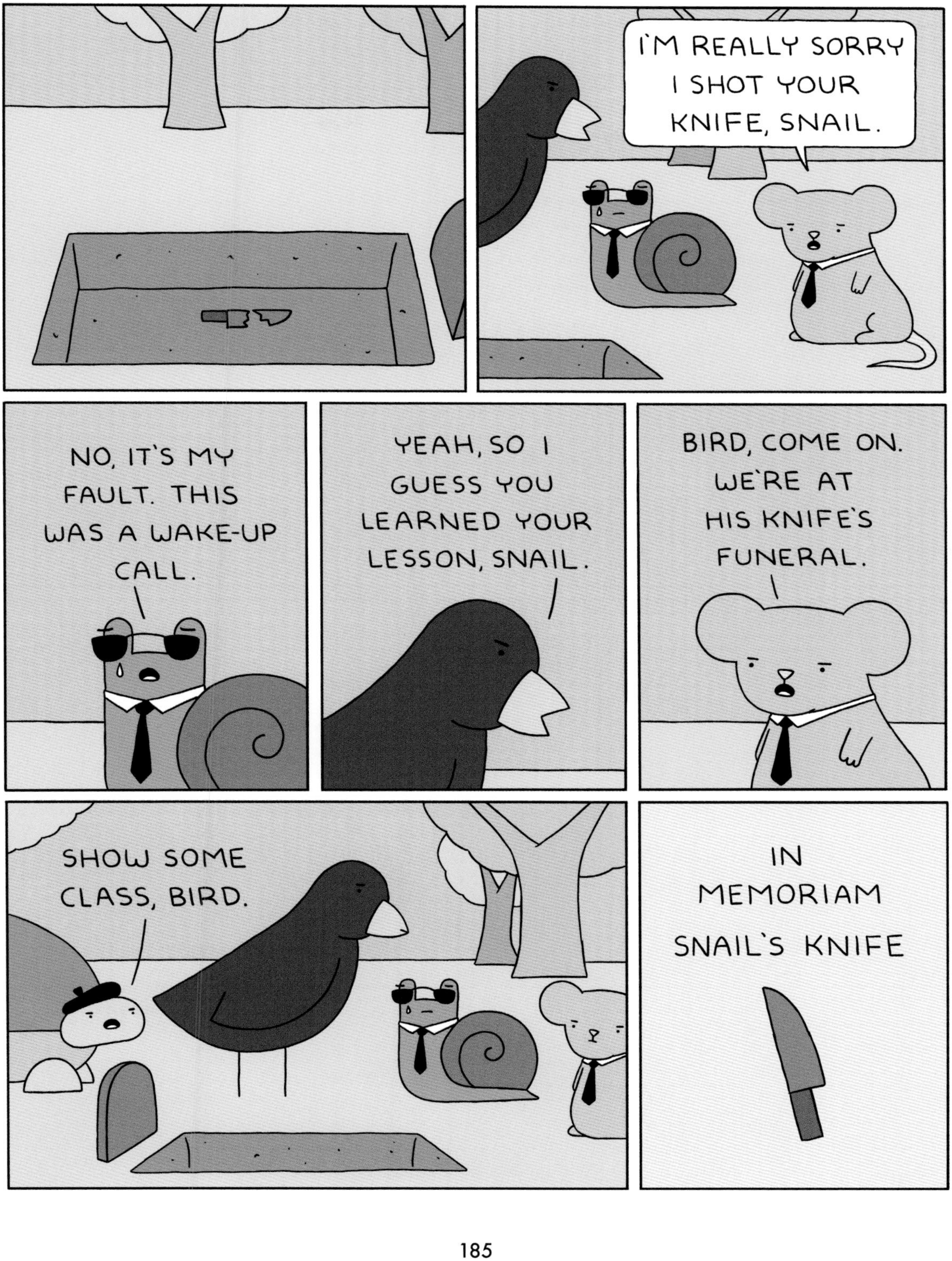
I'M REALLY SORRY I SHOT YOUR KNIFE, SNAIL.
NO, IT'S MY FAULT. THIS WAS A WAKE-UP CALL.
YEAH, SO I GUESS YOU LEARNED YOUR LESSON, SNAIL.
BIRD, COME ON. WE'RE AT HIS KNIFE'S FUNERAL.
SHOW SOME CLASS, BIRD.
IN MEMORIAM SNAIL'S KNIFE

Older

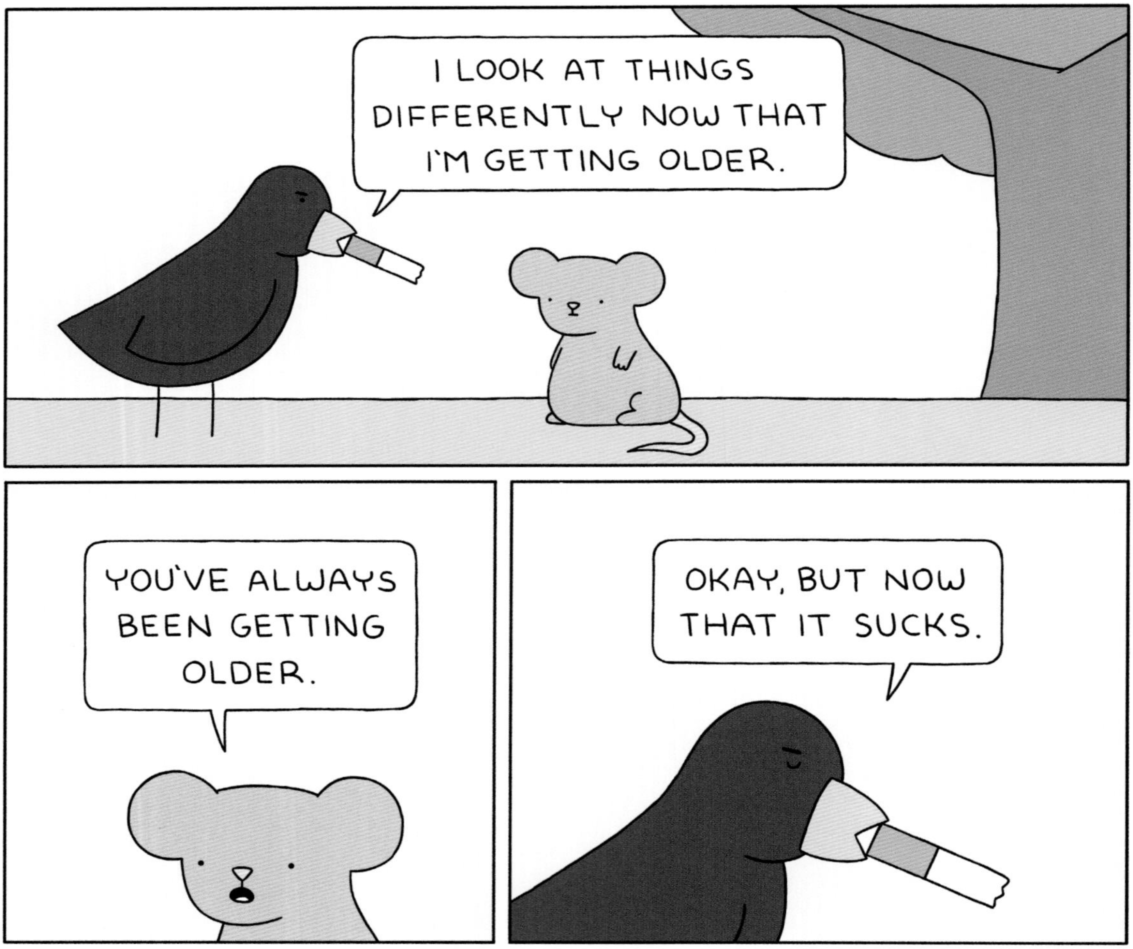
I LOOK AT THINGS DIFFERENTLY NOW THAT I'M GETTING OLDER.
YOU'VE ALWAYS BEEN GETTING OLDER.
OKAY, BUT NOW THAT IT SUCKS.

Excuse Me

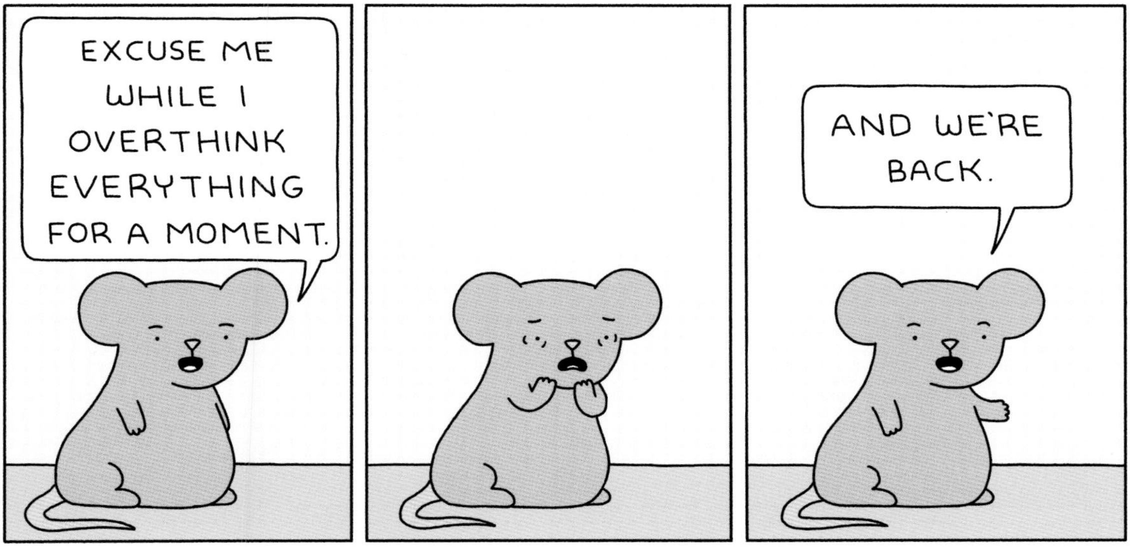
EXCUSE ME WHILE I OVERTHINK EVERYTHING FOR A MOMENT.
AND WE'RE BACK.

Unreliable

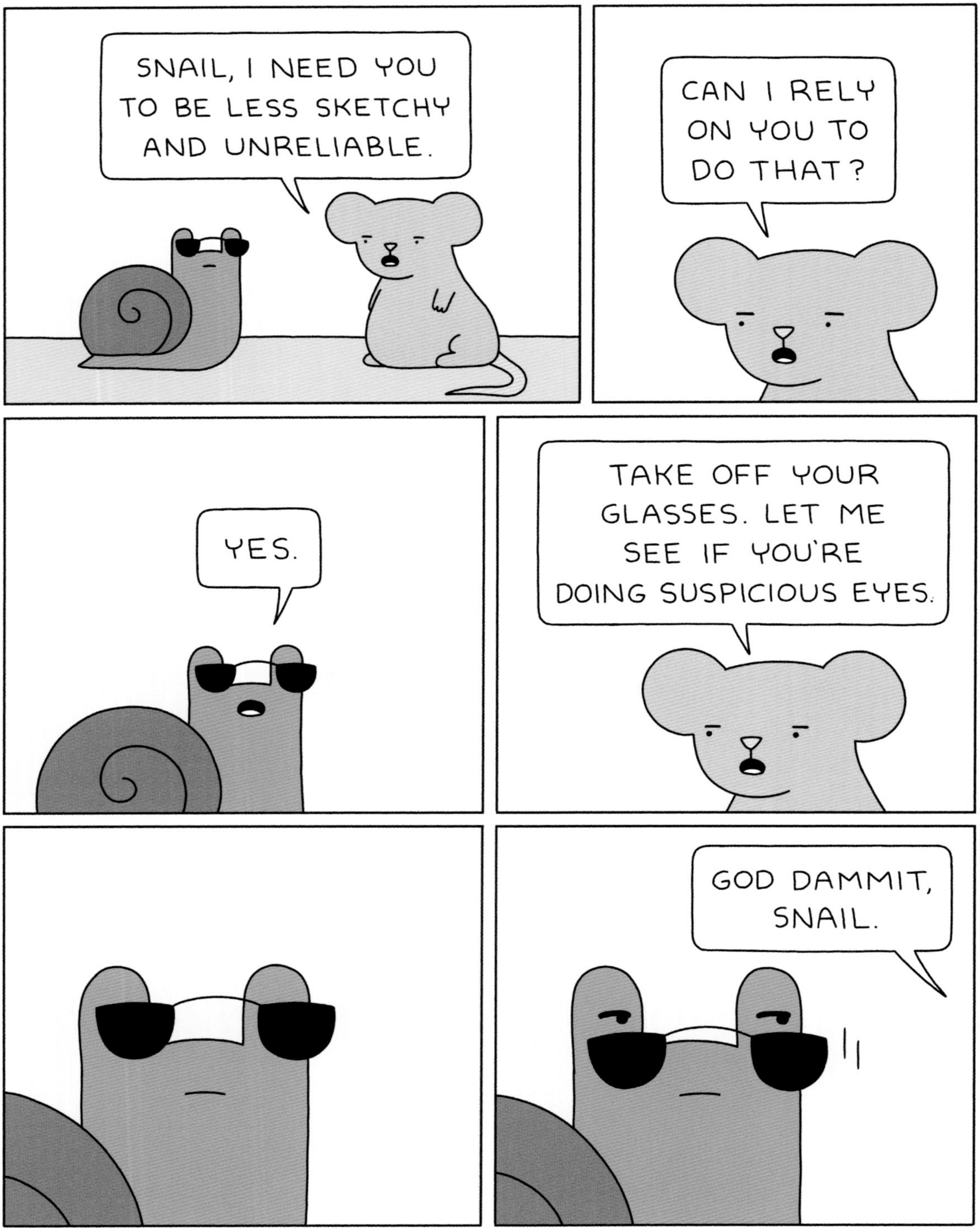
SNAIL, I NEED YOU TO BE LESS SKETCHY AND UNRELIABLE.
CAN I RELY ON YOU TO DO THAT?
YES.
TAKE OFF YOUR GLASSES. LET ME SEE IF YOU'RE DOING SUSPICIOUS EYES.
GOD DAMMIT, SNAIL.

Your Issues

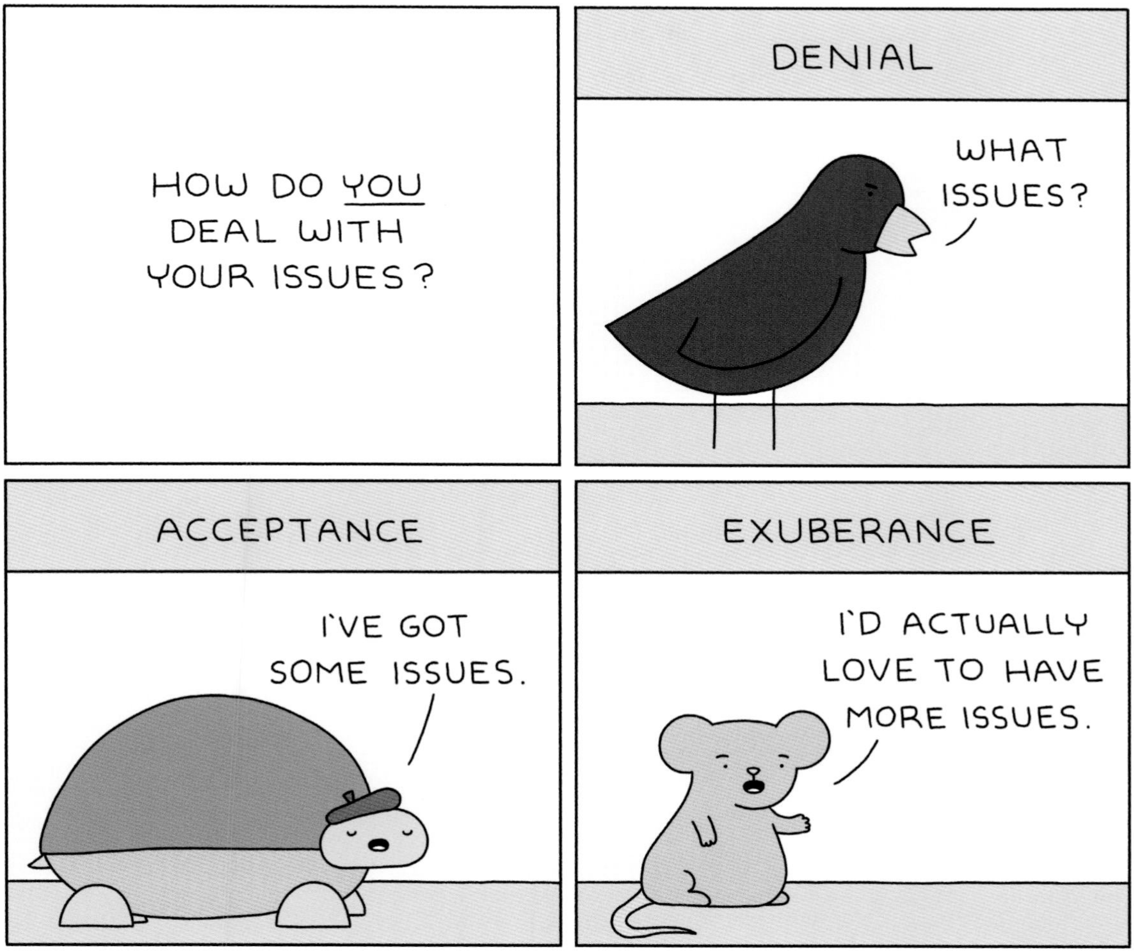
HOW DO YOU DEAL WITH YOUR ISSUES?
DENIAL
WHAT ISSUES?
ACCEPTANCE
I'VE GOT SOME ISSUES.
EXUBERANCE
I'D ACTUALLY LOVE TO HAVE MORE ISSUES.

Favorite Things

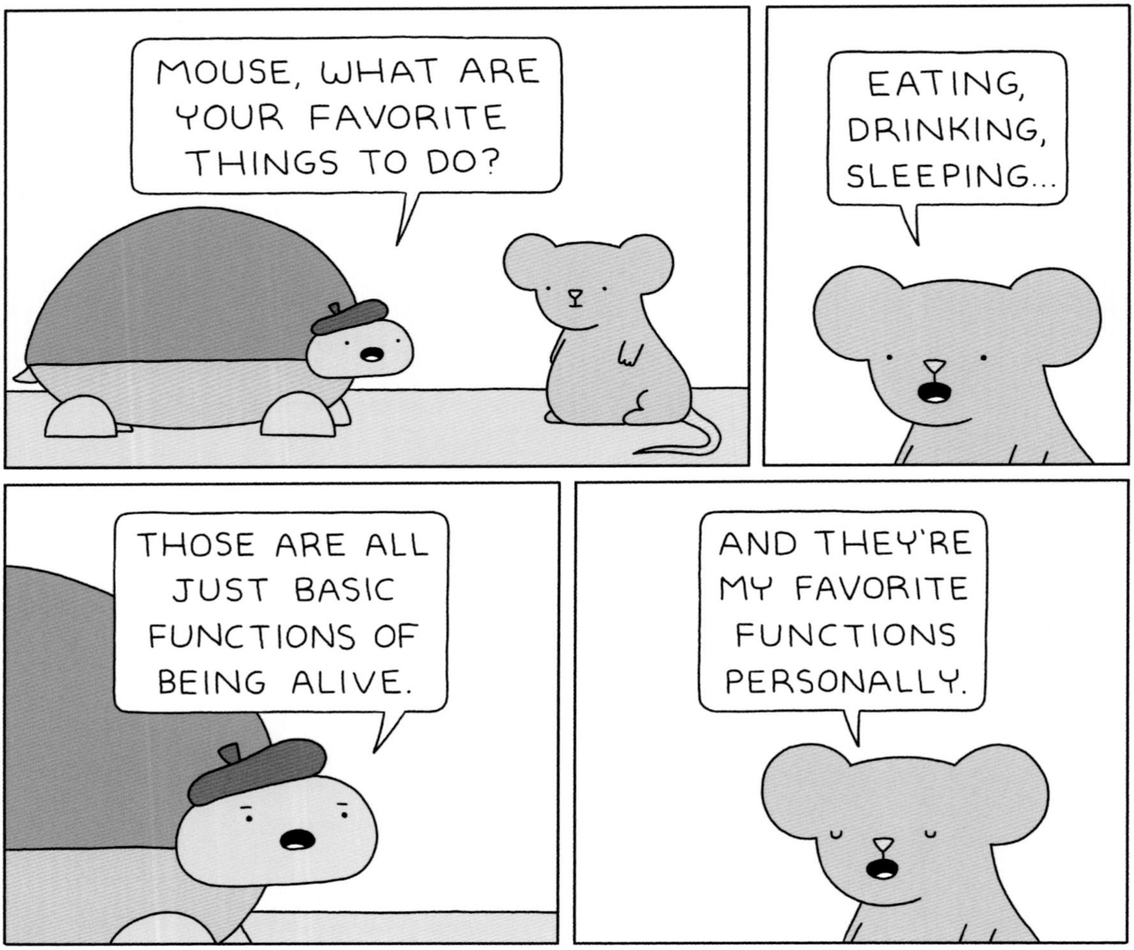
MOUSE, WHAT ARE YOUR FAVORITE THINGS TO DO?
EATING, DRINKING, SLEEPING...
THOSE ARE ALL JUST BASIC FUNCTIONS OF BEING ALIVE.
AND THEY'RE MY FAVORITE FUNCTIONS PERSONALLY.

History of Humans

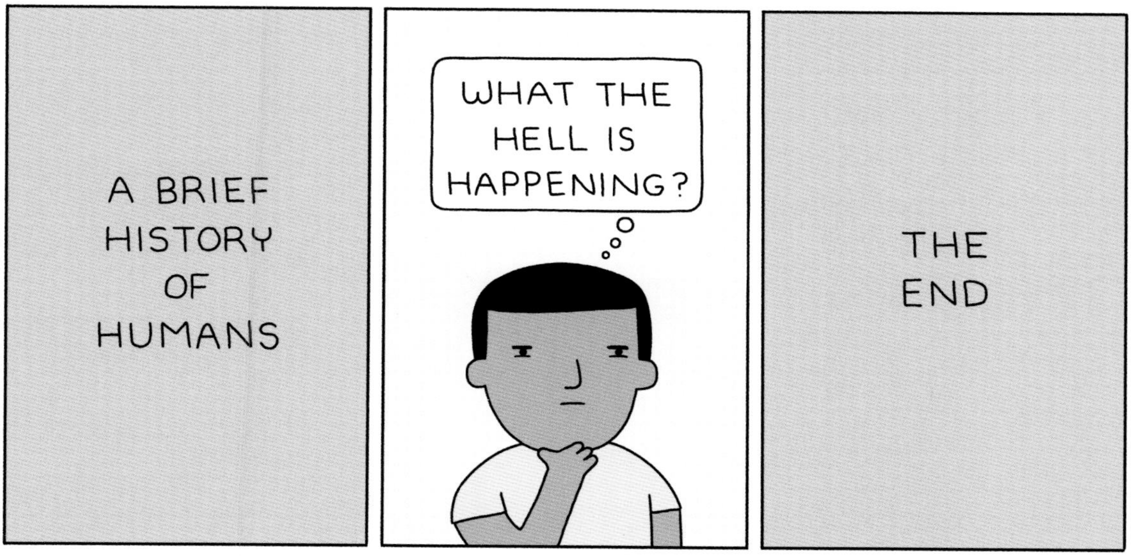
A BRIEF HISTORY OF HUMANS
WHAT THE HELL IS HAPPENING?
THE END

Thinking About

TRASH BIRD, WHAT ARE YOU THINKING ABOUT?
ISSUES.

Won't Sit

I WON'T SIT AROUND DOING NOTHING!
YEAH!
I'LL MAKE THINGS WORSE!
NO!

Turtle Sunset

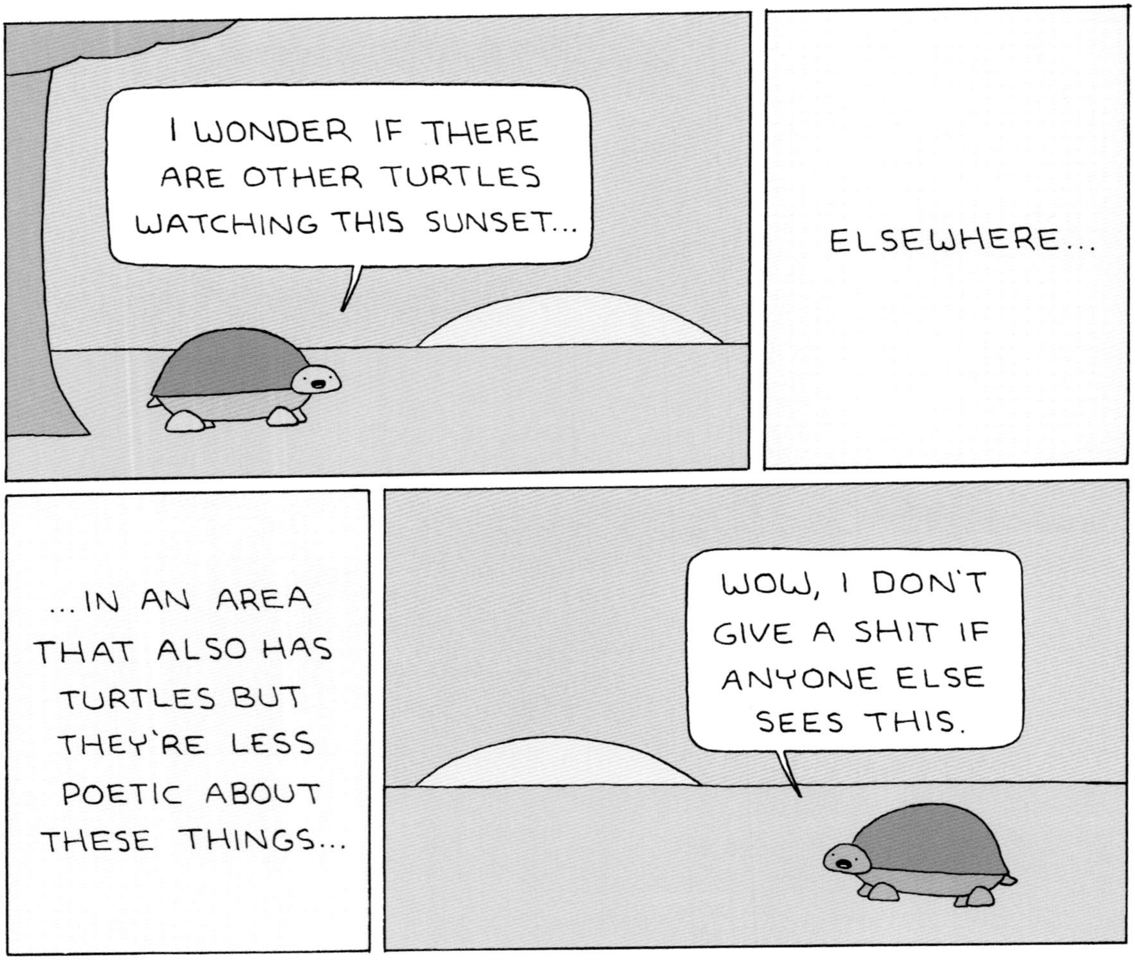
I WONDER IF THERE ARE OTHER TURTLES WATCHING THIS SUNSET...
ELSEWHERE...
...IN AN AREA THAT ALSO HAS TURTLES BUT THEY'RE LESS POETIC ABOUT THESE THINGS...
WOW, I DON'T GIVE A SHIT IF ANYONE ELSE SEES THIS.

Something New

I WANT TO TRY SOMETHING NEW
FOOD? OR AN INTERESTING LIFE EXPERIENCE?
TO ME THESE ARE THE SAME.

Haunting

GHOST, ARE YOU HAUNTING ME?
NO, I'M HAUNTING YOUR HOUSE.
I LOVE ARCHITECTURE.

Your Story

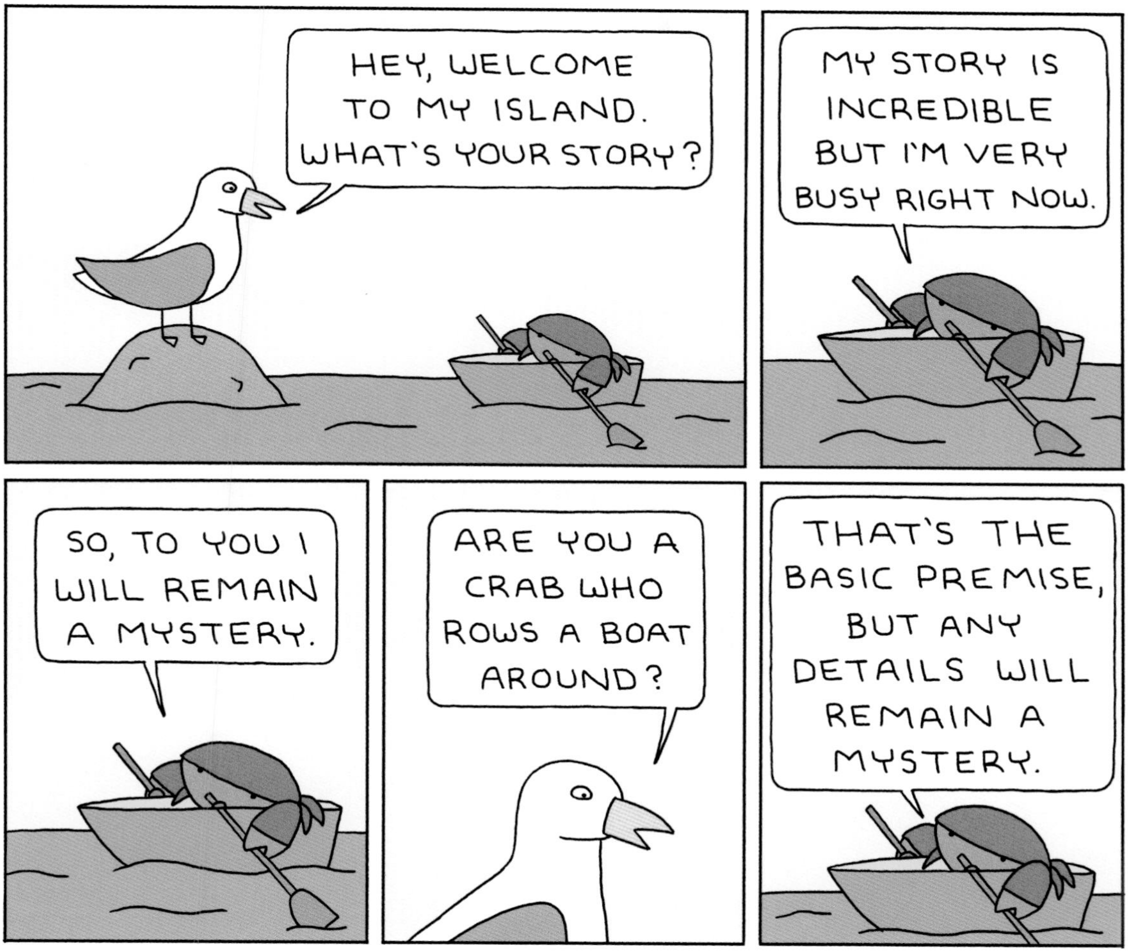
HEY, WELCOME TO MY ISLAND. WHAT'S YOUR STORY?
MY STORY IS INCREDIBLE BUT I'M VERY BUSY RIGHT NOW.
SO, TO YOU I WILL REMAIN A MYSTERY.
ARE YOU A CRAB WHO ROWS A BOAT AROUND?
THAT'S THE BASIC PREMISE, BUT ANY DETAILS WILL REMAIN A MYSTERY.

So Many Ideas

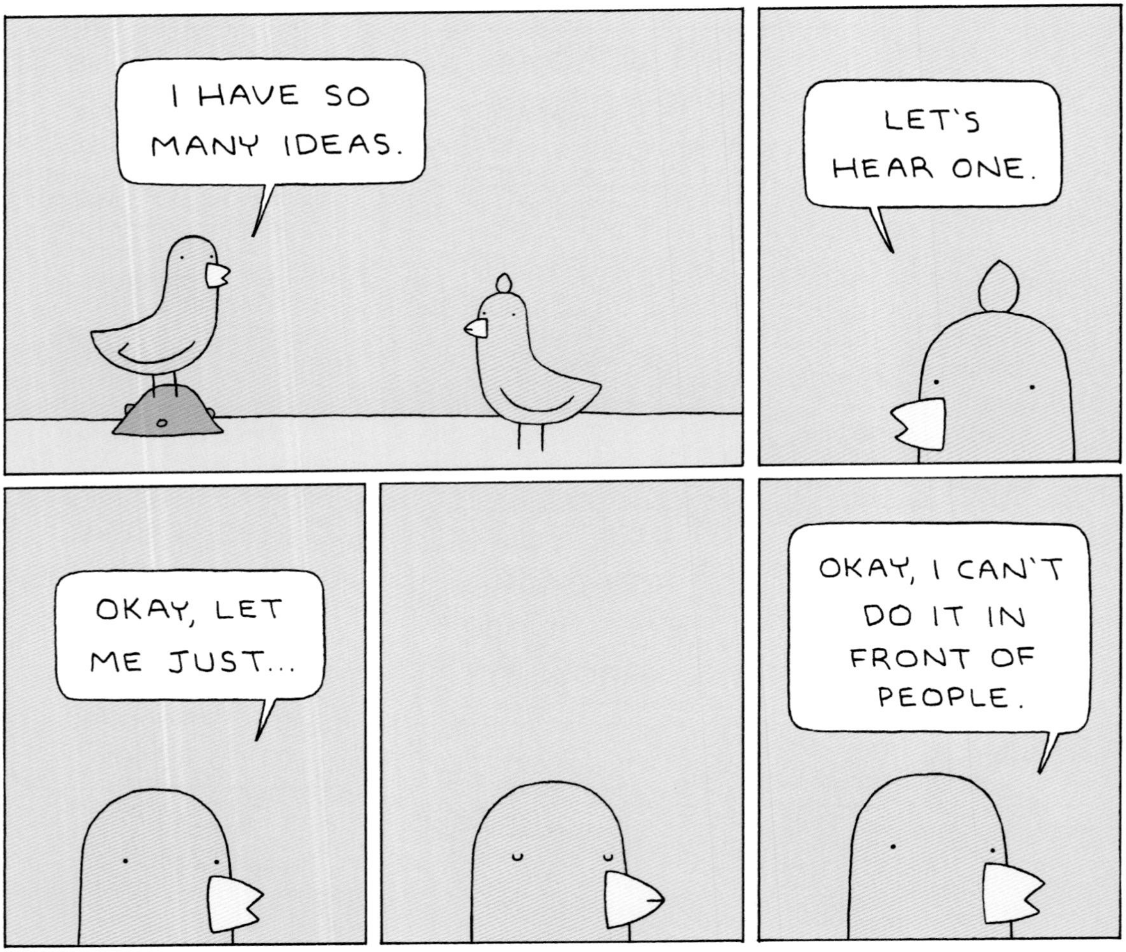
I HAVE SO MANY IDEAS.
LET'S HEAR ONE.
OKAY, LET ME JUST...
OKAY, I CAN'T DO IT IN FRONT OF PEOPLE.

Fights

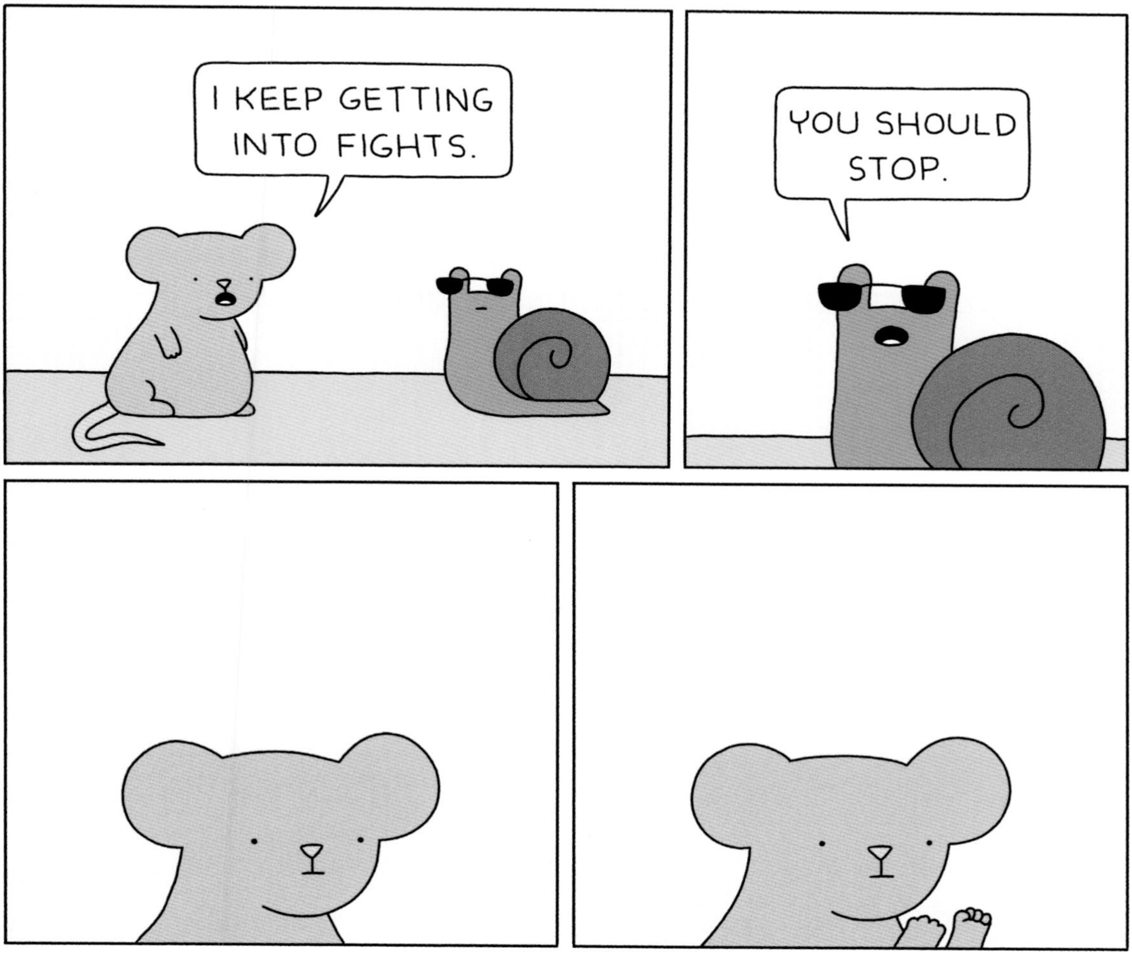
I KEEP GETTING INTO FIGHTS.
YOU SHOULD STOP.

What's Wrong

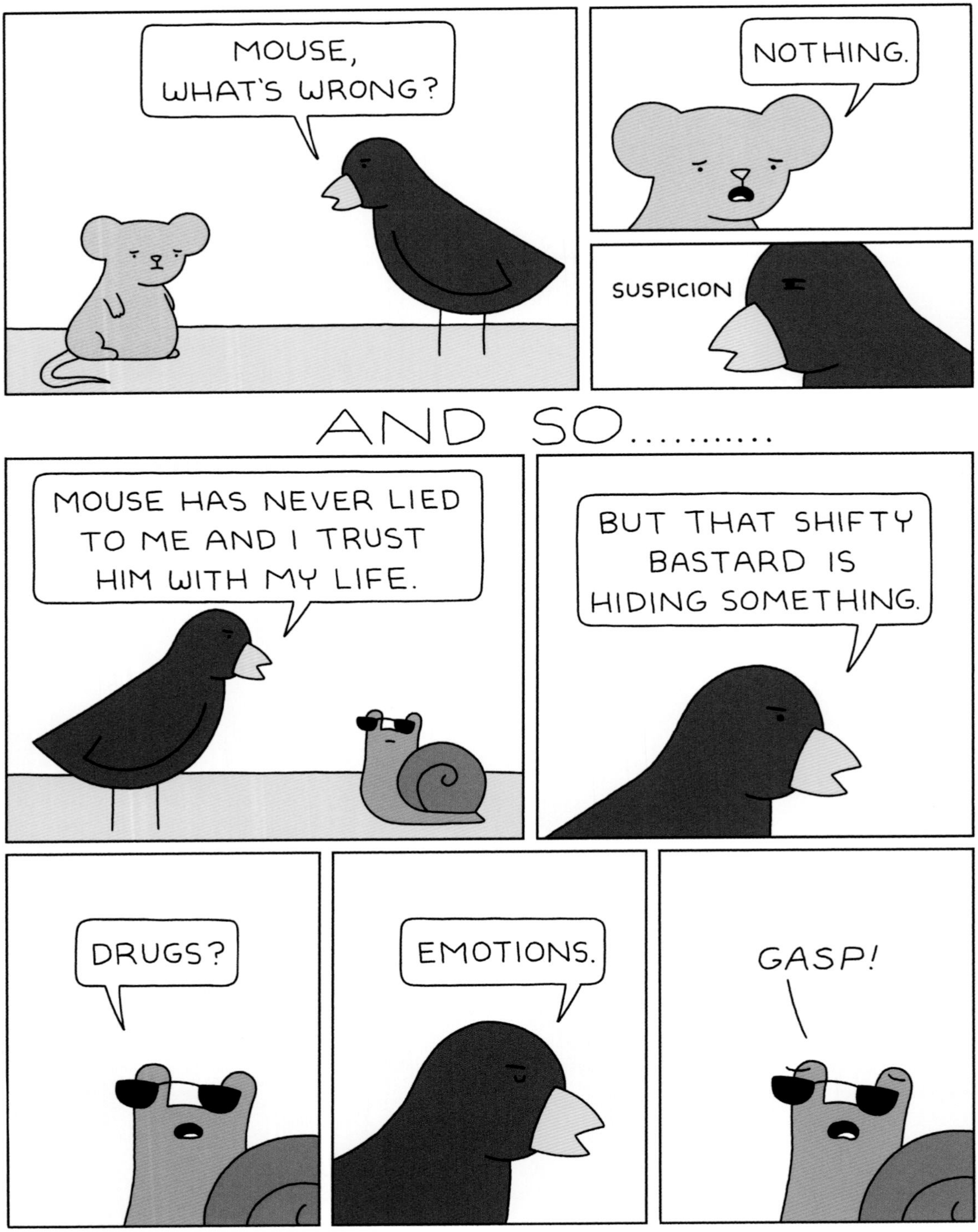
MOUSE, WHAT'S WRONG?
NOTHING.
SUSPICION
AND SO..........
MOUSE HAS NEVER LIED TO ME AND I TRUST HIM WITH MY LIFE.
BUT THAT SHIFTY BASTARD IS HIDING SOMETHING.
DRUGS?
EMOTIONS.
GASP!

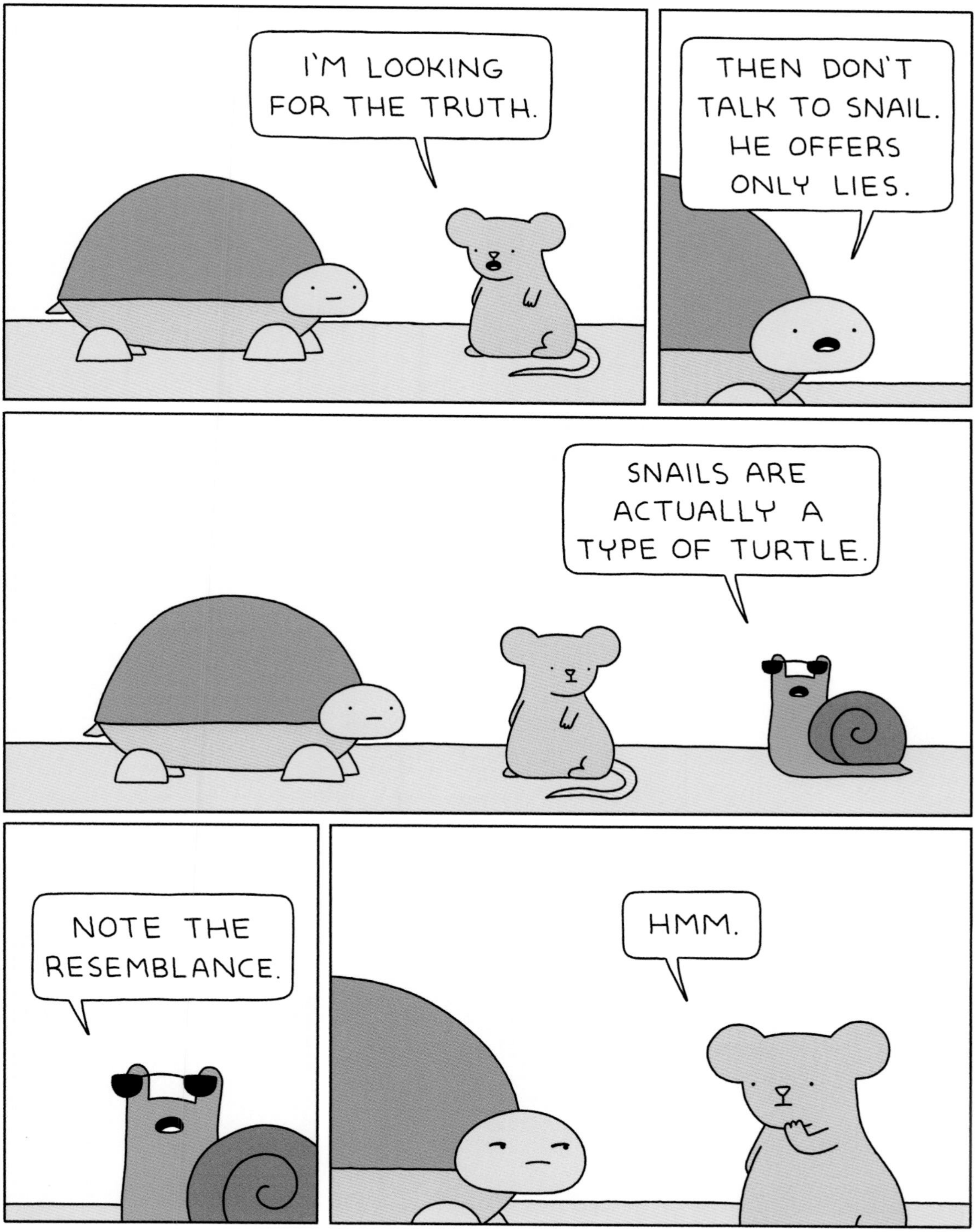
I'M LOOKING FOR THE TRUTH.
THEN DON'T TALK TO SNAIL. HE OFFERS ONLY LIES.
SNAILS ARE ACTUALLY A TYPE OF TURTLE.
NOTE THE RESEMBLANCE.
HMM.

Fool

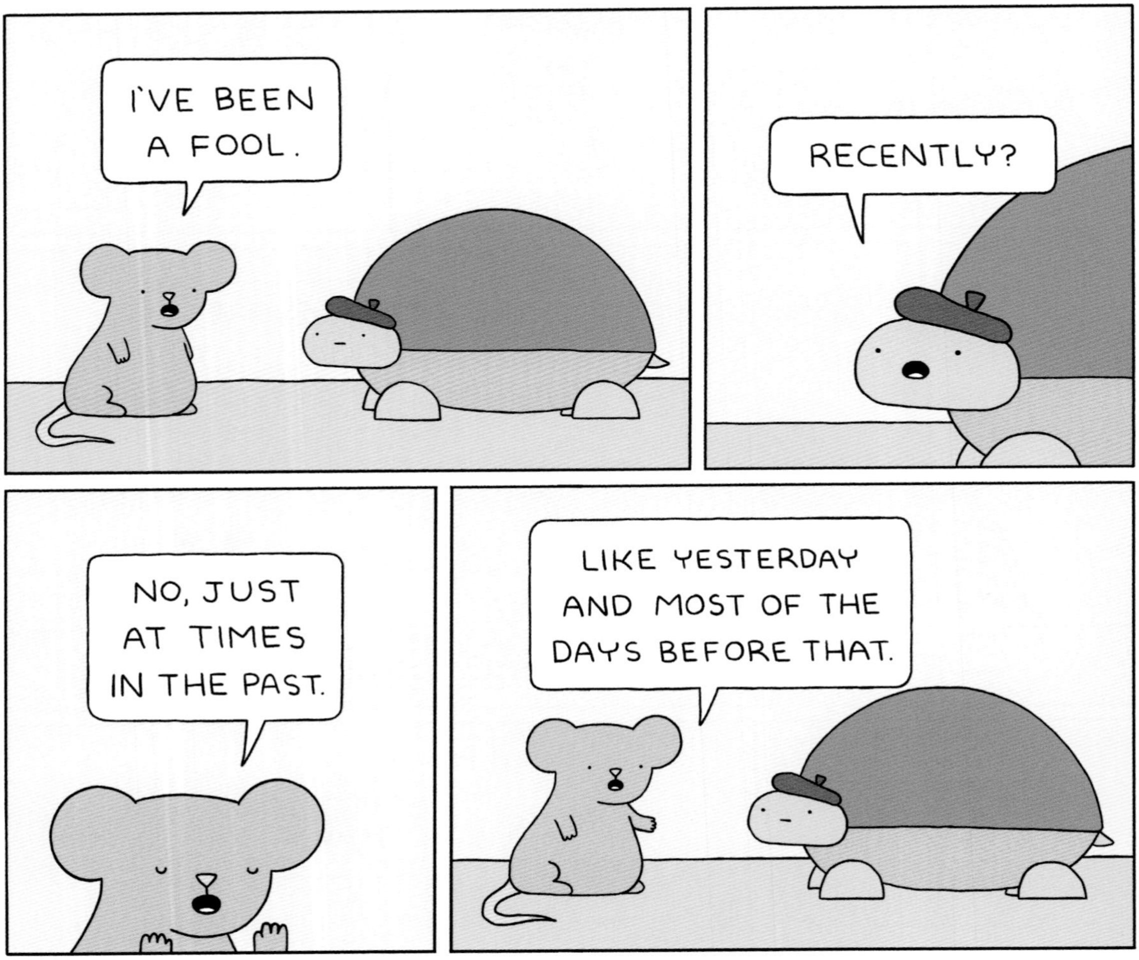
I'VE BEEN A FOOL.
RECENTLY?
NO, JUST AT TIMES IN THE PAST.
LIKE YESTERDAY AND MOST OF THE DAYS BEFORE THAT.

Focus

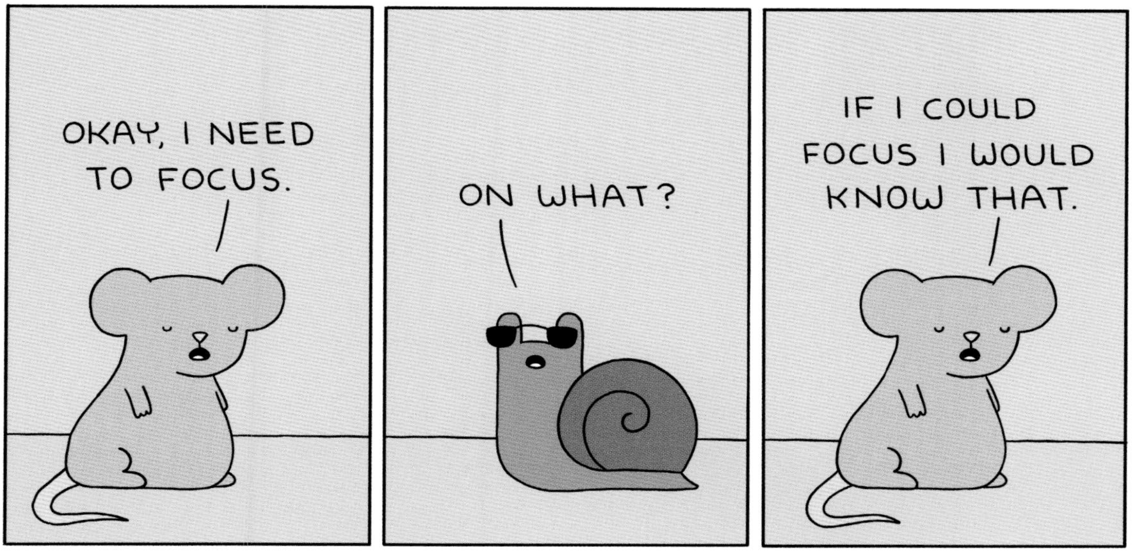
OKAY, I NEED TO FOCUS.
ON WHAT?
IF I COULD FOCUS I WOULD KNOW THAT.

Conflict

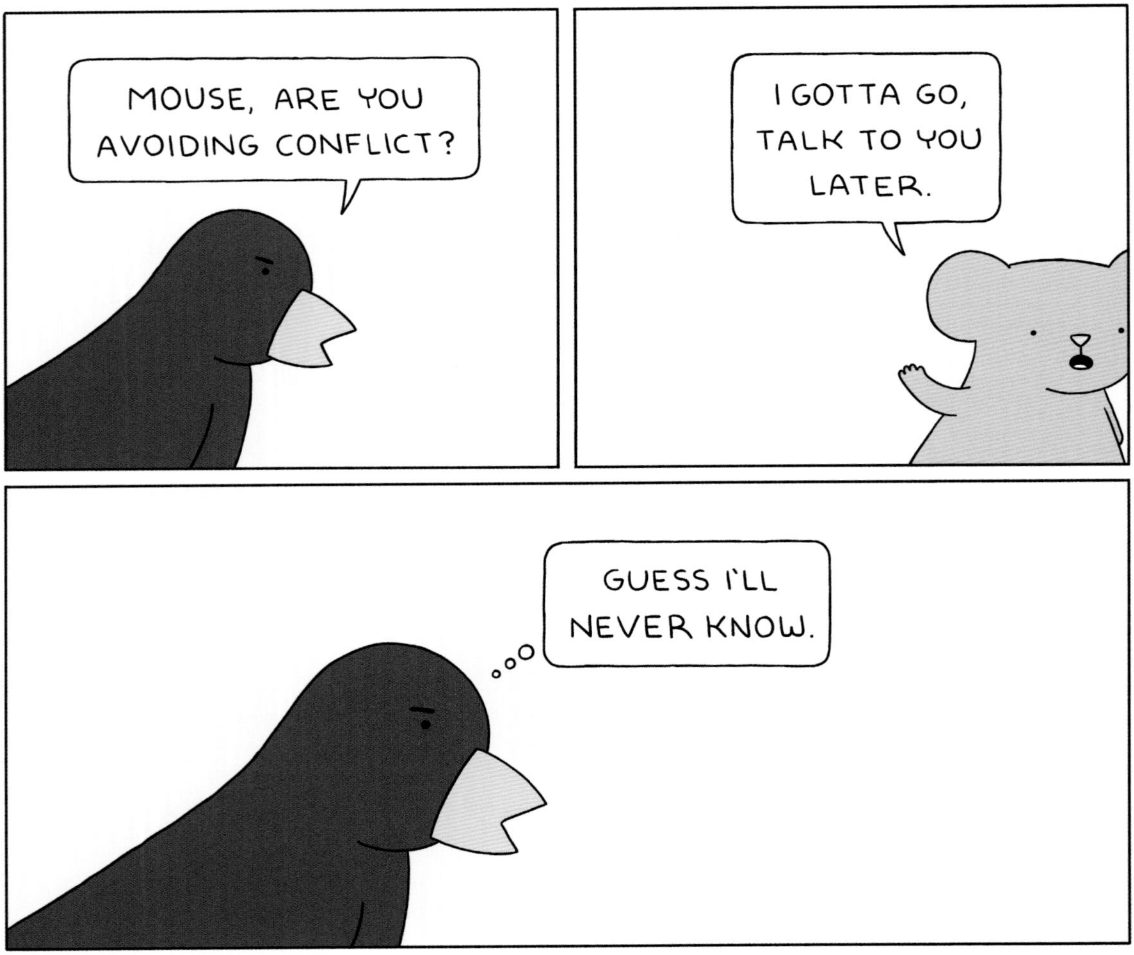
MOUSE, ARE YOU AVOIDING CONFLICT?
I GOTTA GO, TALK TO YOU LATER.
GUESS I'LL NEVER KNOW.

In Life

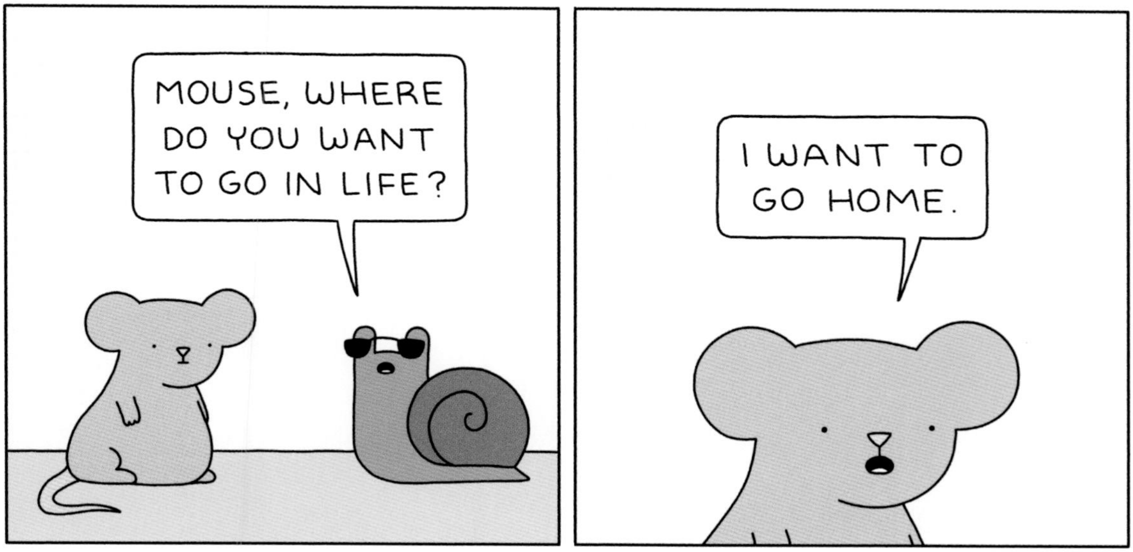
MOUSE, WHERE DO YOU WANT TO GO IN LIFE?
I WANT TO GO HOME.

HOPE IT ALL WORKS OUT!

Andrews McMeel Publishing
a division of Andrews McMeel Universal
1130 Walnut Street, Kansas City, Missouri 64106
www.andrewsmcmeel.com

24 25 26 27 28 VEP 10 9 8 7 6 5 4 3 2

ISBN: 978-1-5248-9389-7

Library of Congress Control Number: 2024933267

Editor: Lucas Wetzel
Art Director: Diane Marsh
Production Editor: Brianna Westervelt
Production Manager: Chadd Keim

ATTENTION: SCHOOLS AND BUSINESSESS
Andrews McMeel books are available at quantity discounts with bulk purchase for educational, business, or sales promotional use. For information, please e-mail the Andrews McMeel Publishing Special Sales Department: sales@andrewsmcmeel.com.